BREAK CONTACT—CONTINUE

BREAK CONTACT—CONTINUE MISSION

RAYMOND D. HARRIS

Pennsylvania & Yorkshire

Published in the United States of America and Great Britain in 2024 by
CASEMATE PUBLISHERS
1950 Lawrence Road, Havertown, PA 19083, USA
and
47 Church Street, Barnsley, S70 2AS, UK

First published in 1990 by Paladin Press.

This edition © 2024 Raymond D. Harris

Hardcover Edition: ISBN 978-1-63624-500-3
Digital Edition: ISBN 978-1-63624-501-0

A CIP record for this book is available from the British Library

All rights reserved. No part of this book may be reproduced or transmitted in any form or by any means, electronic or mechanical including photocopying, recording or by any information storage and retrieval system, without permission from the publisher in writing.

Printed and bound in the United Kingdom by CPI Group (UK) Ltd, Croydon, CR0 4YY
Typeset in India by DiTech Publishing Services

For a complete list of Casemate titles, please contact:

CASEMATE PUBLISHERS (US)
Telephone (610) 853-9131
Fax (610) 853-9146
Email: casemate@casematepublishers.com
www.casematepublishers.com

CASEMATE PUBLISHERS (UK)
Telephone (0)1226 734350
Email: casemate@casemateuk.com
www.casemateuk.com

All photographs are from the author's personal collection.

MAY YE HAVE WARM WORDS ON A COLD EVENING
A FULL MOON ON A DARK NIGHT
AND THE ROAD DOWNHILL ALL THE WAY TO YOUR DOOR.
Old Irish toast

The "Golf Course," looking southeast, 2 November, 1969.

Author and Kehn on the Golf Course Trail, planting vibration sensors. Looking north.

Preface

The Military Assistance Command, Vietnam, Studies and Observations Group, was a very small unit in the war.

I don't know how many Americans died. Two hundred? More? How many maimed? Four hundred? More?

I don't know how many Yards, Cambodians or Vietnamese died. Six hundred? A thousand? Who cares today? We care.

I do know twelve Medals of Honor were awarded to SOG members and others they worked with. At least fifty-five Americans are listed as missing in action, but back then they took such things in stride. SOG was a phantom child, awarded a Presidential Unit Citation, a full twenty-nine years after it was disbanded.

Our three main compounds were among the most highly decorated, for their size, in the entire war. Five of those Medals of Honor came out of Command and Control Central (CCC), out of Kontum. Casualty rates hovered high for years. My friends and I were oh so lucky.

Survivors raise the collective cup and take their sip. They stand, and laugh, and cry, and drink, telling tales to one another, remembering all too well the younger men they were.

This is not just a dedication, but a toast to all the boys: to the lifers and short timers, to the living and the dead, to ones we left behind across the fence, to the men of MACV-SOG, what WE called the Special Operations Group.

Raymond Harris drinking rice wine at the village.

The Author in full battle gear, coming back from an eight-day mission on the Golf Course in Laos, early December 1969.

Author's Note

Does history or fiction tell a stronger truth in life? Almost all events depicted in this book actually happened. Some I took part in, many I did not, or was on the edge as a participating witness, but this is not *my* story. It's theirs.

I was in my share of firefights, but none as ferocious as some depicted here. Actions were expanded or contracted in service to the novel. Do changes alter underlying truths? I doubt it. These events spread across several years, in a world that once actually existed. Truth is also in the meaning, and not in just the telling.

One truth is that from 2007 through the end of 2010, I was a civilian security contractor in Iraq and Afghanistan. For two of those years I was in charge of the military gates at Camp Falcon, south of Baghdad. It was night shift, and one unit stationed at Falcon for six months in 2009 was the North Carolina National Guard.

I met a Montagnard kid born in Kontum. His parents were from the very village most of my team came from. Special Forces at Fayetteville have sponsored Montagnard families for citizenship for decades. I gave them information on my team through their son.

They told him, a year after Saigon's fall, a company of Vietnamese soldiers took the village and called out a list of men by name. They marched these men away from the village, and executed them. One was named Dom, who was our interpreter we called Dominique.

So, thirty-nine years after leaving Vietnam, in a small compound in a foreign land, I learned the truth of his death thirty-three years before. SOG was cancelled in 1972, and they had three years to destroy all evidence of its existence to protect its indigenous members; three years to do the right thing before North Vietnamese tanks rolled through Saigon.

Dominique died because Americans left a trail of informational bread crumbs for the new government to follow back to his village, where he and other former members of CCC were murdered. Finding out about such a tragedy in such a way is so improbable that it must be fiction, but it's not.

This novel was originally published in 1990. Some characters were woven with the threads of many men I've known, while others were cut from different bolts of cloth. If all were vibrant flesh and blood, is the collective vision false? I doubt it.

My desire is to show an atmosphere of living and of dying, of fear and hope. Napoleon perhaps said it best. "What is history, but a fable agreed upon."

Ted Garner's Prologue

Twenty-one-year-olds are pretty naive. It takes years to earn wisdom. They say we grow stronger at the broken places, but in the middle of the night another world calls to me. A world where the broken places still spike with pain, anger and resentment. These are places where time has not smoothed the wounds into rounded scars of resignation and acceptance.

I thought I was rushing into growth, hardening, learning lessons of ten thousand years of war. I learned pain is the handmaiden of compassion, but the knifing taught me knowledge is just a list of choices. Wisdom comes by deciding which to keep, which to throw, and which to ignore in peril of searing the soul. The choices haven't stopped. They never will. Maybe knowing that is wisdom in itself.

I always guessed that when I got to The Nam, I'd simply be added to a Special Forces unit as a new, but extra member. Damn I was proud of that beret. Still am. I didn't find out until later that I'd replaced a specific man on a specific team, who died a very specific death. Here it is. Someone told it, but please, you didn't hear it from me.

Begin

Rain dribbled to nothing. The jungle popped with glints of silver as thick leaves with sharp tips channeled quick runoff, preventing the growth of fungus. Water sluiced from crowns ninety feet up, to middle and then lower canopies, until finally soaking into a foot-thick carpet of mulch.

Popcorn clouds dropped half an inch of water, and the air sparkled as they rumbled west, whites and grays against cobalt blue. It was a brief shower in the highlands, unlike monsoons, clustering low for weeks on end later in the summer.

Scattered through the mulch, green lumps hugged boles of trees or nestled under brush; a fairy ring of ten toadstools squatted in sodden remains of yesteryear. The ring circled thirty feet across, and started moving.

Water, glistening in folds of ponchos, ran rivulets of shock down necks and crotches as they removed the cowled weather gear. After sitting through the shower for forty-five minutes, the heavy rubber trapped smells of sweat and rot. Surrounding jungle filled with a gauze of steamy evaporation.

Some pulled metal tubes out of pockets and reapplied paste, confident with long practice and consideration. Lighter green went to hollows of the eyes, offsetting darker shadows, while deep gray worked the shiny forehead, cheeks and nose, making the face a flattened mask to hide behind.

Hair plastered with oils and dirt, while three of the ten had six days' worth of growth on their faces, catching dissolving clumps of camo paste that later dribbled down their chests.

Ponchos went into the rucksacks, beneath extra magazines, grenades, cans of C-rations, extra water and a claymore. They stood up, shouldering the sixty-pound canvas bags, hands buckling and adjusting. Then, they considered the tall team leader, who pointed south along the hillside. One of the smaller ones flashed a red and gold-capped grin, then turned his back and headed out with the others in tow, all weapons at the ready.

They crept south for an hour, stopping every few minutes, listening, skirting both densely packed brush and great open cathedrals of trunks rising sixty feet to the first branch. Breezes high above rippled webs of shadows, but the wind couldn't penetrate deep where silence and heat made for labored breathing. Salt caked uniforms, and they attended canteens every half an hour.

Occasional clearings bloomed with sunlight, and the leader took notes on size and cover. Maps were marked. Several conferred, nodding. Then the line snaked off, staying with three-to-five-meter visibility.

In the late afternoon, a speed trail blocked the way. The point man motioned, and the leader came up, peering in both directions. It climbed left, turned at a clump of wait-a-minute vines, and was quickly lost. To the right, it descended for twenty meters, then dipped. He sensed steps cut into the hill.

The leader listened, nodded, and the point man crossed. Second and third Montagnards followed. Then the leader moved out with another small one right behind. The big radio man was next, but he hesitated. There were voices, and he pulled back.

Four Orientals dressed in green sauntered down the hill, laughing, relaxed, wearing similar canvas rucksacks, AK-47s slung muzzle down on their shoulders. Nonchalance jarred each step, making tire sandals slap staccato rhythms. "Flap, flap. Flap, flap." One puffed a home-rolled cigarette, acrid smoke from crude tobacco grown on thin soil.

The team was cut in half, and shakes built with the sweats. The leader tracked them with his weapon, releasing pent-up breath as they passed, grateful they took no notice of faint scuffmarks crossing the two-meter-wide trail. He motioned for McDaniels to cross. McDaniels nodded back and stepped out, avoiding dead bamboo, that even with the rain, if stepped on, crunched like broken glass.

He took three steps, and jumped at the sight of the new man rounding the corner uphill. They reacted at the same time, but McDaniels was also turning left, and was too late and knew it.

The eight-round burst rolled up and to his right: first caught his left hip, blowing out the ball socket and femoral artery (knowledge hit like the bullets, no pain), second was five inches up, left of his navel, taking parts of intestines and stomach, third was mid left in his lung, fourth missed his heart, but caught the aorta and blew out the spine, fifth was just right of his nose. The back of his head exploded like cherry soda. A sixth creased his skull, and then buried itself eight inches deep into bamboo dregs on the other side of the narrow ravine. The seventh and eighth rounds impacted higher up the hill. They weren't needed. The six that took him were all killers.

A peaceful death is seen as an unfolding process. Signs abound: labored breathing, glazed stare, cold skin, until it's surrendered to with a sensual release as life ebbs away, like a light dimmed with a rheostat.

Not so for a construction worker crushed in an instant by a mishandled five-ton slab of precast concrete, or a housewife in a V.W., broadsided by a drunk at seventy miles an hour in the intersection. The essence of Bill McDaniels was gone before he ever started falling.

Two weeks later in a base camp four miles west, the colonel presented Nguyen Tran with the Brave Killer of Americans award. The officer shook hands, calling him, "Comrade." Tran's wife's eyes shone as he held her close. Eight months later, they were both in turn obliterated by a B-52 Arc Light bombing run on the road. She thought she was pregnant, but hadn't told him yet.

1

Garner jumped awake as the C-130 cargo plane crossed a north to south ridgeline. The western wall of rock and trees baked in the late afternoon sun and the updraft lifted the plane a good ten feet. He'd been lightly dreaming, but couldn't remember what about.

He was sitting in a sling canvas seat, twenty or more feet long, strapped in with a shoulder harness. This was where paratroopers sat while approaching the drop zone. Then, as the tailgate lowered and the wind began its banshee howl, they'd unbuckle and stand at the order, "Stand Up." Then they'd hook parachute lanyards onto the overhead cable at the order of, "Hook up." Then, at "Go" both sides would shuffle to the back and step into the void, praying the men who packed the parachutes knew their jobs.

This time the belly of the C-130 cargo plane was loaded full, with crates and boxes stacked into six-foot cubes, wrapped tight with nylon bands. They marched back to back on their oversized pallets, on rollers in the floor, all the way down the length of the plane. More nylon bands strained against their moorings in the deck, as the engines roared and the aircraft canted down and to the left. The only light was what filtered back through the cockpit to the stairway and behind. A few red security bulbs, instrument and radio lights added to the sunlight coming through the windows in the side doors.

The Loadmaster sat at his station beside the short stairway to the elevated cockpit. He stood up, stretched his arms to steady himself between the piled supplies and the side of the plane, and then lurched back towards his only passenger on this milk run.

He yelled above the roar of the engines. "Garner! We'll be landing in Kontum in a couple minutes. Might want to brace yourself."

Garner yelled back, "Why?"

"Blackbird pilots are hotdogs. They always have plenty of runway, but they constantly pretend they're landing on short strips, in case of emergency. As soon as we touch down, Jim will reverse props and hit the brakes hard. Anything not nailed down gets thrown forward, ass over teakettle. Keep your harness on."

Garner gave a thumbs up. "Thanks."

The Loadmaster smiled again. "This your first tour?"

"Yah. Just got in country."

"Well, you look it. Who talked you into joining SOG?"

"No one. They just said there were slots open, and the job was interesting."

"Interesting? Didn't they tell you it was an all-volunteer unit?"

"Well, yah, but—"

"Hope you got a clean past. If you can't get top secret, we'll be flying your butt back to Nah Trang next month. You sure wouldn't catch me out there doing that kind of stuff."

"Doing what kind?"

The Loadmaster smiled again, then straightened. "Stay buckled up. I guess some guys will take you in when we unload." With that, he turned and wobbled his way back to the front of the plane, where he sat at his radio controls and strapped back in.

The C-130 lurched three more times as it dropped. The shift in Garner's belly increased. Then came a hard bounce and a squeal of rubber, tied in with an even greater engine roar as the props reversed. He was thrown left, into the restraints and pummeled against the seat's framework, as the plane slowed. Then it turned left, and the afternoon sun shifted angles through the windows, like prison spotlights probing the dark.

Momentum stopped, and the engines fell to an idle. The ramp at the back of the plane cracked open, and an eye-tingling brilliance flooded the cargo bay. Garner stood, gathered his duffel and laundry bags, and headed for the exit. Right behind him, the Loadmaster and his crew undid the straps for the last two bundles of supplies, and started breaking them down.

An army deuce and a half backed up to the ramp, and the two men in it initially ignored Garner as they jumped out and dropped the tailgate. Then one in civilian clothes yelled, "I'm Sergeant Jack Tone; this here is Bill Day." The other man in jungle greens gave him a quick nod as he walked up the ramp. Tone yelled, "Throw your bags up front and help us load this stuff. Now!"

Garner, being an E-4, did as he was told, helping Day, Tone, the Loadmaster and the other crew members unload supplies. Ammunition, both 7.62 and 5.56 caliber, C-rations, lots of C-rations, truck parts, movie reels, and fifteen thick waxed cardboard cartons brimming with ice under their covers, were piled in.

Finally, Day checked off on loaded material and jumped in the truck, starting it up with a roar. Tone climbed in, hacking a smoker's cough as he pitched the duffel and laundry bags into the back, on top of stacked C-rations. Garner was last in the open cab.

They lurched to the gate as the Blackbird headed to the runway and parts unknown. It turned from the tarmac, picking up speed as props edged out. Reddish dust billowed while it jumped to forward pull, and Garner watched over his right shoulder, as its wings caught lift and punched away from the swirling cloud behind.

Tone asked, "What's your name, poncho?"

"Garner, Sergeant! Spec. Four Ted Garner."

"Welcome to Kontum, Garner. We'll make your stay as pleasant as possible."

Garner watched him turn and give Day a broad wink.

Day wheeled toward the gate and gunned it as they approached a gaggle of Vietnamese children that had been watching the unloading. Garner gripped the dash as they picked up speed. Then his mouth dropped and he leaned away, as Tone reached beneath his red and blue madras shirt to pull out a .45 automatic pistol. "Here, I can't stand in the middle, take this," he said. "The dinks will climb all over the truck if Bill slows at the corner or has to stop. Take it!"

"Jesus." Garner looked dumbfounded as Day glanced over.

"He doesn't mean shoot 'em. Just fire in the air if they get on. Last month they boosted a carton of steaks. Pitched it over the side. Split wide open. The little bastards grabbed handfuls and ran like hell. Probably sold most on the black market in Kontum and took the rest home to momma san."

He took the pistol, and watched the back with eyes like saucers, as Day gunned through the crowd. Several older boys grabbed on when second gear popped out. Garner jumped, yelling, but Day goosed it back to second and powered into third. The boys dropped in the dust, cursing the rapidly disappearing Americans.

He breathed deeper, tremoring as he turned towards Tone who studied him with an evil-looking grin. He'd been had. Garner pushed the weapon sideways towards the other man, saying, "Take it," as he sat down.

Tone chuckled like a file rasping tin, and Garner studied the surrounding countryside, resolving to keep a stronger grip on himself. There were people here who would use unguarded moments against him.

"Those older ones are cowboys," Day said above the engine. "Most of 'em have a motorbike hidden someplace. Run in packs. GIs are okay sticking together, but going downtown unarmed is just asking to get stomped. They're wiry little bastards, and all have knives or pistols."

Garner took in the view. Shacks and paddies stretched wall to wall inside the four-mile-wide valley. The colors were fresh for him. Greens of every shade assaulted his eyes, and he remembered people talking about the colors of the Caribbean with blues of all ranges that could never be captured on film, let alone be described properly. It was a visual feast he guessed the others no longer savored.

They bounced along the pock-marked road, and Day swerved three times to miss two mopeds and an old French Citroën. "Jesus," Tone said, as he held the top of the windshield with a bloodless grip. "These people drive like they're playing bumper cars at the state fair. I've always wanted to turn the wheel right into them."

Day swung across traffic again, missing a girl on a water buffalo wandering off the side. "Did you just get in country?" he asked.

"Yah, three days ago."

"What made you choose Command and Control Central?"

"I don't know. Folks in Nah Trang said it would be interesting."

The other two laughed, and Day looked in his rearview mirror at the receding children. He was pensive for a second, and then glanced over with a smirk. "Yah, interesting. My former team sergeant, Howard Billings, is head NCO for Recon now, but I was with him seven months ago when he chased a truck loaded with NVA troops, pitched in a claymore and set it off. Blew the hell out of all of them. It gets interesting all right."

"Where in the hell—"

Day cut him off. "I take it you're out of Training Group at Fort Bragg?"

"Ahh. No, they stuck me with the Seventh Group just after graduation last August. I put in for transfer and finally got approval to get out of that nut house."

Day said, "Out of the frying pan so to speak. You know there aren't any slots other than Recon or A-Company open for new guys."

"Yah, I heard that in Nah Trang."

They came to the Dak Bla bridge, and traffic slowed. Up ahead to the right was a ten- or twelve-year-old black-haired girl, screaming in the road. Her water buffalo collapsed in the traces of a grossly overloaded cart, and it kicked its legs in feeble attempts to rise. Eyes glazed with heat stroke, and its shrunken hindquarters twitched as bluebottle flies swarmed around sores that the trace lines had worn in the animal's back.

They drove wide, passing as Vietnamese bridge guards pushed it to the side. One screamed, waving an automatic pistol, while the little girl searched for help wherever. Garner's eyes locked with hers, and saw the terror of a world collapsing. He wrenched away, studying the metal webbed bridge.

They rattled across, and he vaguely heard Tone's sarcastic comments that the guards looked like roosters, strutting in their tall boots. Down by the water, barbed wire enclosures protected the bridge supports, and Day said honking geese were the best defense against enemy sapper teams floating late at night. The trouble was, the human guards up top always eventually ate them.

Half a mile later Garner shook free of his thoughts, asking. "What do you guys do? Are you on Recon?"

Tone dropped his hand from the windshield. He stammered trying to find an answer. Then Day broke in with a laugh. "No, not any more. We're Crispy Critters. We're off Recon now. I'm the Recon gofer and Jack here gets to play with radios down in the commo bunker. We both quit last month."

Tone found his voice and bore in. "We ran hard and fast for over ten months. Put it in with the best of them. Billy and me were good Recon men."

"Whoa." Garner held hands up in mock surrender. "I just asked a question, Sergeant."

Tone settled back, chewing on his lower lip while staring straight ahead. Then he popped a warm beer and concentrated on it.

The driver glanced over. "Hey, Garner, you gotta understand something. Combat slots are primo here. It's the big stick. It's hard to quit and turn into a Rear Echelon MF overnight. Right, Jack?" He nudged the darker man so hard he jumped. "Lighten up. New guys don't know the score."

"People gotta learn to have respect," Tone mumbled.

"Jack, you take it too personal. Only the dead get automatic respect. Everyone alive has to earn it day by day.

"Ya see, Ted, when you start out, either with A-company or on Recon, fear is pushed down, and for a while it doesn't matter."

Tone said. "But it comes back later on. Man, it comes back hard, until it's the only thing to cope with."

"Yah. When all you think of is survival, then it's time to quit." Day said. "We did our stint. Now it's your turn."

"I guess, Sergeant Day. My turn."

Finally, Tone looked up and said, "Well, laddybuck, here's your new home."

As a military base it was not large by any measure, maybe thirty acres, half on each side of the road. Six rows of barbed-wire entanglements rippled around the compound, like waves from a stone dropped into a millpond. Peering from behind were flat-topped bunkers, side by side, staring out with gun slit eyes. Highway QL-14 pierced the camp like an arrow through an orange. It was a tactical weakness having the road run through the camp, but like many things in Vietnam, the CCC compound was a jury-rigged affair.

Four hundred feet from the forward wire they passed vendors' stands, shacks and girls. The crazy quilt buildings of stolen boards haphazardly nailed together sagged. Discarded C-ration boxes and split oilcans covered the sides. Tone waved and yelled to one of the girls outside. "Hey, *te te co*! Be back in forty minutes."

She looked about sixteen, wearing a white blouse and miniskirt as black and shiny as the hair falling to her waist. She smiled, waved back, and looked over her shoulder as she rolled her buttocks sensuously.

Tone laughed. "Man, if you want to get your ashes hauled, this is the place for it. Mama Nie over there at the Green Door cooks up some pretty mean soup too." He pointed to the left, where a garish green door hung loose.

Day added, "You got to get used to VN food in these places. Some of it tastes pretty good, but don't look at it. They cook up a lot of tripe. Bad water gives you worms too."

Garner shucked a tightening of the gut, and remembered chow halls at Fort Bragg with all the ice-cold milk you could drink.

"The girls here are pretty good, but they're young and small."

Garner laughed with the others as they passed. "I hope I don't get that horny."

"Oh you will, you will. Promise."

He smiled, looked straight ahead and turned silent.

They drove past the outside wire and the inner bunkers connected by serpentine trenches. The barbed wire turned inward, running along the road, making a woven corridor through camp. Guard posts and barricades were on the right, next to a tan truck with slab sides and slit windows.

"What the hell is that?"

Tone nodded, "Oh, that's an old French armored car. We've got another one on the south side of the compound, and use them to close the road at night. Of course there's guards and barricades and all added. They don't run, we just roll them out."

"Oh, will that plating stop an M-16 round?"

"Yah. They tested M-16 and Chicom 7.62, but .50 cal cuts it like cheese."

In the middle of the corridor, gates on both sides stood open, making an intersection. Day turned left, past a flagpole and a small assembly area. Fifty feet further, he completed the loop, grinding to a halt, facing a small wooden building. Chest-high sandbag fragmentation barriers stood six feet out from the door, and on the sidewall was a sign stating, Recon Company, Snowden Hall.

"Well, here you are. Welcome to CCC, Command and Control Central," said Day.

The eastern half of the camp reminded Garner of an Old West "circle the wagons" type layout. Buildings were one story, about twenty-four feet wide with chest-high cinder block walls. From there to the eaves, wooden posts were spaced every six feet with mosquito screening allowing any circulating breath of air to drop interior temperatures from broil all the way down to bake. Push out awnings lowered for rain, or the necessity to lock up.

He only saw the roof of a north perimeter building and half of the eastern one. Both were barracks, 150 feet long. Brown men loitered by doors punctuating every twelve feet. Closer in were smaller huts. "Photo Lab" was the sign on one, and a tall antenna on the other side announced the commo bunker. The larger building closer in had "TOC" (Tactical Operations Center) posted over the door, and farther down another read "Lt. Col. Frederick T. Anders. CCC Headquarters."

The jumbled buildings south of the assembly area angled different directions. He made out a motor pool, supply area, latrine and weapons cleaning station along the wire next to the road, but the other buildings were nondescript. Names of states like Kentucky, Hawaii, and Arkansas, were emblazoned above the doorways he could see. He guessed many others were hidden on the buildings farther back. All together, the gray and black no-nonsense look gave it the charm of a prison camp.

"Hey, let's go." Garner jumped, as Day stood by the front fender looking at him. "Get your duffel. I'll take you to the sergeant major. The CO is out for a week or so. Come on."

Tone walked away, calling over his shoulder, "Welcome aboard, Garner. I'm gonna grab a bite to eat. I got a hot date tonight. See you." Puffs of red dust floated in his wake.

"See you later, Sergeant Tone. Nice to meet you." Garner watched Tone walk off, while biting his lip at the shallow lie.

Day took him to the TOC, where the sergeant major skimmed his records, saying that it was too late to process in properly. Supply would shut down soon, and briefings for S-1, S-2 and S-3 simply took too long for time available. Instead, he sent Garner straight over to Recon for team assignment and a bunk for the night. He could finish up the next morning.

Day led him over to Recon, where they edged around the sandbag barrier and walked through the door after a quick knock. The windowless room was dim, and so cold Garner thought he saw his breath. To his left was a growling air conditioner. Beneath it, a water stain the shape of Florida glistened down the rippled plywood.

In the back was a closed door, and Communist weapons, AK-47s and SKS rifles, hung on the side walls. Otherwise, the room was bare, except for a bulletin board, a desk, and the dark-haired man rising from the chair behind it. He loomed large, menacing the little room as he reached out and shook Garner's hand.

Day made introductions to Sergeant Howard Billings, and got permission to off load the truck. "Good luck, Garner. Welcome aboard. I'll see you in the club." Day gave a thumbs up sign, while backing out. The Recon NCO was already examining the papers in Garner's record file.

"You're a day late. How come?"

"Well, Sergeant. I got into Cam Ranh Bay three days ago, but final detailing got delayed because of shortages in the grunt lines. There were rumors they were yanking SF qualified personnel, and sticking them with regular units." The thought turned Garner quiet.

Cam Ranh Bay was the main dispersal point for incoming soldiers, and it was known that prior orders for Special Forces personnel had been rescinded before, just so warm bodies could plug holes in regular combat units. It was the Army's version of Shanghaiing someone. Official requests could be made for transfer back to SF, but chances were slim, and a callous reshuffle like that was their worst nightmare come true.

"I came over with a guy I knew in Training Group, Bill Curlin. We sweated it out for a full day before they gave our papers back and granted clearance to report to the Fifth Group in Nah Trang."

He wouldn't admit they spent three agonizing hours over a bottle of bourbon, deciding what to do if their orders were changed. Nah Trang was just twenty miles north along the coast, and lights at night were close, calling for action, calling for them just to leave and show up at SF Headquarters, pleading stupidity.

But the decision never had to be made. Their orders came through and they reported in a day late.

"Where'd your friend go?" Billings's deep bass brought him back to the present, and he looked into the man's black eyes.

"To Command and Control South, down at Ban Me Thuot," he said.

"Damn. I'm still six men short, and losing eight more next month, if I'm lucky. Come on, I'll give you your briefing and then put you with a team."

Garner followed him through the back door. Billings was an imposing, seemingly self-assured man, and Garner had the feeling that his exploit with the claymore that Day mentioned was just one of many he could recount.

The briefing room was larger than the first, about twenty-four wide by thirty. Rows of chairs faced a low stage against the right-hand wall, which was covered by a map of South East Asia. There were no windows, but Garner's eyes locked onto an item in the very back.

It was a hand-painted insignia three feet high. A skull wearing a Green Beret grinned out with black eye sockets; its gaping mouth was filled with bloody fangs. Surrounding it, jagged rays of light extended outwards, like the sun exploding through broken clouds. Beneath the skull, a banner proclaimed MACV-SOG. At the top was a pair of Air Force wings, while at the bottom were the flukes of a Navy anchor. He stared at it, as Billings stepped to the platform and pointed at the map. Three small flag pins clustered in the middle, where chunks of terrain were blocked off with various colored pastels.

"We are part of the US Army Special Operations Augmentation Command and Control. This compound is Command and Control Central. C and C North is in Da Nang, and C and C South is down where your buddy went. Our mission is to gather intelligence on activities and strength of Communist troops in areas currently denied to regular United States forces. We have a—"

"Sergeant Billings?" A buck sergeant opened the door, poking his head through with an uncertain air.

"What is it, Hagland?'

"Papers, Sergeant, sorry to bother you, but Lieutenant Wilson at commo said to find you and have you look them over ASAP. Sorry, Sergeant."

Billings muttered while walking toward the door. Then he turned and glared, saying, "Stay put."

The back of his leathery neck bulged. It was worn and cracked from too much sun, like coffee at the bottom of a boiled-out pot. Garner turned to examine the map.

Borders of all countries, Laos, Cambodia, North and South Vietnam, China and Thailand were highlighted in red marker. Vietnam was a long sliver, curving down along the coast of the South China Sea, and contour lines showed that except for some isolated pockets, the southern half of the country was flat rice land.

However, eighty miles north of Saigon stood the crumbled ramparts of the Central Highland Mountains. Contours writhed and turned back upon themselves, with valleys and ravines cutting deep into the uplifted mass. Toward the middle was one of many brown blots marking a population center. It was labeled "Kontum," and Garner leaned in closer.

The Kontum valley was a wobbly spear of flat land jabbing ninety miles northeastward, into the heart of the high plateau's stumpy mountains. The tip began far north near Dak Pek, and was carved out by the rushing headwater stream called Krong Paka. The valley floor widened to a mile by the time it reached Dak Seang, twenty miles south.

Highway QL-14 ran along the east edge of the roiling water, and the valley grew out in a flare further south at Dak To, where three tributaries joined to wander the rare flat land strip. Rice paddies and vegetable fields crowded wall to wall, and deep sediments, improved by over two thousand years of human gardening, belied the poor soils of the surrounding jungled mountains.

Twenty miles south, Krong Paka joined the Dak Bla, coming from the east, around the southern edge of Kontum City. The valley exploded to four lush miles, and then continued another thirty, eventually emptying out on the open plains surrounding Pleiku, the focal trading area of the lower Central Highlands.

The river, however, lost its track before reaching Pleiku. Because of some secret buried deep within the geologic past, it broke out of its own valley, cutting westward through steep gorges, moving through Cambodia with the name of Se San, finally merging its waters with the great mother river of all South East Asia, the Mekong.

Down south, red borders separating Vietnam from Cambodia ran over flat land on arbitrary lines, or along rivers. Up north, the ridgelines of the higher Annamite Mountains separated the countries like a serrated knife. They squirmed along the tops of different watersheds, then plunged down valleys and up the other side. Laos was to the northwest and Cambodia was to the southwest. Less than thirty miles from where he stood was the meeting place of all three, the Tri Border.

Billings came back as Garner contemplated the flagged pins and the chunks of land that were colored different shades of orange, red and yellow. The twenty or so outlined areas fit together like a puzzle, and together, formed a long colorful comma that arched down through the Central Highlands to the Cambodian flats.

They were of various shapes, but all were about twenty-five square miles in size. Each had a one letter and a one number designation inked into the upper left hand corner, like India-Six, (I-6), or Juliet-Nine, (J-9). Finally it sank in, and Garner realized the target areas were west of the squiggly borders. Two pins were in Laos, and the third was in northern Cambodia.

He whispered, "Dear God," as hair began rising on the back of his neck.

"Garner, you've been granted an interim top secret clearance to receive this information."

He could see a faceless someone checking police files and asking discreet questions.

"Charlie has a web of road systems coming down from North Vietnam, through Laos and into Cambodia. This so-called Ho Chi Minh Trail allows them to constantly resupply the Viet Cong through numerous break off points, where materials are brought across the border.

"Both these countries are technically neutral, and deny that North Vietnamese troops control a thirty-mile strip all along their eastern edges. We can't send in full military for political reasons. However, our compound and two others like it, regularly penetrate this corridor with reconnaissance teams.

"Our mission is to gather information on supply and troop movements coming down the road. We also attack targets of opportunity as they're located, and bring back prisoners whenever possible. Other objectives are area recon, linear recon, point recon, bomb damage assessment, rescue of downed aircraft personnel, and destruction of those aircraft." He shifted away from the map.

"Teams are made up of three Americans and five to seven Montagnard tribesmen living here in the compound. For larger targets we have A-Company, with fifteen Americans and about a hundred Montagnards. Their mission is strictly for disruption and interdiction of enemy supply lines. They often go in on targets originally identified by Reconnaissance teams, which are just too small to exploit the opportunity.

"Sometimes the company goes in on high points overlooking the road, shooting up anything trying to squeeze through. Then, when the enemy gathers troops, we call in air power and lay waste to several square miles of jungle."

Garner's jaw was open in surprise. The US claimed no official missions existed. Excursions across the borders were blamed on soldiers who couldn't read their maps in such mountainous terrain. Down south in Cambodia, where it was mostly flat, there were few landmarks; so the official excuse makers in Washington had it both ways. Flat or hilly, American soldiers evidently couldn't read maps as competently as they did when they were Boy Scouts.

"We're in violation of some international agreements, just as the North Vietnamese are. However, this is how the real world works, Garner." Billings's black eyes bored in.

"I understand, Sergeant. Where am I assigned?"

Billings stepped to the listing chart on the opposite wall and ran a finger down. "You'll go on Team Iowa, with Lieutenant Larsen and Sergeant Dodge. They lost their radioman last week, and are first in line for replacement since Larsen is leaving soon."

"Lost, Sergeant?"

"Killed. Technically missing."

"Oh."

"Now, Garner." He turned back toward the map. "The code name for Laos is Prairie Fire, Cambodia is Salem House. Up until two months ago that name was Daniel Boone, but—" He turned, staring hard. "Some sonofabitch leaked that, along with details of operations, to *Newsweek* magazine. They wrote it up, and denials flew from here to Washington." Garner withered under the stare.

"Whoever dropped that information conducted a disloyal act. Do you understand me?" His voice rose as Garner nodded. "Anyone caught divulging information to unauthorized personnel without a need to know, will be thrown so far behind bars they'll feed him with a slingshot! A top secret clearance has responsibilities a soldier must accept. Let the politicians deal with the small print."

"Yes, Sergeant; no problem here."

"All right. A mission normally lasts seven to ten days, depending on target and objective. Once the team gets back, they get a week of stand down. That means you can do whatever you want, no formations, no police call, no physical training. If you can catch a ride on a Blackbird, we'll cut orders for a trip to Saigon, Taipei or Bangkok, so you get out for a while. After stand down, teams train every day except Sunday, until the next mission.

"Since we launch out of Dak To, twenty miles north of here, we maintain an emergency reaction team there, ready for immediate insertion in case another team gets in trouble. We rotate these teams once a week, and the code name for that duty is Bright Light. Any questions yet?"

Garner just stared. "Ahh, no, Sergeant."

"Good. The code for team leader is One Zero, the second in command is One One, and the radioman is One Two." He stood there looking at Garner, then stopped and straightened. "The colonel is in Saigon for the week, and Captain Simpson, the Recon CO, is in Pleiku. Come on, I'll turn you over to one of the members of your team. Leave everything here."

They approached a junior officer, a lieutenant, and Garner shot a stiff salute at him. He appeared startled, and then returned it while he regained composure and passed them by.

"Forget that." Billings said. "We don't salute here."

"What? We don't salute? Why not?"

"It gives Charlie a chance to spot officers and possibly snipe at them."

Garner glanced around, for the first time understanding no one was safe, not even in the center of their compound. Snipers abounded. The enemy was everywhere, but nowhere. He'd seen no violence, just the residue of fear.

"Sergeant, how long have we been going across the borders like this?"

"Since late sixty-five. Overall code name is Shining Brass, but that's not used much now."

"May I ask how long you've been doing this?"

Billings swiveled, looking cold and mechanical. "From near the beginning."

Unlike the courtyard effect of the east side, the western half had a handful of buildings crowding the gate. They crossed the road. A medical dispensary spread south on their left, but they turned right along a wooden walkway, toward a cluster of buildings added onto at different times. Chest-high sandbag fragmentation barriers stacked around everything, adding black accents to the gray, white, and tin silver buildings.

Finally, they turned left and entered a large screened room with sixty or so folding chairs facing a stage and movie screen in the far left corner. Immediately to the left was the entrance to the mess hall, and ahead was the door labeled "Club." They crossed between the chairs and stage that bulged out, and stopped before entering.

"One thing, Garner. We don't talk about missions in front of Vietnamese. We've got mechanics, barbers, truck drivers, hooch maids and bar maids all over the place. At least one in five is probably a VC sympathizer."

His eyes went wider. "Yes, Sergeant."

"Good."

They entered, and got hit by a wash of hoots from within. Garner waited for his night vision to adjust. He swept the paneled and red brick room, where a bar spread along the far left wall. It was twenty feet long, with mirrors and shelves behind. Glasses, mugs, and half-filled bottles glimmered in colored points of light.

Four-man tables filled the twenty-four by sixty-foot room, and straight across, a bright doorway announced a game area with pool and ping-pong tables. The Beach Boys played a tune off to the right on a battered multicolored jukebox.

In the middle, a crowd of twenty men clustered around tables, drinking, laughing and smoking. The very center held undulating forms, and as his eyes became accustomed to the dark, the shouts increased in pitch.

A laughing man was on the floor on his knees, masturbating a glassy-eyed German Shepherd. He yelled out, stroking faster as the dog jerked back and forth with its tongue hanging out. Finally, it convulsed and exploded in a milky ejaculation. The yells and drunken laughs were deafening, and several soldiers were chanting, "Go, Go, Mo Jo. Go, Go, Mo Jo."

The man stood up, yelling in triumph. Then he put out his left hand and collected money from most of those standing nearby, as they slapped his back and ordered more drinks from disgusted Vietnamese barmaids.

Then some saw Billings, and backed away.

"Whoa. Shut up. Back off." People yelled in all directions, until it spread that Billings was there. They jumped up and elbowed others into silence. The big man approached with Garner in tow.

"You like dogs, Dodge?" Billings roared.

Dodge was one rank below, a few years younger, and twenty pounds lighter. He took one step back, then stood his ground and flashed a drunken grin, but Garner could tell he was ready.

"I like winning money, Sergeant!" he yelled back. "They bet me I wouldn't do it, but you get the odds you like, you'll do damn near anything. At least I will!"

Billings's discomfort and temper visibly dwindled. Garner guessed he'd seen worse and probably done worse, but this was awkward, because he had to step in the middle and make introductions.

"This is, Spec. Four Garner, first name's Ted. He's your new radioman." His powerful left arm pulled Garner forward, until he stood five feet from Dodge in the center of the circle. Garner was an inch taller, but the other was a gristled boxer. Broad, well-muscled shoulders rolled under the shirt like boulders covered by rushing water, seldom seen, but always recognized by the power of their presence.

His hair was curly, and the strong nose canted to the right from a blow delivered long ago. Dodge was older, and the eccentric glint in his eyes complemented a twisted smile. Anyone who did what he'd just witnessed lived by a totally different set of rules. Billings was strong, square-jawed and hard, but Garner understood Dodge was the first erratically dangerous man he'd ever met.

The boxer smiled a toothy grin while stepping forward, raising his right hand to shake. It was the hand he'd jacked the dog off with, and the challenge was made.

Garner whispered to himself, "Oh God, you bastard."

He was caught. These were men he'd live with, and there was no time for other considerations. He groped momentarily for a way around, but there was none. He finally looked Dodge in the eye and stepped forward, taking the sticky hand in his right and squeezing with the same pressure he was given.

"Good to meet you, Garner. Hope you like Kontum."

Glued hands pumped up and down.

"I'm sure I will, Sergeant Dodge."

Dodge's eyes gleamed as the crowd started yelling and applauding. Even Billings stepped back, smiling. The Beach Boys played on, and Garner saw Sergeant Bill Day, standing in the background, drinking a beer and giving him a thumbs up sign.

2

First mission out was said to be two or three weeks away; it was enough time to learn fast-action drills, brush up on first aid, body carries, rappelling and marksmanship. It also gave him a chance to know the team and let them know him. Teams were tight, and he learned right off that confidence in abilities and character had to be established fast. People seldom risked their lives for strangers.

The death of Bill McDaniels two weeks before had cast a pall over the team. He found out that McDaniels was a favorite with the Yards, because when he was in school he'd been president of a Magicians Club, and had dazzled the simple tribesmen and their families by making coins disappear, or cards pop out of a deck.

For Dodge and Lieutenant Larsen, the hurt was more professional. North Vietnamese troops had come at them from both directions, and although Dodge and the last element of the team successfully crossed the trail, they couldn't retrieve the young American's body, or the main PRC-25 radio he carried. It was too open, and the firefight was just too strong.

They were chased by the better part of a company, and escaped two ambushes, coming out after finally using the emergency radio just before sunset. McDaniels had been in country for three months, and his body would never go home. That type of fate was a fear that all Recon members shared.

The Yards were five inches to a foot shorter than most Americans, with dark skin and raven hair. Many sported Beatle cuts, with bangs sweeping just above the eyes. Smiles were fresh and genuine, showing glints of gold or gaps of black. Garner learned the differences were many between the tribesmen and the wily Vietnamese.

Dominique, the interpreter, passed on instructions to the others in a halted fashion, but they all tried learning a little English, and everyone encouraged, helping out. At the same time, the Americans tried picking up Bahnar words and phrases. Jokes passed back and forth, but everyone depended on Dominique for better understanding of each other.

After four days, Garner began getting into the camp's daily rhythm. Morning formation, police call and physical training were over, and they walked back across the compound from the assembly area to pack equipment and load up. Now they were free to follow their scheduled day of training.

"You know last year for a time the idiots tried to have us run in formation up and down the road." Dodge said.

Garner didn't take the meaning.

"Yah. They had us out there running along, calling out the old dirty airborne cadences. It was like I was back in Jump School, by God."

"So?"

"So? So? Do you realize what a fat target a column of jogging, unarmed men would make for a sniper? Hell, a three-man ambush could take out twenty, if not the whole lot."

Garner got the point. "Jeez, Phil. I'm still not totally tied to it. I've been in country a week, and haven't even heard a shot fired, except at the range. What the hell happened?"

"Well, a couple of us kicked up a stink. We never ran far, just along the camp road and maybe a hundred yards either end, but someone would've gotten killed. Too tempting. Charlie came right up in the middle of the day, and took pot shots at guys on stand down who were catching rays in lounge chairs up on the bunkers. Charlie's gutsy, Ted. Don't ever underestimate him."

Larsen was at the team room, and they loaded up for training. As usual, packs were up to mission fullness. They strapped on pistol belts with flat suspenders. On the belts were two canteens of water at the kidneys, a coiled six-foot length of rope called a Swiss seat, with two D rings attached, and six antique Browning automatic rifle magazine pouches, three to either side of the center link buckle. Each held three M-16 magazines, eighteen rounds each, two below the maximum to keep from weakening the spring. Behind the neck where straps connected was a canister of blood expander. Front suspenders had two fragmentation grenades each; a knife was taped upside down on the upper left, and a strobe light on the upper right.

Rucksacks were loose, without a frame. Each held sleeping gear, an extra shirt, socks, a plastic ground cloth, seven days' rations, a claymore mine, machete, fuses, det cord, one stick of C-4 plastic explosive, one white phosphorous grenade, a cleaning rod, four full canteens, two hundred extra rounds of ammunition, bandages, and six more grenades, two smoke and four high explosive.

A signal mirror hung around the neck, along with a compass and OD neckerchief. Front pockets held pen flares, pen flashlights, maps, camo tubes, insect repellant, and dayglo colored signal panels. Side pockets had the small emergency radio, and someone always carried the camera and extra radio battery. Sixty pounds at least were carted around mountains with forty-five-degree inclines. Dog tags stayed in footlockers. No one wore them across the fence.

Garner cursed the weight, but Larsen demanded realistic training. If they had wounded, he wanted to know the strength of each. The new man always carried the main PRC-25 radio, 25 pounds of hell. Even after shifting materials to other members, Garner's pack still weighed much more than any other. They locked up and met the Yards at the truck.

The thirty-acre range was two miles south, along QL-14. Off on the eastern edge were three broken trucks and two helicopter bodies, which were used as props or targets depending on the day's training. Just south was the rotting sixty-foot tower, where teams, using ropes and gloves, climbed up and rappelled down, time and again.

This day they worked "fast-action" drills. They walked in file, with Whean on point, Kuiet next, then Phe and Larsen, Garner and Dominique the interpreter. Behind came Djuit, Dodge, Kui and Kehn. The radio and interpreter always stayed close to the team leader, the One Zero.

They patrolled east. Then Larsen shouted out a warning and blew his whistle, signaling retreat. The team unraveled like a zipper to either side, and the point man opened up, firing to the front with three- to four-round bursts. He fired empty, then turned, shuffling back through the split team, ejecting the magazine and ramming home a new one. The second man opened up as soon as the first cleared, then he also turned and ran. Each opened fire and retreated, until they turned the line of march inside out, and were heading in the opposite direction of the contact.

After lunch they practiced ambush to the side, one half of the team firing and leapfrogging backwards, under cover fire from the other half. Targets were set up so aim was always practiced with the movement. Otherwise, thousands of rounds were used for nothing more than sound effect.

By late afternoon they bundled in the truck, hot, wet, tired, and headed home. Larsen and Dominique sat up front. All others sprawled in back, and as they bounced along, Garner noticed several Yards putting extra ammunition bandoleers into cloth bags. "Phil? What are they doing?"

Djuit waved stop to the others, and looked at him with apprehension. Then the Montagnard looked to Dodge for what appeared to be guidance.

Dodge motioned with his left hand and said something in Bahnar. They went back to stuffing ammunition, as Dodge gave Garner a huge smile.

"They're not doing much, Ted. I let them take a little extra ammo out of the compound sometimes, so they can shoot monkeys and stuff like that. No big deal."

Garner started adding. "Phil, we're not supposed to do that and you know it. I count about sixteen hundred rounds stuffed in those sacks. That's not piddly-assed ammunition. What the hell's going on here?"

"Nothing, Ted, I swear. A lot of teams do it. It's not much. No one notices. Don't sweat it."

"Does Larsen know?"

"Why should he? Like I said, it's no big deal. Forget it. Trust me." He smiled with open-faced honesty, and motioned for the Yards to stop. Extra ammunition cases closed up tight, and Garner felt them staring at him.

They bounced along the road in silence. He fought to take his mind off what he saw, and wondered loosely if the road's cheap mix of asphalt was due to embezzlement of funds. Chunks of stone and tar stuck to the tires in the heat of the day.

"Hey, Ted, tell me, is the Seventh Group back at Bragg still a hell hole?"

"Pretty much. I thought when I got out of Training Group I'd go somewhere, do something interesting. All I got was KP twice a week or more! A bunch put in transfers for the Fifth Group in Nah Trang, but headquarters just sat on the requests. The Seventh wasn't letting anyone out." He felt tension in his neck start to loosen, and he relaxed a little.

"How'd you finally get out?"

The Yards sat in the back of the truck, talking to each other, quietly eyeing the half full ammunition cases.

"A bunch of us went to up Fort Belvoir for Advanced Engineering Training. Six weeks. One day a couple of us skipped class to find Mrs. Alcott at the Pentagon. We begged her to get out of Bragg."

Dodge looked startled, and said, "What? You've met Mrs. Alcott?"

She was a legend, a middle-aged goddess for soldiers of Special Forces. She was one of those lucky mistakes in governmental bureaucracy that comes along so seldom that affectionate stories of her achievements took on the aura of a personality cult.

"I wonder how they got a lady like her in charge of SF assignments. I've heard a lot of bigwigs get mad, but she's wedged in tight and tells them to take a hike."

It was understood that if a soldier made a reasonable plea, she'd sometimes help him out, and submarine the lower levels by approving a previously ignored transfer. That's what happened when Garner and four others worked through miles of corridors to her unpretentious office in the Pentagon's third ring. They stood there awkward, asking to get out of the spit and polish of Fort Bragg, and go to Vietnam.

Garner said, "A lot of guys would rather take chances over here, than stay in that nut house. We had half the class request the Fifth Group at graduation, and almost no one got it."

Dodge nodded, and the wind flecked his curly hair. "I know what you mean. This is my second tour, and I don't like the thought of going stateside next October." He sat with the rifle propped between his knees. He looked pensive while considering the blackened barrel.

"When you get stateside everything turns to garbage. It's the typical military attitude over there, 'Mind over matter, I don't mind and you don't matter.' Over here it's free, loose. You understand?"

"No, not really. I hear you, but I'm scared right now sitting in this truck. I heard there were three sniper incidents on the road last month. I don't know if the trade off's worth it." Garner examined Dodge's scuffed and calloused knuckles wrapped around the rifle's hand guard.

"It's worth it. At least it is to me. You want nuttiness at Bragg? Here's one I heard when I first got there a couple years ago. Back when Kennedy made the Green Beret official headgear for the forces, he made a special trip to Bragg, to review the troops and let them show off their stuff. The fort commander, the general, goes nuts, and has the place so clean they're using Brasso on the bottoms of garbage cans.

"Well, Bragg has got pine trees all over, you remember? The old man, who's not Special Forces mind you, takes one last review. He sees everything clean and tidy, and notices all the pinecones have been policed up. This he thinks does not look pretty and natural. So, he sends five hundred troops out into the woods, collecting pine cones to spread out under the trees at the fort."

"That's insane," said Garner.

"Yah, I know, but it proves a point doesn't it? Anyway, what's Mrs. Alcott like? I've never run across anyone who's met her."

"Well, I guess she's about forty. It's hard to tell those things."

"Yah."

"She's thin, good looking, and what got me was she was nice to us. I didn't expect that. I couldn't believe we even found her."

Garner had heard a lot about Norma Alcott. She had a GS 14 ranking, and was as Dodge put it, wedged in tight. The rumor was that she couldn't figure why so many bright good-looking boys wanted to go to Vietnam and get shot at. Eleven months total training went into these soldiers. When they made their way to her office seeking help, Garner had heard she was impressed with the initiative and personally flattered with their attentions.

Each was a volunteer, and most of the new ones had some college. Requests for Vietnam came in a steady stream, and she was sure it all had more to do with a foggy grasp of dangers involved, rather than a desire to defend Vietnam. Rumor said she considered them all her boys, either running to or from something. She would try to help.

Garner knew most were short timers, like himself, and wouldn't reenlist. The new ones were good quality, but he also knew to career Special Forces members, they represented a debasement of the Green Beret they wore with unimaginable pride. For them, Special Forces was a career goal, not something to be given to someone who was in for just three years. It was a small, very elite unit. But, with the buildup in Vietnam, the role of SF expanded, and more members had to be recruited. He knew old timers didn't like it much.

Training Group Cadre visited Airborne units or Airborne Infantry Training groups throughout America. Garner's was at Fort Gordon Georgia at a small camp in the woods called Camp Crockett, where he heard speeches, inviting all soldiers to take a battery of tests. About five percent passed.

Even at those levels, Training Group swelled with new recruits, and a double class system emerged. It was not hostile nor totally open, but the old guard was on one side, and the short timers were on the other. Mrs. Alcott knew all this, and within three weeks Garner and four others who went to the Pentagon, had their orders for Vietnam.

The truck rumbled north. They passed the wire, the bunkers, the second armored car, and Larsen turned right into the Recon half of camp, stopping briefly as the others rolled out. Then he drove on to turn in the vehicle.

The end of each day was like the beginning in that it was steeped in its own more informal rituals. When teams came in, the Yards cut loose to eat and drink in their own club, or possibly go home if families lived nearby. Since the Americans didn't have the luxury of going home, they were restricted by curfew, and only had the options to eat and drink.

Each Saturday they grilled steaks outdoors, and every night they had a movie. Bar maids shuffled constantly between the theater and the club.

Garner learned that Special Forces camps found collective ways around, through, and over problems. Networks of trade were extensive, and they took pride in being the masters of scrounge. They had odd, sometimes horrifying duties, but they ate steak on Saturdays, played pool, watched *Star Trek* on T.V., enjoyed hot showers, used indoor toilets, and slept in air conditioning. Not many true combat units could make similar claims.

3

The next day was Sunday, no formation, so Garner overslept, working off the accumulated stress of the prior week coming in. By noon he was in the mess hall for lunch, and recrossed the compound when finished, fully intent on going back to bed. However, as he entered the eastern gates he noticed a pick-up basketball game by the Recon head shed, just south of the assembly area. The rotting backboard held a netless hoop.

There were no official lines to call bounds on, just dust. If there had been any, they would have only added grist to the constantly churning mill of arguments roiling around the court. Besides, everyone understood generally what was in and what was out, but everything else was open for discussion, especially the fouls. At any given time, a game was on between Shirts and Skins.

Shouts increased as they neared, and Garner searched for the few faces he recognized. Overall, the people he'd met were friendly, and he breathed easier once getting past the initial assault of quick handshakes and smiles. Nicknames like Troll, Red Devil, Stinky, Snake, Squirrel, Hammer and Zoomer, added to the confusion. All too often, the name and face just couldn't come together. Not yet.

He'd met Lieutenant Larsen the second day in camp. He was twenty-six, from Eagan, Minnesota, a six-foot-two-inch Norwegian, whose parents got off the boat in 1939. They had thick Scandinavian accents that Dodge called "hurdy-gurdy," and their son trailed a small lilt in his voice, hinting at the Nordic heritage.

Garner hadn't met the colonel though. He was still down in Saigon, and wouldn't be back until the next day. They said he wanted to shake hands with every new member, and Billings growled he'd set up a meeting as soon as the Old Man's time was clear.

He headed for the team room as a voice called out behind. "Hey, Garner, how about some B-ball. Jackson's gonna wuss out and go clean up. We need another shirt out here."

Sergeant Jackson was walking off, and shouted back. "Day! Who you callin' names, boy? I'll get your young ass out here an whip it one on one. I'll run you ragged round this court, boy." The black man's teeth glittered porcelain white through a liquid, laughing smile that held nothing but affection for the curly blond-haired man.

"Tell me. Tell me, Jackson. I'm from Kentucky, and they play hard B-ball down there."

"Bull! You from Saint Louis, you peckerwood."

"Yah, but I was born and played in Louisville, and that's serious basketball country."

"Well I'm from Philadelphia, an' they got a hoop on every corner, an' I been—"

"Knock it off!" yelled Tone, the only other player that Garner knew. "Get out here and play one on one sometime. We got a game now. You wanna play? Get to know some of the guys."

"Ah, yah."

"Do you want to play?"

"Yah, yah, sure, sure. He skittered to the side, dropped the jungle jacket, but kept his olive drab T-shirt. It was four on four, and everyone was antsy to get on with it. He turned around, and jumped as Tone pitched the ball hard into his stomach from ten feet away.

"Take it in. Come on. Let's go."

He did, and the game was on. The other Shirts were Day, a tall boy about six foot four, evidently named Jones from the surrounding yells, and another shorter man about thirty, who he recognized as a helicopter pilot with the 57th Assault Helicopter Company. He thought he heard someone call him, "Sir."

They played rough, and he got chewed out three times for having the ball batted away. It was like the earlier games, but it still took awhile to catch on to the higher level of aggressive play. He drove in, passed off, bullied under the basket, pulled a pass from Jones and flipped it in.

The Skins were ahead by eight, but the gap was closing. Everyone soaked in sweat, and since of course there was no clock, they'd play until dropping dead tired. It was understood.

Tone passed to a tall Skin: dark haired, awkward kid. He could barely dribble, so he stood post-like in the middle, passing and shooting. He was a good shot. The other two were smaller, five-six to five-eight, but they were built like darting fireplugs. He remembered fast moving guards in high school, who were great shots but far too short for college play. The awkward center might make it, but greater talents of the other two could never overcome the handicap of height.

Both the small ones were bona fide jocks, even though at least fifteen years separated them. They were all over Garner, and the holding, slapping, stripping of the ball was part of their game, but not his.

He blocked a pass from Tone, popped the ball and dribbled three times, as the older jock's right hand came down, hammering his wrist. He fell on his knees grappling for the ball, and came back up covered with caked dust, half swinging at the smaller man.

"Goddammit, stop fouling me, you sonofabitch!" He took two steps toward the shocked player as the dust swirled.

"Sorry!" he said. "I play rough ball."

The others stood straight, in dead silence. Dust settled. Then things went fuzzy with sensory overload as they all began babbling at once. Six arms grabbed, turning him from face to angry face, as all the words of the English language seemed to fall on the court in a jumbled clump.

Through the fog he heard bits, pieces, "dumb sonofa," "stupid," "didn't know," "new guy." The word "sorry" pierced the verbal fog rhythmically, like a string of ducks popping up at a shooting gallery. Finally, it hit when he picked up the word, "Colonel." Then his vision retreated, and it sounded like they were yelling at him down a long tube.

He whispered, "Dear God in heaven, he's back a day early. I'm a dead man."

It was slow motion, looking over shoulders, past flapping mouths, and across sweaty backs of those talking earnestly to the startled jock ten feet away. The older man looked up, their eyes clicked, and he knew he was dead meat ready for 358 days of KP or burning crap in a barrel.

The small hard man cut through them all and stood before Garner, ready to start chopping. Instead, he smiled, put out his hand and said, "You must be the Garner Billings told me about."

"Ahh, ahh, Yesssir, Yesssir." He took the hand and was afraid to squeeze.

"Come on, boy. I won't bite."

He squeezed.

"Men." Hands dropped, and the smaller man turned to the clustered circle. "He didn't know who I was, so I can't be mad. I play hard basketball, and when I strip off that shirt the rank goes with it. I'll kick the butt of anyone who plays like a pansy because they're scared of me. Anywhere else, I'm a lieutenant colonel, but I've told you boys before, out here I'm just another player. At least within reason." He turned and winked at Garner. "I can't go around getting decked by my troops. Besides, you were right. I fouled you badly."

Garner began incoherent apologies, but was stopped with an upraised palm. Heart palpitations eased, and peripheral vision came back as his hearing cleared. Finally, almost with an audible "click" in his head, he was back, watching the older man chitchat his leave from the embarrassing situation. The colonel finally said it was time he went and cleaned up.

By the time the Old Man turned the corner, Garner was being pummeled with good-natured blows and harsh whispers of, "jackass," "lucky ass," "dumb bastard," and so on. Of course he was all such things, especially "lucky" since he now learned that Lt. Col. Frederick T. Anders was a rare Field Grade who was considered by his men to be a "damned good troop."

Garner learned a lot about him right there and then, from the others. He was about five-eight, youngish mid-forties with silver hair swept back. If he had a look that some called haggard it was because he was a mustang who served as a Marine NCO in World War II. He was wired tight as a banjo string.

Garner understood the speech under the backboard wasn't hollow. What he'd said to Garner he'd said to others, and meant it. Anders cut the line and never blurred the edges of the cut. He had an eye for quality and an ear that went clear down to his soul. Like Jackson said once, "The dude has class."

He'd been out of the service since '45, but came into the old brown boot army in '54, as a second lieutenant. He became Airborne qualified in '55, and worked his way up. Making lieutenant colonel was a surprise, considering he wasn't a ring knocker from the good ol' boy network of West Point. Full colonel was out of the question, since he didn't have a high-ranking mentor to pull/push him along treacherous political pathways, but the rumor was that he had second thoughts when he was assigned to CCC.

Before then, the compound was designated FOB Two (Forward Observation Base). It was subordinate under CCN out of Da Nang, and the highest-ranking officer had been a major. With Anders's assignment, the compound became free standing, and maintained its own priorities equal to the others. It was his first Special Forces assignment, and he visibly glowed with the challenge while walking the camp. The paradox was that it was considered a Special Forces assignment, even though it really wasn't.

The men of Command and Control Central were from the Fifth Special Forces Group, but headquarters in Nah Trang did not issue mission orders or have anything to do with running the compound. The soldiers were instead on temporary duty status with Studies and Observations Group out of Saigon, SOG, and their intelligence data was mingled with other splinters of that organization. Every Saturday morning, the bull colonel in charge of the overall unit spent an hour briefing General Westmoreland, and with the later change over, General Abrams.

Garner had been trained for the normal Special Forces mission, going into rural areas largely ignored by the Vietnamese government. These areas were prime targets for Viet Cong recruitment, because the government's grip was as weak as the people's loyalty.

Teams set up camps and helped the locals, always espousing support for the Saigon government so very far away. They built schools, hospitals, and homes. They designed sanitation facilities, taught personal hygiene, brought in electricity, captured springs, and dug wells. They formed villagers into military units that patrolled the countryside, stopping confiscations of rice and other staples by the Viet Cong.

They provided frontline public relations for the government, and thereby stopped many Vietnamese from joining the enemy. They also suppressed rebellion among half a million Montagnards in the Central Highlands, who hated the Vietnamese.

The Yards were loyal to Special Forces, because the Americans treated their religions, their women and their lifestyles with genuine respect and affection. Many men wearing the Green Beret also wore Montagnard friendship bracelets, or even more importantly and much more rarely, the loincloth of an initiated tribal member.

SOG, however, was not involved with winning hearts and minds of people. Treating native populations with respect was a basic tenet of all Special Forces training, but the fundamental mission of SOG was to gather intelligence information. They didn't dig wells. They ran Recon.

The colonel came in just six weeks before Garner, and people said half that time he walked the compound with a grin. He was proud to command men he called Sneaky Petes, and his good mood surrounded him like a mist for most of the year.

The men watched for signs. Lifers smelled out officer qualities right away, but Anders confused them. He was tough to read, and they'd never believe that to get answers, all they had to do was ask questions. Like a stiff shot of bourbon, he was straight up.

Short timers took to him right on. The lifers, having been betrayed before by other commands, kicked back and watched. But Garner didn't need to watch. He'd skated whispers of ice, and crossed a freezing void that could have swallowed and drowned him. If the colonel said, "Charge," the only question he'd ask would be, "What direction?"

4

On mission day they boarded two helicopters on the pad outside camp, and flew north along the river to the launch site at Dak To. The crews were with the 57th Assault Helicopter Company stationed at Camp Holloway down at Pleiku. Every morning, six Hueys and two "Pink Panther" Cobras blew in and picked up teams.

The turbine's roar mingled with the "whop, whop, whop" of the swirling blades overhead, making any kind of normal speech impossible. Instructions or observations had to be screamed from one man to another.

Garner marveled at the panel full of round dials facing the pilots, informing them of every condition of their ship. Door gunners' flight suits snapped in the wind, as half the team sat on the floor Indian fashion, cradling weapons, squinting at changing patterns of the young sun as it burned off upper wisps of fog, leaving thicker mantles below.

Mountains surfaced in receding layers to an indefinite horizon, like the staggered humps of a thousand dragons swimming lazy through a misty sea. As they flew four thousand feet above the highlands on a February morning, he puffed his own dragon breaths at the monsters below, and shivered while leaning out to track the valley.

It lay flat and green, split by the mahogany river that webbed and twisted wide, but five miles north, it narrowed and the hills closed in. Two years before, one of the most vicious battles of the war had been waged here. The Battle of the Highlands lasted from June until December 1967, and the 173rd Airborne Brigade fought hardened NVA troops time and time again, earning the Presidential Unit Citation for bravery.

Intelligence figured many thousands of NVA were killed with round-the-clock bombings, but bodies were frustratingly hard to find. Finally, Charlie simply left the fight. Where they went no one knew for sure, but the guess was back across the fence, to lick their wounds.

The only thing certain was they'd never been back in full strength. Surrounding hills were full of roving bands, but they'd failed at set piece battle, and now concentrated on stealth and ambush.

Unlike Kontum, the Dak To airfield was right in the middle of a military base. It was secure, and the CCC compound of three buildings and some bunkers, bubbled like a blister on the west edge of the airfield, was hemmed in on three sides with barbed wire.

A ten by sixteen-foot radio shack ran east and west with two open doors on the south side. It was loaded with radios, maps, C-rations, extra supplies, water cans and equipment. Inside, along the side wall, was a cot for the regular radioman, who monitored calls and relayed command information back and forth from the decision makers at CCC in Kontum.

The middle building was a twenty by thirty-foot barracks for the Bright Light team. It formed a western wall, and cordoned off a small assembly area. Then there was a roofed tower just south by the strip, loaded with equipment. It was large and squat, and closed in the little compound.

Posted signs on a thin wire barrier restricted the area, and although it was in the middle of a base, the buildings were isolated and alone. They flew along the runway, and Garner wondered what the surrounding grunts thought about the choppers constantly flying westward, toward the nearby border.

They landed along the edge, and the team unfolded, waving and smiling while crossing small bridges over empty drainage ditches. In the wet season, those ditches would be full, breeding mosquitoes. They gathered in the assembly area, where Larsen had them line packs and web gear against the barracks wall. Then he and Dodge went to the radio shack to get an update on weather, fuel, and the location of the small airplane they'd need as a spotter and radio relay during insertion. All Forward Air Control planes were simply known as "Covey."

"Hey, Garner, going in to break your cherry, huh?"

Danny Dravos on Team Texas came out of the barracks, scratching his head and yawning. He walked up, stripped to the waist, holding a steel helmet full of water in one hand. The other had a razor and a miniature can of cream he was using to scratch the top of his head with.

"Yah, Dan, they figured three weeks of day training and night drinking was enough orientation for anyone. No more slacking. Time to earn the pay."

Dravos gave half a smile and wandered to the tower, where he squatted in the shadows and began shaving.

Garner caught them coming out. "What's up, Sir?"

"The Covey, Broken Bottle, four, two, eight, says he'll be on station in thirty minutes, and we might as well meet him there. Looks good for insertion now."

They walked back to the equipment, and were shouldering web gear and packs as the turbines started building. Garner thought of the tractor on grandpa's farm, and the starter kicking in and out, until the first of four cylinders caught, burping a belch of soot. Then more cracked the lethargy of under use, blowing out carbon until everything sat there, purring in a mechanical mess, making him wonder why it didn't fly apart.

In seconds the turbines were up to force, and snapping blades brought him back, "whop, whop, whop." They crouched, trudging to the ships, boarding awkwardly under the weight. Texas was out in force, yelling and waving. Dravos caught Garner's eye, gave him a wink, and then started buttoning his jungle shirt.

The ride was fifty minutes to the northwest, and Garner enjoyed it the best he could. Side doors lay open in the freezing cold. This was real time. No more practice. He shivered, and examined the green velour stretching forever north. Then he closed his eyes, breathing deep into his hands, keeping hyperventilation at bay. He felt the shift and drop that caught him in the bowels and throat.

They canted down, and he held on as the gunner motioned to Larsen across the deck, on the inside of the spiral. Garner marveled at two full 360-degree descending views, before skittering straight above the trees. The transformation was a miracle. High concepts of color distorted, becoming ones of texture, which in turn mutated into reality, where trees and brush snapped past with jagged tops.

The Hueys carrying the team were the only ones to drop. The other four Gladiator crews stayed high and circled. Two were replacements in case of a downed aircraft, and the other two vectored direction and distance to the LZ (landing zone). The insertion helicopters skimmed above the trees, taking direction from those above.

Looking ahead, Garner saw a break in a small valley, a hole with long grass and brush. There was no reason for its existence that he could see, but there it was, large enough for the Hueys to come in side by side. Then he noticed the second one come up and fly parallel. Dodge was in the door with Djuit, smiling big, thumbs up. They slowed and dipped again, dropping to the bottom of the kettle, while "Pink Panther" Cobra gun ships scoured the sides, prepared to fire, but it was clean, no muzzle flashes, no people. They hovered down, and Garner jumped with others, into three feet of soggy grass. It was a spring seepage, and larger trees wouldn't hold. He steadied against the skid and pulled his feet through the bog.

They wallowed to the side as the chattering Hueys lifted. Then the team moved two hundred meters to the west and sat in silence, listening to them circle far off south. After ten minutes, Larsen was satisfied, and signaled "Good day" on the radio to Covey. The Hueys and Cobra guards swung around in one more circle, and then began heading back to Dak To. They were on their own.

The target was Juliet-Nine, a twenty-square-mile area that Dodge described as being as hot and edgy as a woman's temper. Besides roads passing through, there were at least two battalion-sized staging areas, supply depots, three suspected truck parks, and two fuel dumps. Charlie repeatedly used and abandoned facilities up and down the trail, since overstaying any site invited discovery by the teams and destruction from the air. That's why some targets grew hot and then went cold. Everything rotated, except Juliet-Nine. It always seemed hot.

It was an area recon, and they were in the southeast corner of the target. Ridgelines ran primarily north and south, and one road was on the western side. Larsen said they'd head north, and then come back through the middle, and head north again along the western edge, like the letter S tipped over. Two days on each leg should be enough. He motioned up, and Whean headed out.

They moved at a pace that averaged one step every two seconds, placing feet with care, watchful of making noise, while swinging their heads side to side, looking, smelling, listening. Weapons pointed forward, slung over outside shoulders, taking the weight. Every few minutes they stopped, specifically to listen to the sounds of the jungle, for thirty seconds.

Waxy, dark green leaves added to the sense of weight and silence. Garner thought of home, of the reds of autumn and lime greens of spring. He found no such captivation here. Seasons were defined by rains, and only slightly by the cold. The jungle was old and hoary, full of secrets. He wondered why the colors of the mountains and fields hit him so hard that first day on the road into camp, and then realized that fear had not been a factor in that observation. He gripped the weapon tight, until the long noonday break.

They sat in a circle, facing half in. C-rations were dug out and the packs reslung, used as backrests while settling down to eat. Folding can openers grated, and they were fast spooning ham, turkey or some other pressed and mutilated meat that long ago lost any nutritional benefits. They ate for bulk, to stave off hunger.

Others looked perfectly at ease, but Garner fumbled with the P-38 opener, spilling turkey juice down his open collar. It mingled with his sweat, and disappeared beneath the shirt. After whispering a curse, Dodge looked up.

"Hey, Ted," he whispered. "How do you like it on the ground so far?" He was working on a pasty-looking cracker.

"I don't know yet. Ask me when we're out. I'll say this though, it's depressing as hell in here, claustrophobic. I thought it would be beautiful."

"Don't worry. It's in your mind. It is beautiful. First time out, it kind of gets to you. Later, it all changes. Trust me!"

"I'm settling in okay." Garner willed his hand still, and ate the rest of the C-can only when no one was looking.

Cans were repacked, and spoons licked clean and stored. They listened for twenty minutes, reported in by radio, and finally dozed for forty minutes. Then they were up and moving, making sure no evidence was left of their stop.

The afternoon wore old, and they crossed three east–west footpaths. The fourth one wasn't noticed as they took a later break. As usual, they sat in a circle, and after twenty minutes, Larsen motioned up. Whean stood, then froze, and started waving back and down with his left hand, like he was patting a child on the head. He slumped, and others stiffened, lowering in response.

Garner searched face to face, his heart pounding in his ears like water surging through pipes. He panicked and couldn't hear, but Dodge's face was fixed and staring forward, telling all there was to know.

Twenty meters north were bobbing heads and helmets, moving left to right, up the ridge toward the border. They flickered among the leaves, branches and dappled shadows, and he cursed not applying more paste on the break. He shuddered lower, gripping his weapon, and then instinctively started counting: sixteen, seventeen, eighteen. It stopped at fifty-five.

Then came bicycles, one man each side, pushing and pulling the heavily burdened but unseen vehicles up the hill. Twenty-two in all were grunting and struggling with the loads. Some called out and cursed. Others laughed, and banter passed around. They were at home, and as Garner's hearing cleared, he understood their secrecy was still intact.

The passing company looked to either side in idle curiosity, searching for different plants or things that moved. Fresh meat was always a consideration. Garner felt vacant stares gliding over him, unhurried and unknowing, leaving an ooze of fear that grew with every sweep. He squeezed his eyes to hide the corner whites, but dared not look away. If eyes caught and locked, then only timing could save his life.

They all squatted reptilian still, and he felt hyperventilation building. He panted, overfeeding lungs with oxygen, but he couldn't stop and couldn't move. What if they should hear? The thought screamed at him. Eyes watered, and he grew dizzy trying to control his breath.

Then they were gone, disappearing like the narrowing tail of a snake in the foliage. He slumped with the others, all of them panting, as if finishing an easy mile run. They settled back, collected themselves, and listened for ten more minutes before finally crossing like the shadows.

The next day, continuing north, they crossed the ridge when it turned and swept west. Then they moved down the other side to the valley bottom, where the stream raced and another trail hugged close. They crossed and climbed again, finding abandoned bunkers on the northern hill. Fire beds held charcoal undissolved by rain, or covered by leaves and trash. Paths were packed and clear.

After taking pictures and moving on, Garner remembered the father of a girl from high school. A boy soldier of the Wehrmacht who told him, in broken English tinged with Scotch, that they could tell how far away Russians were by the warmth of their shit in the snow. The mother stood embarrassed, chiding. The father groped for someone to tell old tales to, laugh with, and understand. Garner drank it up in fascinated silence while the girl waited, turning mean.

The third day, after checking maps, they headed west for an hour. Explosions far to the south broke the silence. They were mixed and overlapped, like muffled thunder behind a bank of clouds. Larsen whispered into the radio, and mouthed "A-Company" to the others. Right before the noonday stop, they turned southwest on the first curve of the search.

Noon sit-rep was nothing much, and they crossed three trails in two hours. Then they were back into the connecting valley found the day before, fording the fast stream, crossing the main trail and moving up the other side. Halfway up the hill it started.

Whean was the first to spot the problem. They climbed a steep incline and found a wooded ledge ninety feet wide, like God's own seat on the side of the mountain. Cliffs fell into the valley on the right. The ledge ran down the ridgeline, and after a quarter mile, they came up to the backs of some huts, and smelled the cooking rice too late. They froze and backed away, then froze again as a man walked toward them from between the crude buildings. He fiddled with his fly, paused, let the stream go, then looked up, registering horror as he stopped up short.

Whean brought a finger to his lips. A prisoner was welcomed any time, but the man broke away, screaming, and was shot by the first four members of the team. Two others turned the corners, armed, and were also shot. Then Larsen motioned forward, and they skirted left of the huts, keeping their backs against the mountain wall.

It was a rice depot, but there was no time to destroy it. Alarms were sounding down below, so they hurried on. Yells increased, and as they passed, Garner eyed the crumpled men, grateful he was too far back to fire.

Reinforcements surged in, finding strewn bodies and the careless trail left by the running team. The track was on. Thick jungles never allowed a team to literally run. A fast walk was more like it, increasing to a trot when foliage opened up. Trade offs were always the same. Faster movement made for greater noise and a sloppier, more easily followed, trail behind. Stealth and silence, eyes and ears, were what the business was all about. No one but the crazy ones wanted combat.

Larsen gave instructions, and Garner whispered into the hand mike as he trotted. "Leghorn, Leghorn, this is Operation Blackjack. Blackjack. Over."

The reply came back. "Ah, roger, Blackjack. This is Leghorn, read you five by. What can we do for yah, partner? Over."

"Leghorn, this is Blackjack, we need an extraction. We have a Prairie Fire emergency. Over."

"Ah, roger that, Blackjack. Will contact Dusty for permission and call ya back. Over."

The team moved south along the ledge, and knew they had to leave it, so Whean took a faint path heading south-west, down the rock face. Roads and trails coursed everywhere in the jungle. A team on the run never moved continuously in one direction, otherwise they'd be flanked, and stumble into an ambush along their line of march. Unpredictability was essential to survival on the run.

"Ah, Blackjack, Blackjack, this is Leghorn. Over?"

"This is Blackjack. Talk to me, Leghorn. Over."

"Ah, Blackjack, Dusty says if you don't have wounded, you're supposed to break contact and continue the mission. Sorry about that. Over."

"What?" Garner motioned, and Larsen slowed up to listen in. Leghorn repeated the message as Larsen's eyes went wide.

His whisper exploded. "Did you tell 'em we've got people on our trail? They were yelling and screaming at us just twenty minutes ago. Over."

"Look, Blackjack, I told them, and they told me to tell you to lose them. You've only been out three days. Do you know how much an insertion and extraction costs? Over." No one ever stayed more than four days in Juliet-Nine.

The map showed general roads, but it couldn't pinpoint all the trails wandering through the woods. They headed south and west in a saw-toothed pattern, changing directions every three hundred meters. The ledge above petered out, and they ran along the side of the mountain. They did not want to back up against the road, which was further west, so an hour later they did a complete twist, and headed east, up the ridge, to get lost. After two hours, they took a break to listen, and forty minutes later they heard it.

Garner whispered, "What do you think it is, Sir?"

It was infrequent, staccato, and high pitched.

"Maybe apes?" Suggested Dodge.

Larsen searched a middle distance with his ear, looking off into space. "Nah, they scream constantly when they get shot up or scared. This is on and off. Kind of—" Then Larsen snapped up, and the Yards turned towards him with eyes wide. He turned to the center, shaken.

"Jesus, I shoulda picked it up. I heard them do this once with bears way up by Duluth one time. Never thought I'd hear it here. We've got dogs on our trail."

The others rocked back, now listening with a reference point. The sounds came again, far off.

Dodge said, "Wait a minute. There are things called barking deer over here. I've heard them. They've got a mating call that sounds like a dog. Besides, these jungles have all sorts of other weird-sounding animals. What about the 'fuck you' lizards and the peacocks, and the apes."

Everyone sat back and listened once again. The sounds continued growing louder, and Dodge said, "Oh, no." They were the bays of large lop-eared hounds, hot on a trail.

Everyone rolled to the side, staggering with the weight. Larsen motioned east, and Whean started moving out when Dodge signaled stop, and looked to Larsen for permission. He got a nod, threw off his pack and dug out an unrigged claymore mine.

He ran back where they entered the rest area, and began looping a green trip wire between two saplings. He pulled folding legs down, aimed the device along the back trail and set it firmly in the mulch. Next, the blasting cap and trigger assembly were inserted, and the trip wire pulled snug, just five inches off the ground. When all was set, he covered it with leaves, reslung his pack, and moved out with the others. Their back trail was all but invisible to the naked eye, but the first creature to successfully follow it, dog or man, would be shredded and spread out over eighty square meters of jungle floor.

The claymore had a directional blast, and looked like a folded Polaroid camera. Along the slightly bowed front were seven hundred quarter-inch steel pellets, and behind was an inch and a quarter slab of C-4 explosive. All this was wrapped in a green plastic mold with folding stick pin legs on the bottom, blasting cap holes and sight on top, and instructions for use on both front and back. When detonated, the pellets cut a killing zone of sixty degrees. It was a horrid device wrapped in a handy container.

They climbed through heavy undergrowth for thirty minutes, crossed a trail, then turned south for thirty minutes, crossed another trail, moved on, and finally stopped in line, listening. The western sun disappeared behind the next ridge, as Larsen radioed the sit-rep.

The radio relay site came back. "Blackjack, Blackjack, this is Leghorn. Over."

"Roger, Leghorn, this is Blackjack. Over."

"Blackjack, Dusty says you must be kidding. They've only heard of them once before. Over."

"Well, we've got them, and I don't know where the hell I'm going to RON [remain overnight]. I want the hell out of here. Over."

The Yards jumped at the explosion a mile northwest. They grinned, looking around, flashing white and gold teeth.

"Damn, Leghorn, I think we just got them with a little surprise we left behind. Over."

Everyone was patting shoulders and snickering, while glancing north. Larsen finished the official coded report about the trails, and signed off.

They sat down, waiting and listening until sunset. No dogs. Then, right before dark, they stood and started moving one last time, finally bedding down for the night two hundred meters west, down the side of the mountain.

It was standard procedure to move just before nightfall. There were many human trackers across the fence, sitting on landing zones, or picking up a team's trail during the day, and following silently till night. If they didn't move one last time at sundown, the position might be closely fixed, and they could be surrounded by morning. So they moved.

Claymores were placed like the spokes of a wheel, but no guards were posted. None were needed. Each man slept little, if at all, and movement at night in the dry season jungle was as jarring and loud as a kid running down the street dragging an empty gasoline can behind him on a string. They were confident, and Garner slept with a smile, hopeful that his constipation would be over in the morning.

Dawn creeps through the jungle. Each team member drifted in and out of consciousness five to seven times in the dark. The rhythm was, sleep, shake loose, listen, listen, breathe easy, drift off. Over and over the pattern repeated. It was familiar, reassuring. Sleeping too sound was danger, snoring, suicide. At any time two people were probably awake.

Light grew. Indistinct forms turned into men, who started packing rucksacks with plastic ground sheets and retrieved claymores. Teeth were brushed with spit water, as necks and privates were checked for rubbery leaches. New bug repellant got squirted everywhere. Wet socks were changed out. Camouflage slathered over old dirt. Cigarette cravings were swallowed hard with gum substitutes. The field was a hard place to quit.

Morning sit-rep was given. Ham and eggs C-ration cans repacked. Lousy stuff. Find a stream today. Five quarts each, almost dry. Waiting in the gray-green dawn, it happened.

Howling. Howling close by, coming in fast.

Dodge jumped up. "They found where we crossed the last trail. Dogs are on the run this time. We musta got a handler with the claymore yesterday. Let's go."

Larsen struggled up, and the team coagulated in line of march, getting set to bleed out south, fast. On the run.

"We can't beat dogs. We'll have to shoot 'em," Garner panted.

"We'll move and shoot on the run." From Dodge.

"What if they hold back and follow? We're flanked."

They ran along the hillside, at an angle.

"No." Larsen directed more southeast. "They'll come straight on. Dogs just run. We'll shoot 'em, but we'll get triangulated. They've got us. Phil, get an LZ."

Dodge dug his pockets for a map, as he ran.

"Ted, get Leghorn. We need a Covey and a Prairie Fire. Those bastards."

In five minutes the dogs were on their heels, coming fast. Larsen turned on the run, spreading them out. "Get 'em all!" Brown forms, lunging, blocked by jungle, in, out, strung along a line, heads down, ran howling into a barrage of 122 rounds. Too much and too little. Four went down. One more bayed with wounds. The last followed like a howling Irish curse.

They hit a trail, running across en masse. No time checking it, breaking brush, but it was clear. Then they were moving up, almost parallel to the ridge along the flank, climbing east. They got hit from the top, up on the left.

"Jesus, get down!" Dodge yelled. Three grenades pounded, and small arms rattled. Two more concussions, and Kuiet was bleeding from the ears, two fingers gone, in a daze. His left leg twisted beneath at a funny angle.

"Djuit, help him!" Larsen yelled, while reloading a third magazine. The entire team worked with one rhythm. One, two, three. Aim, fire, move, aim, fire, move, aim, fire, move, semi-auto. No reloads. No resupply. Four hundred rounds went fast, then out for good. Larsen yelled, "Move him now, dammit!"

Two Yards pulled Kuiet back and down, back and down. Fire was everywhere. Hiding behind the trees, they got his pack and picked him up. Dodge was in front, as planned in fast-action training, moving southwest and down, away.

"Where's Covey?" From Garner, covering the rear with Kehn and Larsen.

"Go, go, Ted. Follow Dodge! Get an LZ. Get Covey. Go!"

Forms were moving down the hill now, right at them, dodging in and out of the foliage, wearing green helmets of cloth with centered stars. Pith helmets, not steel. Like African explorer movies come to life. Twenty? Thirty? More? Five down, maybe six. Breathe slower.

"Garner, move!"

He pulled the hand guard against the bark and aimed around the tree. Two deep breaths, and he lined sights on the first life he'd take. No thought, just training. Two squeezes, one, two, "pop, pop." The chest jerked, and the back exploded, while the man twirled down in a fluffy clump of green and red. Garner didn't even feel the weapon kick his shoulder.

Then he pulled a fast swivel ten degrees to others just in front and to the side. "Pop, pop. Pop, pop." Like pins they started twisting, falling, spinning. He screamed. What fun. "Pop, pop. Pop, pop." Then out. Reload. Come up. Swivel hard. Line up. "Pop, pop. Pop, pop." He fired and fired again, not hearing Larsen or the sounds of gunfire in his ears. They came. "Pop, pop. Pop, pop." Breathe slow. Then Larsen angled in and kicked him with his boot while flying past, down the hill.

"Move, damn you!"

He swiveled and lined on the closest pins. "Pop, pop. Pop, pop." Then he was shouting as if at a football game. End run, touchdown, big grin. The pins swiveled slowly in the mottled green and brown. Blood was pumping now. He moved back and down, screaming with a raging bloodlust.

The attack slowed, the escape quickened. Packs exchanged. Two carried Kuiet, with tradeoffs on the run. Larsen moved to the lead, ripping Kuiet's pack. Ammo, water, grenades, radio battery taken, and throw the rest.

They moved down to water. The valley was full of noisy brush, but there was no choice. No time for a claymore surprise. Not yet. Dodge worked on a rig. Eyes and ears were looking, listening, everywhere. Then water, thin water, a stream, rocks. They skipped down one to one, then stopped and filled up two quarts each. No time for more. Voices raged in impotence behind and up the hill.

Covey was little help. Fast movers were elsewhere, and A-1E Spads were thirty-five, forty minutes out. Prairie Fire was cleared; they were coming. The LZ was eight hundred meters away, back across Charlie's ridge. They moved down the stream, southwest.

"Dammit!" Larsen looked up from the map. "Over the next ridge west of us is the road. No good. The LZ is southeast."

They jumped rock to rock, splashing water. Buckles and sling swivels were taped down and dark. Black spray paint dappled olive drab jungle shirts. They were moving shadows. Just grunts of work and aching shoulders marked the passing.

Further down—a klick?—the valleys ran together. Charlie was to the north, behind. The road was west, and soon it curved ahead. The valleys merged. The road was there. They were running into the maw, and had to turn east across the ridge they were attacked on. Did Charlie split, moving south, or were they all on the following trail?

Who should ask the question? Even Garner knew the answer. They split. That's what any trap would dictate. Larsen stopped the team. They listened. He motioned east and up, and took his chances.

Kuiet passed to fresher arms. More packs were pulled apart and dumped, as Dodge readied his surprise and aimed it up the stream. Quiet now; they listened. Lots of rocks at the bottom and twenty-meter line of sight, but on the sides it was thick. They clustered in and disappeared. Up and slow, quiet, listening.

Kuiet was chewing on a stick, awake, aware, shot full of morphine, patched and stifling groans. They moved up, up the forty-degree incline at an angle, slow and quiet, stop. Compass checked. Listen. Brush was breaking down below. Up above was the lazy drone of Covey, waiting for the ships, the team, the Spads. Reassuring sounds.

Compass checked okay with Dodge. No divergence in opinion on the course, 125 degrees, up and over the top and five hundred meters to a hole in the trees.

"Covey says twenty minutes to Spads on station. Taking longer than he was told." Garner listened to the muffled speaker.

Larsen motioned up and quiet. The ridge had to be hot! They moved, staying in thick cover. Then the package left behind went off, and filled the narrow valley with a blast of powdered smoke, and the sounds of ten explosions echoed off of only one.

Looking back, two hundred meters down and to the right, was a growing white powder haze, where four men went down. The only thing left behind of one was his name. The others scattered, wounded, screaming, puking and crying. Dodge added a surprise to the package. Powdered CS.

Rice can't be killed. Blow it up, and Charlie picks up the pieces one by one. Burn it, and the rice cooks. It stores dry and won't rot. It's super food, but it can't get away from powdered CS tear gas. It goes into the meat, ruining it. Most teams carried plastic bottles to spray in rice depots and bunkers. Dodge

CHAPTER 4

added three to the front of the claymore. No dog would follow a scent down that back trail now.

Larsen held them crouched in line, quiet, listening. Screams behind, babbles, random shots. Now, "aha," voices were ahead on the ridge, passing by, running along the top from left to right. The North Vietnamese were looking, listening, but noisy, very noisy, just thirty meters away, up.

"Will they leave sentries?" Garner whispered.

Larsen shook his head. "They'd shoot themselves in confusion. They're mad, plenty mad. First ambush broke too soon." How many? Thirty? Forty maybe. They passed. "Let's go."

Up and up. Up and up, slow. Twenty meters, ten. There was the beaten track of their passing. Look both ways, like kids crossing the street. Fast cars. Look out.

Then down the other side and out of the trap, and east with a collective sigh of relief increasing with the pace and distance. Down but quiet. Kuiet muffled groans of despair. Gratitude was in his eyes as the stick in his mouth turned pulpy with the pain.

"Covey says Prairie Fire five minutes out."

Larsen nodded to the whisper. They reached the hole in the trees while giving a sit-rep. It was a lousy LZ, but sounds of helicopters far off made it look better. Nevertheless, it had to be cleared. Two eight-inch-thick trees clogged the middle, high and thin.

"Covey, Covey. This is Blackjack, Blackjack. Over."

"Roger, Blackjack. This is Triple Nickel, five-five-five. Read you five by here. Glad to hear from you boys. Thought for awhile you decided to walk out instead of fly. Over."

"Not this time, Triple Nickel." Larsen winked at Dodge and grinned at the Covey's southern drawl. Smiles were all around. "Would like a cool flight home, but bad guys are on the west ridge looking down at us, and we're going to have to make noise clearing this LZ. Can you help? Over."

"Ahh, roger, Blackjack. I have cavalry circling three miles away. Will you pop smoke. Over."

"Roger. Popping smoke. Over."

Dodge dug into one of the remaining packs, and threw a red smoke grenade out in the middle of the clearing.

"Ahh, Blackjack, I see red. Over."

"Roger, Triple Nickel. We have red smoke on our position. Again, there are bad guys on the west ridge, our side towards the top, two hundred and fifty meters away. Over."

"Ahh, Roger, Blackjack. Keep your heads down. I'm bringing in good guys south to north. Over."

Dodge, Kui and Phe dug out strips of C-4, and prerigged blasting caps with thirty-second burn fuses. They hovered low in the wood line, watching the Forward Air Controller in the small plane go to work. Fat-bellied single-engine A-1E Spads, circling south at three thousand feet, peeled off in line, coming ever lower with the long axis of the ridge, firing rockets and cannon. They guessed the bombs were 250-pounders.

Then, as debris, bark, shrapnel and smoke came rolling down the hillside in a lazy fall, Dodge and others rushed to the clearing and set charges at the base of each tree. They took only the largest, because Huey blades could handle the small saplings. Larsen stayed on the horn, spreading the rest of the team out in a crescent on the west side, to give covering fire if necessary. It wasn't. The trees blew down in two shattering explosions that successfully opened the hole.

"Triple Nickel, this is Blackjack. Over."

"Blackjack, read you five by. Over."

"Triple Nickel, we have cleared the LZ and bad guys are yelling and screaming up on the hill at you. I think your boys are right on target. Over."

"Roger that, Blackjack. Thanks for the info. I'll tell the boys. I know they'll be so happy they'll want to do it again. Over."

And sure enough, the five planes came screaming in, pistons popping, south to north once more, as the Hueys hovered down under the protective umbrella, scooping the team out of the hole in the trees. They were up and out, going home, leaving behind smoke, fire, and an unknown number of dead and wounded. The next day at debriefing, they gave the hungry number crunchers in Saigon a guess of twenty-two of the former and sixteen of the latter. Larsen said, "What the hell," scratching the back of his head in lazy pleasure.

5

The club was rowdy, and Garner drank with Dodge and Day at a couple tables pushed together. Lieutenant Don Glass and Sergeant Bill Buckman sat across, and Tony Sardo of A-Company fiddled with his glass at the end closest to the bar.

"I'm telling you," he said. "It was the damnedest thing to read. I've got the paper over in the room. It bit the guy on the ass, and tried to drag him off and eat him."

Stinky Sam came wandering back from the bar with a drink, and sat down, yelling to the waitress. "Hey, Canada, you're slowing down, honey. I'm having to get my own now. Better shake it up."

The pretty girl looked over, nodding and smiling perfunctorily, while passing drinks at the third table over. Then Samuels asked Tony, "Now who ate whose ass?"

"If you're gonna leave for drinks, you're gonna miss the stories," said Dodge.

Tony waved the objection away. "It was a tiger. *Stars and Stripes* says it carried off one of the guys on the APCs guarding the road between here and Pleiku."

"Really?" Samuels was trying to concentrate through the alcohol. "Did it get the guy?"

"Nah. One of the other guards heard him yelling. They said it was at dusk. Anyway, he hears the screaming, grabs an M-16 and gets off five or six rounds while the thing's running to the woods with the guy in his mouth."

"Jesus." Samuels sat riveted, and Day sniggered at the other end.

"I guess he hit it a couple of times, 'cause it dropped the guy."

"We saw tracks one time down in a stream bed. Remember, Bill?" Lieutenant Glass was the One One on Minnesota.

Buckman, the One Two, said, "Oh yah, Sir. I remember. Big as dinner plates." He motioned wide with his hands.

It was Garner's second night of stand down, and his first chance to buy his own drinks. The night before was a celebration for breaking his cherry in combat. They poured beers on his head, and he swelled with acceptance as an equal. The fact it took killings didn't matter.

He studied the subtle shame and pride in taking other lives, but it was war; they had their chance. He'd think about it later.

The chewing out was not much either. Larsen braced him up for not moving on command, but he sensed the leader took it light. Crazy things were done in heat of combat, and Garner pledged to keep a better grip. Larsen shrugged and simply mumbled, "Good."

The waitress hovered near. "You say you want drinks now?" Her heart-shaped face glowed with a creamy luster of youth, and was framed with black hair falling past her shoulders. She stood slightly bowed, smiling, refusing to acknowledge hard returning stares that roamed her body. Almond eyes, glinting like ebony, flashed each face as she took instructions one by one. She was natural, coy and flirtatious, and Garner sipped her vision like spring water.

The blue print blouse was clean, but frayed, with shoulder straps revealing shapely arms, and a tattoo high up on the right. He blushed when she caught him staring. It read "Canada" and was crudely done by rubbing gouges in the flesh with charcoal.

He sat swirling a new bourbon/water with a finger, while looking around the room, where stories flew among the tables. The club was a churning mill of rumor, fact and fantasy. It was the town hall, where every bitch and moan was fully aired to sympathetic ears. It was more than just a watering hole. It was the life's blood and connective tissue holding the camp together. It was the focal point, and drinks were stiff and cheap.

He tilted back, smiling with the burn of bourbon. Then, over the glass rim, he saw Sergeant Ed Morrison enter the club. The burly black-haired man shuffled, dragging invisible chains like Marley's ghost. He scanned empty seats and crabbed two steps to the right, finally sitting with a thump, next to Day.

"Well, I just got away from Billings. We've got Bright Light next week." He leaned over, knuckling his chin while contemplating silence. He was the team leader on Minnesota, and the other two members, Buckman and Glass, watched and waited.

"When do you go up?" asked Samuels.

"Next week. We replace Florida. I wish we didn't have it."

"Why not?" Tony asked. "It's a week's worth of lying around. You shouldn't be called up to go into the field. After all, A-Company isn't going back in for awhile. At least it better by God not."

Everyone chuckled at Sardo. The company came out of the field three days before, after fighting to get off their hill and moving seven klicks south, to a suitable extraction LZ. Combat, with green North Vietnamese tracer rounds, provided more than a few good war stories in the club later on. Several Yards were hit, but the massive fire support from eight-inch and 175mm guns stationed at Ben Het just across the border, coupled with air strikes by fast movers out of Pleiku, wiped out North Vietnamese in their line of march, allowing 125 men to come out relatively intact.

"Well, I don't care what you say, I hate Bright Light. I'd rather be training than sitting at Dak To, wondering if we'll get called up to go in and get our asses shot off."

Garner said, "Some people like it, I hear. Of course I haven't done it yet, so I don't know about the tension, but it's got to be less than going in the field."

"Well, I sure don't like it. How about you, Lieutenant Glass?"

Glass looked up over wire rim glasses while running a hand through his thinning hair. He was second in command on Team Minnesota, even though he outranked the leader. In the field he took orders from Morrison, a sergeant, and like it or not, any new officer in Recon put up with it until he had enough missions to split off and take a team of his own.

Three teams out of the eighteen in camp had new lieutenants, and Garner noticed the One Zeros always dealt with their higher-ranking subordinates with a great deal of consideration and respect. Garner didn't care for many officers, but Glass was mindful of the situation, and it was visibly appreciated by the NCOs he worked with.

"I get uncomfortable on Bright Light, but it's all good time." His broad Germanic face lit with a grin as they nodded in response. Any day was one more closer to leaving for home.

They talked awhile, and when Morrison's drink arrived, he swallowed it down.

"I wish to God I was part of this blasted Hail and Farewell party coming up next week," he said.

"How long ya got?" asked Garner.

"One hundred and twenty-four days and a wake up. I'll never make it." He looked down the table. "But at least I'll go home in one piece. Not like Tony here! I bet they send your privates home in a box because of clap or something."

Tony clucked, shaking his head while eying Canada across the room.

"He thinks I'm kidding, Ted. This guy has gotten shot up for streptococcus, gonococcus, staph infection, and God knows what all. You build an immunity to the shots you know. Are you using rubbers down there at Mama Nie's?"

"Nah, hell no. I don't take showers in a raincoat. That's for you Northern European types. Where I come from machismo is a way of life."

Samuels laughed. "Well, you're gonna machees your butt down to the Philippines in quarantine for the rest of your life, if you come up with that black creeping crud we keep hearing about. You know, the stuff that nothing cures and Uncle Sam is scared witless of letting back in the States?"

"Nah, that's just a Hanoi Hannah rumor. They don't want a lot of round-eyed kids running around in this country. In twenty years they won't be able to tell who they're supposed to fight," Tony said.

People circulated among the tables, and a small mountain of a man worked his way along, taking in the conversation from behind Tony. He leaned in, putting a hand the size of a baseball mitt on Tony's shoulder. "Don't you guys go discouraging Tony from going to the Green Door."

Tony looked up saying, "Thanks, Cooper."

"Tony's my room mate, and Fazio's, and Jenkins's. If he doesn't get a little fix at Mama Nie's, he keeps us all up at night whackin' off."

"Cooper!" Tony yelled amid hoots and jeers.

"We even threatened to throw him outside on the bunkers if he kept it up. So don't ya'll tell my little whoppo buddy here to stop. I need my beauty sleep."

Sardo eyed the waitress. "I admit Canada plays with my mind. I got a hard on that could split wood." He shifted, pulling at his groin as they all turned to contemplate the girl.

She floated back and forth, serving drinks, and might have been pleased had she known Tony's problem was a common one; that as she passed, she created ripples of erections in her wake, much like undulating waves of wheat in a wind-blown South Dakota field.

Garner knew she was nineteen, and had to be painfully aware that past twenty-seven, most rural Vietnamese women were hard, drawn and thin. They shriveled, showing sunken flanks, bone, and sinew, like the cattle walking ahead in the fields during planting time.

She dressed western, studying pictures in magazines left in the club. Skirts were going up and up, and there wasn't much to hide anymore. Garner studied her tight skirt, and realized she kept it smooth by not wearing underwear.

Canada was no virgin. It was no secret she'd had her men, both VN and American, but she had to keep herself pretty, sexy, available, but yet aloof, if she was going to get an American to fall in love and take her to the wonderful United States she'd heard so much about. All Americans would take a whore, but none would marry one.

"Down, Sardo," said Samuels, "I wouldn't go messing around. Two years ago she tried to shoot an American with his own pistol, 'cause he wanted to buy her for his interpreter. I heard she fought like a cat trying to get the weapon. I don't know many VN women who like the Yards. They're real prejudiced. Call them *moi*, savages, and all. I'd be careful. I think Italians got some Yard in them."

Tony licked his lips and wiped beaded sweat from his forehead. "No, just looking, Stinky. Just looking."

Conversations roared around the tables with different war stories. Dodge said he once hid behind a tree with a Charlie on the other side. He couldn't shoot, and his first grenade was thrown back at him. He kicked it further down the hill before it went off. Then, he held the second grenade a full two seconds after popping the handle, throwing it as the rest of the four-second fuse ticked off in the air, blowing the Charlie away.

Morrison was surrounded once and popped a smoke, telling Covey to hit everything close in around. It drifted north, popping out of the trees seventy feet away. Then the jets came in and nearly killed them all.

Timmons used the guns at Ben Het one time, and couldn't tell exactly where he was on the map. He said the shells came in like freight trains.

Garner and Dodge took turns about the dogs, and everyone was quiet.

Stories worth telling were repeated many times, and through rotating one-year generations of soldiers, the legacy became lore. A verbal heritage grew, with new adventures added to the old. They offered no footnotes in the pages of serious history, but all were part of a living saga.

The biggest laugh went to the oldest story, and Tone was the one who lived it.

"Hansen was the damnedest guy. You remember him, Billy?"

Day nodded, smiling.

"Well, Hansen had three weeks in country. Just three weeks! He's still running Recon. Pay attention, Garner. Sometimes it's not being new and stupid that kills you, it's being old and cocky. He'd walk trails, sling his weapon, cross clearings. Jesus, he was scary.

"Anyway, last time out he swears he's gonna get a prisoner. They just started the two-hundred-dollar reward thing. Of course the Yards got forty dollars each and a new Seiko watch; they're nuts about those watches, so they wanted a prisoner too. Hansen goes to walking trails. He figures he'll jump someone and yell '*Cheu hoi*,' you know, give up. Well, this dink comes diddy bopping down the trail, and Hansen jumps out, looking like some kind of half-assed John Wayne. He goes to yell '*Cheu hoi*!' and forgets the fricking words." Tone and Day were now laughing at the long-ago incident.

"The dink is startled witless and his AK's low slung. Then Hansen blurts out, "Cheui Uwha!'"

"What?" asked Garner.

"Cheui Uwha. I think it's the name of some town down on the coast. It's like an NVA trying to yell 'Surrender!' at an American, and coming out instead with Sheboygan, or Seattle." Tone wiped his cheeks.

"The guy brings the AK up, and rips off rounds, then hauls ass. Hansen's standing there watching these bullets hit the ground in front, and climb across. One nicks his outside left calf, another goes between his legs, and a third clips his outside right thigh. He got religion real quick. Came back, gave me the team and quit. Just drank in the club. Wouldn't even leave to get laid."

More stories came and went, and Garner snuggled in. Everyone took turns and bragged about the fear. No one hid it. The whole point was to dispel it by getting it out in the open. Everyone had unconscious ratings of one to ten for war stories.

Lieutenant Glass called it a night, and they razzed him good naturedly. Then Garner considered those around him in quiet satisfaction, as Canada passed more drinks. She smiled while collecting club payment coupons. He gave her the coupon wrapped in a blue twenty-five-cent Military Payment Certificate. She acknowledged the fifty percent tip with a smile and a nod, and then was off again on rounds.

Dodge nudged him. "As the Lone Ranger said to his faithful horse, Silver, 'Down big fellow.' What you givin big tips for? You wanna get inside that skirt or something?"

He blushed in the whisky light. "Hell no. It's just that she's pretty, and drinks are so darned cheap anyway, I figured she could use the money."

"Well don't give out big tips in MPC, VN nationals aren't supposed to have Military Payment Certificates."

Garner checked face to face, and Morrison cut in. "If you want to leave tips, give the girls dongs, VN money. Not US certificates."

"Why? Who cares what we give them?"

"'Cause," Dodge replied, "the MPC eventually gets traded around and ends up in Charlie's hands. Then he goes out on the black market, exchanges it for greenbacks, and buys weapons and ammo to blow your young ass away with. That's why. You don't give MPC to Vietnamese for the hell of it. Give them their own funny money."

"Well, can't Charlie buy ammo with piasters, or what they call dongs now? That's money? What the difference?"

"It's garbage money," said Dodge. "It's no good outside of South Vietnam. They don't have any kind of international trade with it, so they can pretend it's worth whatever they say it's worth, even when the country's eaten up with inflation. They're darn near printing the stuff on newspapers. No one wants it. Look." Dodge paused, bowed his head and wiped his face with his left hand.

"Look, Ted. You get paid out on MPC, right?"

"Right."

"You either use it to buy something on the compound or at the PX in Pleiku, or you exchange it for VN money if you go downtown to buy something. Right? You've exchanged MPC for dongs?"

"Right."

"Tell me, what did you get for it? How many piasters or dongs did you get?"

"I got a hundred and eighteen dongs for each dollar of MPC."

"Okay," Dodge said. "You know what the free market exchange rate is for the dong versus our Military Payment Certificates?"

Garner studied ice in his glass. "No, not really."

"Well it fluctuates, but a couple weeks ago, I heard a high was around two hundred dong to the MPC dollar."

"Really? How come so much more?"

"'Cause it's a free exchange, boy. The dong, or whatever the hell you want to call it, sucks. No one wants it, especially the Vietnamese. That's why you get so many for a buck. This official hundred and eighteen conversion rate is garbage. It's a fixed deal between South Vietnam and Uncle Sam, because like I said, they don't trade dongs on any international exchange.

"Step out the gate and go downtown. Anyone on the black market will give you over a hundred and fifty for every dollar of MPC. Hell, they'll give almost three hundred for greenbacks, but don't let the Military Police catch you."

Morrison said, "Most everyone's exchanged MPC on the black market once in awhile, pocket money, or to buy a girl or stuff like that, but I'll be damned if I'd get greenbacks and trade for profit. That goes straight in Charlie's pockets."

"Or some rich Saigon government crook gets it, and sends it off to his numbered account in Switzerland," Tone added.

Then Dodge said, "Ya see, Ted, the greenback is stable. These suckers know if they save these dongs and keep inflating or end up losing the war, then they've lost everything. They buy gold, they buy dollars, they buy MPC. Everything has a price, kiddo."

"Well," Garner said, "the orders are to exchange money only in the club at the regular rate. You mean you guys don't? You mean you use the black market sometimes?" He looked around, whispering, "Isn't it dangerous? Doesn't it kinda make you guys crooks?"

All the others smiled in a nervous sort of way. Then Dodge replied, "Most everyone exchanges a little for pocket money or for girls. Hell, if you need something downtown and you don't have the dong, then you spend what you have. See?"

Garner straightened up at the hypocrisy, and said, "Yah, I see. Kinda like my giving tips to Canada."

Dodge nodded once before conceding. "Yah, I guess it's no different. Giving her MPC tips in the club is the same as using it to buy a meal downtown. You got me."

Then he bristled. "But I'll be damned if I'd ever start trading currency to try and make a bundle. We all might skirt around the edges a little, but no one I know is a profiteer."

All the others chimed in, tangling sentences together in a monkey puzzle of words. Then they stopped as if on a confused cue, and Samuels picked up the unraveling thread of thought.

"Look, Ted. People don't create the black market, the government does. It's just a system of free enterprise in a controlled economy. My old economics professors would be proud of me."

The others sniggered. "We all know it's bad news, but you can't buy a Coke, a meal, or a taxi ride, without getting bugged about exchanging MPC into dongs at inflated rates. Hell, half the stuff they sell in roadside stands is stolen from the PX or brought in on some phantom freighter dodging import taxes off the coast. We're not going to change anything by staying virgins to it."

The black market was pervasive at all levels, but Garner knew it was a cancer mutating the underlying fabric of the nation. It rotted moral fibers of the country, and its subtle stench betrayed itself from the highest offices of corrupted government to the lowest vegetable stands in the field.

Everyone scrambled, pursuing illegal rewards, and all loyalties to a larger national good corroded. It corrupted values for the treatment of all mankind. It was the ultimate homage to the self, and the lessons were clear. If all around are criminals of cynic wisdom, the man of honesty becomes a frightened fool.

The vague sense of all of this was there. It always had been, and they shifted uneasily, until Canada broke the tension by arriving with another late-night round.

She stood at the corner, bending over, passing the first drink, as Tony passed his right hand up between her legs, locking on a pantyless warmth. He jerked again, and she was jumping like a fish on a hook as he went in thumb deep, cupping her to the front with his other four fingers. Then, while the others howled, his eyes rolled back and he convulsed, exploding in size thirty-six, military issue, one each, olive drab boxer shorts.

The tray catapulted straight to the ceiling, raining glasses, cans, toothpicks, napkins, bourbon and beer everywhere. She was jerking, rocking back and forth, trying to dislodge the post impaling her from the floor below. Then, with a shock, she understood, and started turning quick as a cobra.

Tony had involuntary shudders and never saw it coming. The tray clattered to the floor as her right arm swept left, gaining power all the way. By the time she hit him, he was mentally smoking a cigarette, and the force of her open-handed blow knocked him four feet back, sending his chair another dozen or so. He lay in a stupor, spread-legged with a fading tent pole in his loose jungle fatigues, as she scrambled among broken glasses, yelling and screaming.

She found a jagged shard and rushed him, bending over straight-legged, intending to relieve both the doctors of any further concerns, and Tony of the necessity of taking any more shots. As she bent over, the mini skirt rose behind, displaying her good nature for all to see.

Garner's flying tackle blocked a slicing blow, as a huge tidal wave of developing erections roared behind her. He knocked the glass splinter from her hand, pinning fury with his full weight as she writhed, shrieking Vietnamese curses at Tony.

Finally, she calmed, and Garner let her rise, while keeping a close eye on her. Many girls kept box cutters stored in strategic places. However, Canada was content to spit on Tony, who was panting like a sprinter, and with a hard sniff and turned-up nose, she stalked off to the ladies' room, to do whatever needed doing. She received ragged applause, both for the vicarious thrills, and the gratitude that she hadn't taken him apart. Canada's reputation and honor were intact.

6

The second mission was a dry hole, nothing there; but if the hump was more typical than the first, then Garner knew he was in for a true year of hell. It was an area recon in target India-Nine, where nothing more than ten percent of the terrain was flat. The rest was jungled mountains with grades of fifty degrees or better. He was sure if they could spread it out, the twenty-two-square-mile target would more than double.

Trails webbed the mountains, and they found a camp with bunkers, fallen in. They moved with stealth, but found no one. Charlie was no different than any other soldier. When they owned the real estate and were safe, they picked the flattest land to live on. No one liked rolling down hills at night.

The AO (area of operation) was deserted, quiet. The only sounds of interest were single rifle shots of hunters far away, and the screams of apes or monkeys, frightened by the helicopters on the day of insertion.

The radio was twenty-five pounds of misery, which was reason enough to celebrate whenever promotion to second in command occurred.

Each time they came down steep ravines, they filled up five canteens each. Then they'd drink it in and sweat it out by the next ridge top. Coming down the other side, prayers were made that there would be clean water at the bottom. Sometimes there was, and sometimes not.

For seven days they fought the hillsides. At night, ponchos stretched between trees, catching scattered rains that ran down the cowled head covers and dripped into canteens. It was gritty, but it was wet. Dodge joked that their teeth could filter out the larger chunks.

Afterwards, during stand down, Larsen finished putting together materials collected for the Montagnards, and on day three, they loaded the three-quarter ton truck and drove off toward the village. Larsen took the jeep up front with Dominique and two others. The rest jumped in the truck like schoolboys on vacation. Dodge drove, while Garner fingered the souvenir.

"Where'd you get this, Phil?"

"Oh, I've had it a while. It's pretty neat isn't it?"

"Boy, I'll say." Garner was reverently handling a Viet Cong flag that Dodge evidently captured sometime back. The star jumped out from the four by six-foot field of cloth. It was tattered by weather, and Garner could see it hanging from a flagpole deep in the mountains, at some clandestine compound. He looked closely at what appeared to be bullet holes. Brown stains dotted toward the tethered end.

"Phil, I've never seen one of these before. This is really a great souvenir. You gonna put it behind glass?"

"Nah. I just kinda like to keep it around. I like the colors." He snapped gum way back between his teeth, and gave a dizzy grin.

"Well hell, if you decide you don't want it, let me know. I'll work a trade or buy it."

"Nah, you don't want that, Ted. Wait awhile, you'll get your own. Besides, it ain't for sale right now."

They passed the airfield, driving on through Kontum. The town reminded Garner of the Old West, with mountains in the background, wide streets full of dust, and brown, one- or two-story buildings of plaster or splintered wood. Bars huddled on the corners, and shrunken men loitered by doors or peered out through metal-shuttered windows.

Traffic was a game of chicken, and they dodged bicycles, mopeds and buffalo that broke out between speeding cars and trucks. Everything on wheels or hoof pulled out or over without a moment's notice or hesitation.

All along the sides of the road, GIs of various units stood haggling with vendors. Cigarettes, money, soup, it was all for sale; it was one large crazy market, with everything and everyone on the make.

A girl and a GI stood outside a bar, arguing. She was screaming, gesturing wide as he caught her hand, pulling money out of it. She hit him on the left side of his head. Then he brought his fist down as dust covered the rest. They drove on through town.

Further out, they pulled over at some vegetable stands where convoyed engineers were stopping. Larsen went with Dominique to haggle about buying rice. Garner followed, and Dodge climbed out, throwing the souvenir over his shoulder while talking good naturedly with members of the convoy.

In fifteen minutes, a hundred pounds of rice and one squealing pig, half again as heavy, were bundled in. Garner found Dodge behind the wheel, counting a fistful of dong notes. The highest denomination in print was five hundred, or officially just under five dollars.

CHAPTER 6 • 53

"Whatcha doing, Phil? Where'd you get that?"

"Say what?" He started up the truck, following Larsen out. "Oh, I got down back there, and one of those Legs damn near attacked me, wanting to buy my flag so bad."

Garner looked around the cab. It was gone.

"He gave me fifty dollars MPC for it. Can you believe that?"

"I thought you said it wasn't for sale." Dodge glanced over as Garner tried too late to hide the hard look.

"Well, Ted, everything's for sale. That flag wasn't worth fifty bucks, believe me. If you keep your eyes open you can find them. Don't feel bad. It wasn't worth the money. I've seen them around before. You can get them, easy. Trust me."

They drove on in silence. The Yards in the back talked together in Bahnar. Then the trussed pig pissed on Djuit's boot, and gave off a fearsome squeal when kicked hard in the slats in retaliation.

Then Phil said. "I got a hundred and seventy-five dong per MPC dollar back there. Surprising, considering there's got to be a change coming soon."

"What?"

"The guy that runs the stand back there changes money on the side."

"He does? You did? The black market?"

"Yah. Like I told you, I change some over once in a while. I took that grunt's fifty dollars and changed it over after Larsen walked away. He's pretty straight and wouldn't like it."

"Jesus, Phil, doesn't it bother you to change money like that?"

"Nah, not right now it don't." They bounced east, heading out of the city along the Dak Bla.

"Why not?"

"'Cause they're gonna have an MPC change soon. I can almost smell it. That money's gonna be worthless before it trades around and ends up in Charlie's hands."

"An MPC what?"

"An MPC change. That's when they close up the whole country and all the Americans change blue money into yellow money, or into pink money, or into red money. The old color money's worthless, just like that. Click!" He snapped his fingers.

"Why? What is it?"

"Well, like I told you. MPC is only for Americans, but it gets on the black market and starts trading. After a while the big shots figure too much is floating around the local economy, so they change the color. Bingo, suddenly all the black-market money's worthless. It's been over five months since they changed it. I figure we're over due."

"What happens when they change it?"

"All the Vietnamese go crazy. It's like playing 'Old Maid.' Whoever's left with it, loses. Every compound in country is closed up tight. Then you line up, turn your cash in for new funny money, and the old stuff gets used for wallpaper."

"Jesus, that must be terrible."

"You got it. The whole country goes nuts, 'cause the black market loses millions of dollars in one day. That's why I'm surprised I got a hundred and seventy-five dong. Normally, if they're scared of a coming change, the rate drops down closer to that hundred and eighteen fixed exchange rate. Can't say I blame 'em for being scared of the Old Maid."

He chuckled to himself, whistling aimlessly as they drove up into the eastern hills on highway 5-B. Finally, they turned right and drove down a short dirt track to a growing cluster of thatched buildings.

They pulled past the first huts of Dominique's village, and Garner saw a mass of smiling people running towards them. The Montagnard women had long sarong type robes of rough cotton or flax, dyed flat black. Interwoven along the borders were bold designs of red and yellow. They were bright accents giving lift to their generally dour dress.

The vehicles ground to a halt at the edge of the buildings as villagers clustered around, and he looked across a sea of faces radiating smiles of childlike friendship. Unlike the Vietnamese, who were Asian Oriental and unwillingly traced their history back to Southern China, Garner knew the Montagnards were of Malayo-Polynesian decent.

It reflected in their skin, their eyes, their black hair and broad faces. Even languages, which varied from tribe to tribe, betrayed an ancestry and history that saw a small fractured race of people explore and conquer an area from Nepal, to southern India, to Papeete and beyond.

Many of the younger mothers had children up to three years old strapped around their backs or sides with slings. When hungry or bored the little ones reached around, pulling a bare breast to the side, chewing absentmindedly on the nipple.

The younger men wore nondescript green military uniforms. They didn't necessarily serve in a unit, but the uniforms were reasonably cheap in the markets. Elders, still tied to older days, wore black, rough woven jackets and loincloths bordered with the same brilliant accents. Children ran naked, chasing chickens, ducks and pigs with thin bamboo wands. They were excited and the air was full of anticipation. Guests were coming, and that was cause enough to celebrate for a mountain people whose lives turned slowly with the seasons.

The truck stopped in front of a hut five feet off the ground on sturdy teak-like wooden posts. All buildings were built up, with split bamboo sides and roofs of multi-layered reed and thatch.

The village was four miles east of Kontum above the Dak Bla. It was small, about sixty families, and indefensible. Only larger villages with resident Special Forces teams receiving large doses of American aid could stand up to the VC, who regularly confiscated rice and pigs. All the villagers could do was barter with the hated Vietnamese guerrillas or escape to Kontum if there was time enough for warning.

Dominique told them he was worried for his family. He and Djuit and Kui came from this village. Kehn, Phe and Whean were from their sister village seven miles north, where Kuiet now recovered from his wounds. They were all Bahnar, one of twenty or so ancient family tribes scattered through the highlands.

The six Montagnard members jumped down and began hugging shoulders and slapping backs of friends and relations. Their language was not stereotypically Oriental. There was no sing-song rise and fall of inflection. It was harsh and crisp, with many "clicks" and "clacks." Staccato jolts and hard consonants locked together with rolling Rs and guttural stops. To Garner it was harshly masculine and altogether beautiful.

The village was on the side of a hill and the hard-packed avenue ran flat, wide, and unbroken to an open plaza, with a Long House on poles facing them. Elevated huts ran to both sides, and down on the right a quarter mile, the Dak Bla glinted silver through the trees, as it wound back towards Kontum.

The Yards turned from greetings as the Americans stepped down and stood beside Dominique. He turned to the people, giving a small speech with flourish and rhythm.

Dodge whispered, "My guess is that he's tellin' 'em we're whipping the Cong's ass single handed and will make 'em all rich with the stuff we brought."

Garner glanced, saying nothing. The speech, he felt, deserved respectful attention.

When he was done, Dominique turned, saying, "*Trung Uy* Larsen, my people welcome you all. I tell them you good men. Kill many VC, brave men. I tell them you bring gifts. You friends. You help Bahnar. You help Rhade, all mountains peoples. I tell them these things."

Larsen stepped forward and Dodge gave Garner an "I told you so" wink.

"Dominique, please tell your people we are happy to again visit our friends and bring gifts. The American people are as brothers to the Bahnar and other mountain tribes," (Dominique began translating) "and we will do all we can to help." He continued with the rapt attention of all those gathered. Finally, when he finished, a wizened man came forward through the parting crowd. He talked hurriedly with Dominique. Then, giving a deep bow, the boy turned once more toward Larsen.

"*Trung Uy* Larsen, chief of village say he welcome Americans and say, "Come, eat with us, drink with us.""

Larsen turned, bowing.

"*Trung Uy* Larsen—ah—it is good to take hand. To take hand?" He looked plaintive and the lieutenant was puzzled until it hit.

"Ah yes. Ah yes." Stepping forward, he murmured thank-yous and put out his right hand. The smaller man took it, and they both began shaking hard and smiling wide. Then the officer reached down and took out a gift from his bulging side pocket. He was holding it in both hands, and with a flourish formally presented the black plastic box to the chief.

Garner watched fascinated as the old man in the rough woven jacket opened the spring-loaded top. His face flashed from concern, to curiosity, to surprise, and then his mouth opened in a huge gap-toothed smile of absolute delight. He laughingly held the object aloft, and a new Seiko watch with elastic metal band quickly adorned his left wrist. Then a tiny girl of five or six ran forward jabbering excitedly and pointing.

She ran off with the shiny black box as a treasured toy, with laughter and smiles chasing after her.

Eager hands off loaded the truck, and a noisy processional made towards the Long House and plaza. Surrounding Yards came up to his shoulder, and as Garner joined the laughter, he saw Djuit and Kui making off to the side with two ammunition cans each.

Altogether there were almost two million Mon-Khmer and Cham-speaking tribesmen scattered along the mountains stretching from Southern China down through Laos, Vietnam and Cambodia. They were ancient people, and at one time owned all of South East Asia.

Much of the remote mountain terrain, especially in Laos, was totally wild with little evidence of mankind's presence. Trails and roads webbed the jungle, but did little to control it. It was too great for that, and the grip of man was far too weak. It was weak, but very ancient.

Garner knew the Montagnards and other ethnic peoples contested ownership of the land for thousands of years. Empires rose and fell. Those of Funan, Pagan, Chenla, Champa, Khmer, Dai-Viet and others, ebbed and flowed, making and breaking alliances every few hundred years.

He knew from training that at one time the Montagnards' ancestors owned all of Vietnam. They held rich rice lands of the coast, leaving the mountains to elephant, tiger and ape. Then, almost five thousand years before, a slow exodus of refugees came out of southern China, escaping wars and terrors that constantly racked that broken land.

They came steadily for two thousand years until they took their own identity as the Dai-Viet. They fought the Malayo-Polynesians and slowly gained ground in the north. Then in 250 BC Chinese Emperor Shih Huang Ti took note of the coastal plum, invaded and made it his own. The Dai-Viet were broken, but rebellion brewed through the centuries.

South, the kingdoms of Champa, Funan and Khmer grew, and the emperor's arm was not long enough to gather them in. They prospered on trade routes, and close ties to India were reflected in religions, languages and politics.

Eventually, Chinese power diminished in the north, with the Dai-Viet successfully rebelling in the tenth century AD. Pressures renewed against the Montagnard ancestors, the Chams, and the Dai-Viet came slowly down the coast.

West, the rival Khmer, cousins of sorts, also began pushing. The Chams were being swallowed up, and in 1177 AD, they enjoyed their greatest victories by sailing up the Mekong, defeating the Khmer on the Great Lake and going on to sack the capital of Angkor.

A century later, out of desperation they joined the Dai-Viet against the invasion of Kubla Khan, but that was their last great stand of independence. The race faltered, and by the time Columbus set sail, they had totally fallen, becoming vassals in a land that was once their own.

The Dai-Viet confiscated rich coastlands, pushing the "savages" into the mountains, back to a life of the hunter-gatherer. The tribes fractured. Enforced isolation of the mountains stunted them culturally, keeping them many centuries in the past. However, some ancient things brought forward through time were the old religions, the languages, and the long-abiding hatred of the Vietnamese, the Dai-Viet.

The procession jostled along to the plaza, where they split to form a seventy-foot circle, women on the river side, men on the mountain side. Larsen arranged bags and boxes in the middle, along with the rice and tethered pig. Then with another small flourish he turned everything over to the chief.

Dominique strutted as he interpreted for Larsen, and Garner wondered how complete and accurate the translation actually was. Dominique puzzled over words before asking Americans for clarification of meaning. It showed he tried his best. Other interpreters he'd heard were too lazy or too proud to ask, and the messages became garbled. In the field it could be a deadly dose of pride.

Larsen was breaking loose, and after turning things over to the chief, he moved to the circle's edge. Garner watched four men carry the pig to a fire bed that had been prepared for the visit. A stout bamboo pole ran between its tethered legs, and they laid the squealing animal next to the hot coals. Then one of the men straddled the animal, and swung the flat of an axe against the top of its skull, killing it instantly.

They did not bleed the animal or gut it. Instead, they lifted it with the pole and laid it directly on the coals, and there it cooked, with all of its blood in its veins and digested food in its bowels. Garner thought he was going to be sick, but pushed the thought to the side.

He looked back at the ring of people. Gifts were being passed around.

Larsen said, "My folks and other relatives used to do this after World War II. Norway was pretty beaten up by the Nazis. It was a rural country, but the war damned near bled it dry. Back then folks in Minnesota still knew distant relatives over there, and they collected clothing, toys, shoes, almost anything to box up and ship over."

The chief was distributing shirts and pants, bolts of cloth, toothbrushes and shoes.

"So you asked your folks to send this stuff?" Garner asked.

"Yah, and I told them to strong arm the neighbors. My mom got the church to help too. I told them the Yards are dirt poor and could use it. They don't have any rights as citizens. The Vietnamese crap on them whenever they can. They get shot to pieces in the war, and whatever they grow on the little flat land they have is liable to be stolen by the VC. Everybody screws them over. Why not try to even out the odds a little?"

"I'd like to even her out a little," Dodge whispered and nodded.

In the middle of the plaza taking her turn was a teenage Montagnard girl, bowing and accepting the bright red blouse from the chief. She looked to the Americans, bowing again, coming back up with a dazzling smile.

"God, they do have some pretty girls don't they?" Garner said.

"Yah, but they age fast," Dodge said. "You got to catch them young before they dry out. They got a lot of dirt between their toes too, but like Kipling said, 'Boil 'em once or twice in hot water, and they'll come as fair as chicken and ham.'"

Both the others kept their eyes on the girl, but Larsen was shaking his head. "Don't you think about anything else besides Montagnard women?"

"Why of course I do, Sir. When they're not around I think about round-eyed women, and when I don't think of them, I think of slant-eyed women."

"Well, just don't show your ass here. Screw with Yard girls and the tribe will roast you like that pig."

Dodge grinned, saying, "Lieutenant, Sir, this is the third time you've brought stuff out to the village like this, and I want you to know I think it's great. But I've been out here lotsa times with Dominique and Djuit. We go fishing with grenades and stuff. Some of these girls like to present themselves as gifts to us American heroes." He puffed up, posing like a Civil War statue. Then broke it off and laughed.

"Really?" Garner said suspiciously.

"Really. But not that one. I was half-assed joking. You don't know who she is?"

They stood watching the center, shaking their heads.

"I wouldn't touch her for a million bucks. That's Dominique's wife. She's a doll. Makes me horny as hell, but I'd never touch her. She's his wife, and I respect the hell out of that kid."

More gifts were given one by one. Rice was spread to different bowls and the women began other meal preparations. Then, at the chief's signal, all the men clustered toward the eighty-foot Long House with the honored American guests in the lead.

They climbed sideways on steps cut into huge logs leaning against the outside platform. Inside it was cool, and darkly lit by eight fires built up on six-inch-thick beds of clay. Scattered around were implements like knives, cups, crossbows, pipes and bamboo baskets. Beams glowed with the varnish from thousands of cooking fires, and large baked clay urns cluttered the floor, two or three at each fire circle. They were all about ten gallons, and each had a three-foot straw sticking out of the flared top.

"You ever had rice wine before, Ted?"

"No, Phil. I've heard of it though."

"Well, this is the Yards' version of boys' night out. At a feast, the ladies cook food and young boys who aren't initiated help them. Then the men come up here in the Long House and drink stick after stick of rice wine, talk politics, tell stories and get totally screwed up. Sounds fair and reasonable to me. Right Dominique?"

The interpreter started laughing with Dodge. "*Trung Si* Dodge. He likes our rice wine. We drink many sticks together."

They slapped each other on the backs as everyone arranged themselves around the eight low fires, crabbing this way and that, settling in. Then everything went quiet.

An ancient man with a flat-topped hat and wrinkled skin came in from the outside platform. He was dressed in black weave, and sweat trickled down along his nose. He paid no notice, and concentrated instead on the flapping chicken in his left hand and the short hooked blade in his right.

Dodge winked. "This is kinda like Grace."

The shaman waved the chicken back and forth and up and down while reciting long rehearsed words of prayer and supplication. Garner had no understanding, but felt the sense of the words and when the chicken's throat was slashed, he knew the offering was timely and material. Then the bird was taken out and added to the feast. They shuffled on the wood floor, and after arranging themselves, began drinking.

The Yards talked quietly. Many introductions were made. Many bows were given. Many hands were shaken as they circled the jars. Conversations flashed between the loops of men, and Dominique and others offered translations as best they could. All were courteous, and Garner saw them working hard at their hospitality. Finally, the looping straw passed around and he leaned forward, taking it up.

Djuit smiled, winking as he poured fresh water into the neck, bringing it full to the top. A bamboo stick lay across it, and a sliver was broken at the middle, pointing down at ninety degrees. The end of the sliver was shortened to about an inch and a half, and now it was Garner's responsibility to drink until the broken stick popped free of the liquid.

"Damn, Djuit, this tastes pretty good."

They interpreted for the others, and he blushed at the laughter, but continued drinking. The straw went to the bottom of the pot, through layers of rice and leaves, and the continual resupply of fresh water slowly diluted the mixture. But the jars were so large the effect was gradual, and by the next day it came back to full potency as the fermentation process continued.

Their circle held eight men, and after a third round and a third stick, the Yards began getting loud and Garner started slurring words.

"Phil? How iz, how iz this stuff made anyway?"

"I dunno, Ted. Just natural rice perkin' away down there I guess. I don't wanna know what else they might put in it. This pot doesn't look clean enough to crap in let alone drink out of. Ha. Jeez this has a buzz to it doesn't it?"

"Oh yah. That reminds me, Ted. If you have to take a leak, have one of the Yards show you where to go. Don't, for God's sake go around behind the Long House or the other buildings. That's where spirits of the ancestors live. They don't like you pissing on their ancestors."

"Okay, Phil. Thanks. I'll be careful."

Larsen finished his stick, passing the straw left and refilling the urn from the nearest crock of clear water. "Too bad we don't have drilling equipment so we could come and put in a well for these folks. They hump this water three hundred feet up from the river. A well would be easier, cleaner, safer."

"Well, Sir," said Dodge. "If we were a regular SF unit maybe we could do that, but we don't have equipment and who's got the time?"

"Yah, too bad. I'd like to help out. This high up the hill, the water table must be more than twenty, thirty feet down. Can't dig that free hand."

At the next circle, several Yards were telling animated stories. They rocked back and forth, one telling part and then stopping so the other could continue. Those around were laughing in delight, and Garner asked Dominique what was going on.

"*Trung Si* Garnah, they tell stories of long time back about big monkeys in the mountains. Big monkeys like we hear last week."

"You mean those mountain apes or whatever it was we heard?"

"Not same, same. Long time back when few men live in mountains, big monkeys live in tribes." He was motioning wide and tall with his arms.

"You mean apes. Big apes. *Beaucoup* monkeys, not *te te* monkeys."

"Yes. *Beaucoup* monkeys. Many monkey mans live in mountains long time back. Monkey mans come fight Bahnar. Steal *co*."

"What? Steal the women?"

"Yes. *Bacanook co*." He laughed, rapidly pounding his fist into the other open palm several times. "*Bacanook co*."

"Oh bullshit, Dominique."

"No bullshit, Garnah. Steal *co*. *Bacanook co*. *Co* have babysan."

"More bullshit!" Everyone was laughing. "What did babysan look like?"

He giggled. "Same, same, monkey!"

Stories came and went of times long gone and near: tiger hunts, floods, harvests good and bad, elephants and ivory. The afternoon swam by, blurred with tall tales and wine, and as Garner finished his seventh stick Dodge grabbed him by the shoulder.

"Hey, Ted, listen to this."

Dominique was talking. "I try to tell him, *Trung Si* Dodge, but he is old man. Prays to gods. He not listen. He not believe me."

"Well tell him again for me, and be careful on the translation. Ask me if you don't know the words. Okay?" Dodge was looking at the old shaman off to the interpreter's left, saying, "The helicopters are just machines, like cars or trucks in the sky." Dominique began.

"The blades go round and round, and push the air down and make the thing go up." Dodge explained the best he could, using swirling hands to show the truth behind the magic. Finally, the old man stopped him and talked back quickly.

Dominique shrugged. "*Trung Si* Dodge. He say helicopter fans go round and round to keep people inside nice and cool. Pilots have on helmets. He has seen them talk into sticks in front of their mouths. He say they talk to God, and he lifts them up and puts them down where they say. Helicopter men have strong words to God."

"Well." Dodge looked stumped, then smiled. "That's one way to look at it I suppose. Why not? I pray to the chopper pilots too."

A gong rang outside, and the feast was on. Seventy-six men stood in the smoky dark, weaving to various stages of drunkenness. They worked kinks, stretched, and filed out the doorways to the long front platform, coming down the stairways single file.

Outside, they were assaulted by smells of crisp pork and other foods. Garner marveled how hard the hunger hit. He watched others for clues and sat where courtesy toward guests dictated.

The pig was off the fire, being cut up. Feet were black with ash and as he watched, a tribesman speared the animal's side, allowing the gas that bloated the animal to erupt in a flatulent sounding rush. Garner was grateful the fire was downwind of him.

The Americans were served wooden plates with rice, some sort of greenery, and chunks of the pig. Grease ran between his fingers as he muzzled into the fatty flesh.

Two hours later, after stumbling into the truck and jeep, they started weaving back along the road. People waved and cheered. Hands were clasped. Backs were patted. It was a fully satiated day, and twilight was coming.

All the members of Team Iowa muttered among themselves in English and Bahnar. They laughed and drank more wine from filled canteens, trying to stay alert for unexpected ambush.

The Yards took measurement that day, and Garner felt he'd passed. They'd give sidelong glances, talking in muttered tones, and when he'd catch and look at them directly, they'd stop, straighten up and smile like children caught reaching for a candy bar. He knew in general they had their own agenda, their own priorities, their own collective dream, and that they measured all Americans against the hope of it.

He'd heard the dream was for a homeland they could call their own and rule themselves, a country carved out of the hard bones of the mountains where Vietnamese disgust and prejudice could not threaten. They were primitive and gullible, but not stupid. They could not have a homeland without help.

Of course the Communists lied and promised autonomy if they'd turn VC. It was a seductive lie, but most knew they would simply trade one Vietnamese master for another. No.

But what of the Americans? Could they help? Would they help? Garner understood that many Americans driving by on trucks would jeer, eyeing their women, laughing ugly thoughts that needed no translation. The quiet ones scattered through the mountains were different though. They wore soft skull caps the color of mountains in deep shadow. They listened to the people. They helped build things instead of steal, and in those lucky villages where they lived, people had water from metal machines pumped up and down with the hand.

They had *Bac Si*, who could pull a painful tooth like magic or close a gash with thread. They had defenses against raiding Viet Cong, and weapons, ammunition, grenades and explosives to slowly build up and put away for the day of their eventual revolt for freedom.

What of these large white and black men who lived in their midst? They laughed easily, seeming to really enjoy the friendship of the Rhade, Bahnar, Cham, Hroy, Jarai, Krung, Rai and all the other tribes of the highlands. But would they help? It was a well-known hope they would.

Bright Light
RECON COMPANY
SOA (CCC) 5TH SFG (ABN), 1ST SF
APO San Francisco, Calif 96499

SUBJECT: SOP For Bright Light Team

A. Bright Light Assignment
   1. The Bright Light Team will change over every Saturday.
   2. The replacing B/L Team will be alerted on Wednesday mornings for duty.
   3. The replacing B/L Team will train for two days prior to assuming duties. Training will be conducted on the following subjects:
      a] Basic first aid.
      b] Rappelling.
      c] Ladder training.
      d] Hansen rig training.
      e] Destruction of downed chopper and aircraft. (expedient methods)
      f] LZ selections, for any type extraction.
   4. The B/L Team will be checked out by CCC medical personnel 24 hours prior to assuming duties.
   5. The B/L Team 10 will turn in a team roster of personnel and equipment 24 hours prior to replacing B/L Team.
      a] Equipment required for B/L Team.
         1] Minimum five days ration.
         2] All US personnel on team will carry medical equipment prescribed by company SOP.

3] Demolitions—/ 5 Blks. 2½ lbs. C-4/ 10 non elec. lighters/ blasting caps/ 4 ft. time fuse/ 10 fuse 4 ft.det cord/ 2 M-57 firing device w firing wire.
4] Jungle knife—1 per team member.
5] One Hansen rig/ One Swiss seat/ 3 snap links per individual.
6] One pair rappelling gloves, per individual.

b] Equipment available for B/L resupply:
1] Smoke, 2 cases.
   a. red or violet.
   b. yellow or green.
2] 5.56 ammo—2 cases
3] White Phosphorus (WP) grenades—1 case (M-34)
4] Frag grenades—1 case (M-26)
5] Incendiary grenades—1 case.
6] C-4 1 case
7] 100 ft. Det cord.
8] 100 ft. Time fuse.
9] Claymore mines—2 cases (M-18).
10] 100 non-elec blasting caps.
11] Magazines M-16-400. (40 sandbags, 10 mags. each.)
12] Hansen rigs—12 each.
13] Swiss seats—12 each.
14] Snap links—36 each.
15] M-5 medical kit—1 each.
16] Sand bags—12 each. w/3 days rations.
17] 100 Sand bags.
18] Sand bags—12 each w/4 canteens each full of water.
19] Sand bags—12 each w/2 prc-25 batteries.
20] PRC-25 w/1 handset/1 long antenna/ 1 short antenna mounted in rucksack.
21] Mogas—5 1 gal containers/ 5 1 gal containers diesel.
22] PIRs #3 and #5—1 case each.
23] LRPs—5 cases.
24] C-rations—10 cases.
25] Anti contact gloves—12 pr.
26] Rappelling gloves—12 pr.
27] Body bags—10 each.
28] Axes—4 each (If they are available.)
29] Entrenching tools—12 each.

30] The items listed are duplicated in two locations (primary base of operations {Recon Company} and with team on B/L.)
c] Additional equipment prepared by Recon Company as needed:
   1] Mines—M-7A1/ M-16/ catering charge/ shaped charge.
   2] Clothing and individual equipment.
   3] Special operations equipment—weapons/ wiretap/ radios/anti intrusion/demolitions etc.
d] Primary and daily duties of B/L Teams while on Stand-by at Launch Areas.
   1] Police of Launch Area: Bunkers, buildings and area of operations (daily).
   2] Refill water cans for resupply of radio relay sites.
   3] Daily maintenance of vehicles assigned to Launch Area (1st echelon maintenance). Check:
      a)) water, oil, battery, gas.
      b)) brakes, tires.
      c)) clean.
   4] Help in resupply or arming of gun ships.
   5] Care and maintenance of all weapons at Launch Site.
   6] Responsible for accountability and care of resupply items.
   7] B/L Team will train while on location using available facilities, with emphasis on:
      a)) Rappelling, ladders.
      b)) Team assembly and movement.
      c)) Rehearse hand and arm signals.
   8] Responsible for all classified information and equipment.
   9] Know escape and evade (E+E) plan for Launch Area, brief all members of your team.
   10] Inform base location if enemy activity causes damage to launch location or equipment.
   11] Give fuel report to base location at 0700 hrs. daily.
   12] Sign over all classified documents to team assuming duties as B/L Team.
   13] Brief replacing team on all aspects of duties, responsibilities (Enemy Situation).
   14] 1 American and 1 SCU member (Yard) may return to base location nightly. (Except the 10, he will remain at B/L Team stand-by area until he has been relieved by replacing B/L/ Team.) Team members returning to base of operations will

report to S-3 at 0700 hrs. each morning for transportation back to B/L Stand-by area.

15] After B/L Team has been replaced and returned to base of operations, turn in recommendation to recon office on improvement of B/L operation and equipment or Stand-by area.

8

On Wednesday morning, Billings said they had Bright Light coming up, and they changed training schedules. Fast-action live-fire drills stopped at the range. Instead, they climbed the sixty-foot rappelling tower, coming down time and time again on ropes.

They worked with rope ladders and went back over where to plant charges to destroy a downed helicopter or plane. After reviewing procedures and checking equipment, they shook hands with the Gladiator crew chiefs, climbed aboard the Hueys, and flew to Dak To on Saturday morning.

Team Arkansas boiled out of the buildings as they flew in, running over the foot bridges crossing the empty drainage ditch.

"How's it going, Dodge? I heard you guys were replacing us." Tim Hatton was the One Zero. He was five foot eight inches tall, with stomach muscles wrapping tight as electric coils.

"It should be an interesting week for you," he yelled. "The A-Company is kicking ass and taking names down south, but they'll be coming out sometime this week. Two teams are in the field. They're safe and quiet."

Hatton gave Larsen a full briefing, signing over maps and code sheets. Then he got his team aboard two choppers and hitched a ride back to Kontum for three days of stand down.

"Well, Ted, last few times we were in and out of here so fast you couldn't hardly blink. How do you like Dak To?"

"You know, it's funny, Phil, the hills seem closer in, like Charlie's looking down on top of us."

"Well, that's just the way it is. At least that's the way I feel. He's up there staring down at us. Sometimes he uses that elevation and lobs those hundred and forty millimeter rockets into here. The smaller one-twenty-twos will get us too. You never know where they're gonna hit. I guess we're kind of in a bad spot, 'cause a prime target is this line of helicopters of ours." He motioned to the four Hueys and the four Cobras sitting nearby.

They settled in and waited in the growing heat. There was little to do, other than studying SOP sheets and checking truck batteries and radiator water. Instead, they sat listening to Gable monitor the radio, passing on sit-reps from the teams to Kontum.

One team was on a road watch, counting trucks rolling along the trails at night. Many times, on the day of extraction, a team doing that job might try to grab a prisoner or pull some other John Wayne tactic on their way out. It made Garner nervous.

The second team was on an area recon. He hoped the area was dead, like India-Nine. No one wanted Bright Light trouble.

A-Company was another story. They hit scattered resistance earlier in the week, while forcing their way into a Salem House target. Enemy troops were NVA and Cong. They were disorganized, falling back, giving the Company a chance to capture a supply depot, which they held for several days, destroying captured weapons in place. Helicopters resupplying the force extracted all the captured ammunition, however. They were close to getting out, and Garner prayed they didn't step in something while doing it. No one knew what Bright Light held for them.

However, the afternoon was quiet, no insertions or extractions. By eighteen hundred, the teams in the field were bedding down, and Recon called it a day. Larsen and Phe climbed aboard the lead slick as it started up, and within three minutes they were on the way back to Kontum for a hot meal and a shower. Normally, the One Zero stayed all week, and everyone else took turns rotating for the night, but Saturday was the Hail and Farewell Party, and it was Larsen's night to be honored with a plaque and a black satin One Zero jacket, with CCC and the team name embroidered on the front, and the fearsome picture of the MACV-SOG skull and beret embroidered on the back. Those leaving during the coming month were honored with stories and toasts. It was his time, and he would not miss it.

Garner had a first inkling something was afoot by the time stars came out in force. They brought up beer, and a cooler stood near the radio shack, ready for teams coming out of the field. It was winked at as a policy, and he sat under the tower drinking a cool one, looking across the strip to the hills, when he heard scuffling and giggles off to his left near the barracks.

Dodge laughed, but Garner couldn't see the north entrance. He stood up and started walking toward the lights. As he turned the corner, he saw a nicely curved rump in a pink mini skirt disappear through the doorway.

He followed, and found the team inside, spread out before him in a fan. Dominique and Dodge were in the middle, with a five-foot-two tight-bellied hooker in between. She stood there, hands on hips, canting to the side with a look of knowing unconcern on her face. He stopped short. They were all looking at him, grinning like idiots. Dodge laughed through his twisted smile.

"*Trung Si* Garnah," Dominique said. "You like this girl? Garnah?"

"Ah, yah, sure, Dominique. She's good looking. What's she doing here?"

"Many girls stay inside camps at night. Not supposed to, but they have friends. Many friends."

He felt like a bug on a slide under the microscope.

"You want this girl for night, Garnah? She yours."

The girl pursed her lips, almost imperceptibly undulating. He swallowed and it stuck.

"Dominique. Ah, ah, I'm sorry. She's cute and all, but I don't have the money. Recon Headquarters holds our MPC, in case there's a currency change while we're gone. I don't know what she charges, but I didn't figure on spending money up here, so I didn't bring any. Sorry."

"No sweat, GI," She whispered.

"That's right, Garnah. She want one-thousand dong. We make it right. Okay?"

"What? Phil?"

"Don't look at me. I've, ah, enjoyed Suzy up here before, but I've got nothing to do with this. This is the Yards' doing. They want to put you on the spot? I'm not gonna stop it."

"Garnah, no sweat," Dominique said. He took two steps forward, smiling wide and shaking hands. When he pulled back there were two five-hundred-dong notes in Garner's palm.

There it was. No way out. It was Suzy or shame of face and the brand of Cherry Boy. He took her hand and walked outside to the commo shed, as laughter started dribbling out the door behind.

It's not that he was totally inexperienced. He'd dated during high school and two years of college, but times were different then. Young men are not provided instruction manuals for women. He was tentative, and girls were suspicious.

He'd always thought too much. It was one thing to skirt the edges, fondle and kiss, but it was something else to get right down to it and make love. He was deeply ashamed and embarrassed, but he was virgin, and like any male the branded burden of the term was far more difficult living with than the physical denial of the act.

But there it was. No doubt. Virgin. What a hated term. He'd kill to keep the secret safe. Every time he got close the strings of conscience pulled him back. Girls were not fast and loose. He laughed at the so-called sexual revolution raging throughout the States. The revolution had been muted in Rock Island, Illinois. But overall, sitting, pondering, he knew the lacking was in him.

Back home breasts were young and pert, and thighs had opened to his touch. For a young man the gifts were there, but what of a lifetime of loving? What of a lifetime of responsibilities, of careers and children? What of marriage? What of using? What of guilt? What of cheerful, cheated, lustful, selfish opportunity? The fault was his alone. His fault was thinking, thinking, thinking.

Guilts were too strong, and he was four years past the first of many chances never taken up. He held the Vietnamese girl's hand, leading her to the canvas cot, and as he stripped and laid her down, kissing and entering, he thought of others from before, and laughed. That this should be the time and place: supple body, vacant heart, unknown face, bought by Yards, mosquitoes buzzing, canvas burns now building on his knees and elbows, how strange and totally comic. The laugh cut short, and he groaned as she pushed and built. He shuddered deep. Then, reveling in her warmth, he went to work all night.

She was gone by morning, like a lustful dream. He snapped awake to helicopters coming in, and a rough hand shaking his shoulder.

"Hey, boy!" Dodge said. "We tried to let you sleep in but you musta screwed yourself into a coma. Wake up. It's eight o'clock. The choppers are back."

He looked around like a drunk on a bad hangover, trying to place himself, the time, the situation. Then he slipped on clothes, hitting the doorway as Bill Day and Team Wyoming crossed the ditch, entering the small assembly area between the buildings and the strip.

"Hey, Ted. How you doing!" Day yelled.

"Fine," said Garner, really meaning it. "How are you feeling? I thought you'd be crashed somewhere with a splitting headache. How'd you enjoy your Hail and Farewell party last night?"

Larsen walked up behind. "It wasn't his party last night. He's staying here. The dummy extended his tour three months."

"What?" Garner stood there blinking, while Day laughed.

"Yah. Tone damn near killed me. Called me every name he could think of."

"Why did you extend, Bill?"

"Well, I've been accepted to the University of Colorado, and school starts mid-September, but I won't get discharged till two months later, so I'm taking Uncle Sam up on his early out program. I give him three more months here and get discharged late in August when I get back. It gives me a chance to get set up next summer. Gonna party hard."

"Yah, if you don't get your ass blown off. A couple months won't matter if you're dead."

"No sweat. I'm hiding out. I'm just gonna resupply the launch sites, like I'm doing today. Otherwise, it's in the club for me."

"Yah, how'd the party go last night?"

"Well, Tone was bad drunk. Lieutenant Larsen here tried to put the make on Canada again."

"Did not, I was just being friendly," he said, laughing.

"Right, Sir. Billings was swinging his chair around in the air again. Scared the hell out of everyone. Oh yah. They introduced the new Recon first sergeant last night, before presenting the plaques and One Zero Jackets. The name's Donnally. Came up from one of the A Camps down south somewhere. Second tour. He took over Billings's job yesterday. Look at what we got this morning. Sucker jumped off the rolling truck and hit the ground running." He reached into a side pocket and handed over sheets of paper.

RECON COMPANY
SOA (CCC) 5TH SFG (ABN) 1ST SF
APO San Francisco, Calif 96499

SUBJECT: Policy & Information

TO: All Recon Personnel

1. Thanks to everyone I've met so far. I appreciate the warm reception and look forward to working with Recon Company. I will be posting information THINK sheets such as this, from time to time. Please examine the Recon bulletin boards before morning formation. Extra copies will be available through the orderly.

NO LESS THAN 7 LINES IN A SPOT REPORT

2. The following is a recapitulation of Recon Company policies that have been previously published in Policy + Information Letters since 3 July 1968, or announced in formations and meetings. In some cases, in which the policy statements are lengthy, only a reference as to the date of the publication will be made, along with the policy title.

a. (Manning Board). The 10s will ensure the Manning Board, located behind the Operations Sergeant's desk, is kept up to date, reference personnel, schools, weapons, and pass numbers.
b. (Daily Team Status). The Daily Team Status cards, located behind the interpreter's desk, will be posted prior to 0700 hours daily, except Sundays. When a team is on an operation, the personnel status of any individual left at base will be indicated.
c. (RT Status/Location Chart). Located on the Orderly Room door, will be posted prior to 0730 hours daily, except Sunday.
d. (Formations). The following formations are mandatory for all personnel unless previously excused or otherwise stated:

TIME	DAYS	FORMATION
0715	Mon–Sat	All SCU (Yards)(Special Combat Units)
0730	Mon–Sat	Recon Company
0730–0800	Mon–Sat	Police Call
0800–0830	Mon–Fri	PT/DD (10 held)
0820–0900	Sat	A+D (Awards + Decorations)
1000–1100	Sat	Command Info
1500–1545	Mon–Wed–Fri	10s + E-6 + above
1600–1630	Mon–Sat	Staff Conf
0800–1100	Mon–Sat	Sick Call

e. (SCU) Pay). Published 28 November 1968.
f. (Motor Stables). RTs assigned to wall security will pull motor stables on all vehicles assigned to Recon Company prior to 0730 hours each morning. Any deficiencies found will be corrected on the spot. Those that cannot be, will be reported to the Motor SGT and the First SGT
g. (Alerts). See Company Alert SOP, published 9 August 1968.
h. (Bunker Assignments). See P&I Letter dated 12 July 1968, and paragraph 4, P&I Letter dated 26 July 1968, plus Company Alert SOP.
i. (Lost Weapons). First published in P&I letter dated 9 November 1968. Any weapon that is lost, stolen, misplaced, or cannot be accounted for, will be paid for by every member assigned to the RT from which the weapon is missing. If lost while on operation, the RT 10 will determine the financial responsibility, with guidance from S-4.
j. (Training). Training for 10s, plus all personnel in the grade E-6 and above, is held each Monday, Wednesday, and Friday,

from 1500–1545 hrs in the Recon Conference room. 10s are responsible for their RT's training and will post, on the training and location chart, located on the Orderly Room door, their RT's status, daily. In the absence of the 10 the 11 will post it.

k. (Appearance). See paragraph 3 P&I Letter dated 12 July 1968, and paragraph 1, P&I Letter dated 24 July 1968.

l. (Strap Hangers). A "strap hanger" policy was published on 3 November 1968.

m. (Stand Down). Upon return from operation, each RT will be authorized 5 days' free time. This does not include the day returning or the following day, which are taken up in cleaning weapons and equipment, repacking gear, and debriefings. Upon return to base camp, the Bright Light Team will be ready for duty Wednesday morning. If the Bright Light Team has participated in artillery training at Ben Het on Saturday and Sunday, they will be ready for duty the following Thursday. The First SGT will make any adjustments as to time off permitted when questions or doubts arise.

n. (Promotions). 10 recommend their personnel for promotion. 10s will be recommended by the First SGT and CO.

o. (10 Aid Kits). Aid kits will be drawn from the Dispensary on a mission only basis. They will be turned in as soon as possible upon return.

p. (VRs). Upon return from a Visual Reconnaissance, each individual will report to the Launch Site for LZ reporting, and to the S-2 for an intel debriefing.

q. (TOC Admittance). The only Recon Company personnel authorized to visit the Tactical Operations Center are the CO, First SGT, and those other personnel specifically requested for in reference to operations.

r. (Bright Light Team). SOP published 16 July 1968.

William Donnally
1SG Recon Co.

"Man, the guy dug all this stuff up out of the files in one day? What's he like?" Garner asked.

"He seems okay, I guess. Not a bully like some first shirt. I don't think he'll make my extension hell on earth, but he's organized, picky. It shows."

The rest of the day was quiet, and Dodge and Djuit went back to camp. It was Garner's turn the next night, and rotations continued through the week. It was boring, but had the thin underlayment of tension and uncertainty.

"Suzy," as they called her, didn't come around again, and Garner decided he missed her. They wondered if security at Dak To tightened, and she and the other girls who regularly serviced the surrounding Engineering Companies had been combed out of the large compound. They didn't know.

During the week, two teams were extracted and three more inserted. A-Company was still in, and they had taken three wounded and two dead Montagnards off the resupply helicopters.

Thursday morning, it hit.

"Roger Broken Bottle, this is Dusty. Out. Larsen! Lieutenant Larsen!" Gable, the radioman sitting in the shed by the doorway, faced the foggy dials and gauges of the radio. Headset on. "Lieutenant Larsen!"

Garner watched the officer run up. "What?"

"Sir, you may want to get ready. You may have to go in. Team Washington's hit. Miller, the One Zero's dead. The One One's hit bad and so are two Yards. The new guy, Thompson, the radioman is running to an LZ. Covey, Broken Bottle, says they might need help getting out."

Everyone crowding near the door heard the news, and broke out like flushed quail, flying to the barracks and their equipment. They checked the radio and packs, gutting whatever was not needed on a one-day operation. The helicopters started up, and they went over everything two more times in the rush of excitement.

Finally, they were standing at the strip, pointing weapons down, pulling the charging handles back and letting bolts fly forward to strip off the magazine's first round. They "clicked" safeties on, and climbed aboard the first two ships.

Larsen, Garner, Dominique, Phe and Kehn were in the first. Dodge, Kui, Djuit and Whean were in the second. Five minutes after getting the call, they were up over the wire, heading west.

Garner puckered high as Larsen nodded to the door gunner, yelling instructions and information into his ear. Yards were putting on camouflage, and Phe passed him the stick when he was through. Garner started spreading paste as Larsen scooted over on the rippled metal floor. He screamed above the roaring turbine.

"He says Covey wants to try and get the team out on their own without sending us in. They're close to an LZ, but they've got two more wounded. Moving slow. Under fire. They'll try to get out before putting more people on the ground."

They flew west and then turned slightly north. The sky was bright and crystalline, and their plain green uniforms rippled in the wind. In forty minutes they were there. No one said a thing, but the helicopter shifted, and the screaming turbine slackened as forward airspeed dropped.

Down in the green hills were Cobras making runs. From above, their blades spun like pinwheels slashing sunlight. The blaze of miniguns shredded tracks of leaves in the canopy, through the rising blue haze of a smoke grenade thrown by the escaping team. Again, and again, and again they passed, flying north to south, changing passes with instructions from the ground below.

Garner saw the LZ just two hundred meters east. Washington would make it out. They wouldn't have to go in. He looked again. A dead man? Four wounded? Five? They'd never get out. He took three deep breaths, and wasn't surprised when Larsen tapped him on the shoulder.

He screamed, "We're going in. Hang on."

They plunged. The jungle rushed to greet them, and as they lowered into the hole, he imagined seeing all the swirling leaves turn into NVA, with a million weapons pointing at his heart.

He jumped. They fell together, tumbling forward. Then they gathered, meeting Dodge in the wood line and heading in as the Hueys settled down behind. Whean took point, with the rest stringing out.

After sixty meters the helicopter noise slackened behind, absorbed by the jungle. Ahead was automatic rifle fire. Cobras made one pass and then another.

"Whean!" Larsen nodded, signaling "Stop" as he reached the radio. He was watching the front and talking to Covey. "Phil, Covey says Washington is out of smoke and can't show us where they're at. Throw one out west as far as you can. We walk in unannounced and they'll shoot our asses off."

Dodge pitched a red smoke far out in front. Nothing.

"Broken Bottle says Thompson can't see smoke. We've got to move in closer. Keep down. Charlie's right on top, trying to circle. Look out to the sides. Let's go."

They stood up and headed out again. At fifty meters, they threw a yellow smoke.

"They saw it, let's go. Stay down, dammit!"

They moved through the smoke, dodging back and forth, weaving between the trees while nearing the firefight. Leaves and branches came trickling down, and tree trunks sounded like they were being hit with baseball bats as bullets hammered home. Twenty meters on the other side, they found the team, lying low, firing into the jungle further west.

"Thank God. Thank God." Thompson was close to hysteria. "The Cobras are putting up a wall so they don't flank us, but we can't move. We can't move. They'll get us in a cross fire."

Garner laid out flat, examining the carnage. Five wounded, one dead. Miller, the team leader, got it in the head. Doughy brains puffed out where the left ear should have been. Jackson, the second in command, was twisting and clutching his bloody right shoulder.

One Yard, hit along the jaw, bled wholesale; his teeth were dangling loose. The other three were down for good, two with leg wounds and the third on his back, gasping, flooding red along the chest.

Larsen yelled, "Ted, Dominique, Djuit, Kehn, lay suppressing fire. Phil, get the wounded out of here. Take Miller only if it doesn't slow you down."

They went tumbling around with the rest of Team Washington, helping, as more fire came in from the west. Mulch kicked up, and as Garner lay on his right side, changing a magazine, he watched a tree beside him stripping bark in puffs of small explosions three feet up. He rolled over, hiding his face in the leaves, and then came up on his elbows, lining sights.

Once the fighting started, fear of the unknown was down, leaving sheer mechanics and adrenalin. He held his breath, looking for movement. It was everywhere in front. Figures came closer, dodging and dancing through the jungle, popping up and down, firing short bursts before they disappeared. They were just twenty meters out, and like everyone else, Garner fired four fast magazines in short bursts, hitting half a dozen of the enemy. Then he scooted back around the slender tree.

Larsen signaled, and they pitched grenades forward in a fan. Explosions rocked, and shrapnel whizzed around as they jumped backwards, retreating thirty meters, where they turned and fired again. Moving, stopping, firing, moving, stopping, firing, they ran leapfrogging back to the LZ, always keeping the wounded up ahead in sight.

Larsen threw a yellow smoke twenty meters to the west, and told the Cobras to hit it. Suddenly, the billowing stream came flying through the air, landing back between them. Charlie knew the meaning of the smoke. Larsen went rolling, grabbing a fistful of insulating leaves as he picked up the burning canister.

He came up, throwing as two forms lunged through the smoke that wrapped him like a shroud. He saw his death, and let it go as Garner fired fully automatic, turning them into paper dolls with jointed limbs. They danced backwards, twirling and popping as he aimed from one to another. Then the bolt flew back, locking empty, spent and open, and he changed it out as the bodies tumbled in the yellow mist.

The team backed away. Cobras passed, hitting the smoke, and the rest of the team reached the LZ as two Hueys took off fully loaded. The second pair came in firing, taking the rest. They were out, and Garner's senses reeled with the explosion of adrenalin. The smells of fuel and sweat hit him, and in response he sucked in huge gulps of cold mountain air. Colors vibrated, as he laid back and started getting control of the hyperventilation shaking his body.

Friday, the next day, was no better. Larsen was quiet, pensive. A-Company was hit hard, and they off loaded eight wounded, three dead. All but one were Yards.

A hole in Cooper's high left thigh was the size and shape of a football. The upper left of his head was gone, along with the arm. They couldn't recognize his face, no jaw, just pulpy bits of matter. No one wore dog tags across the fence, and uniforms were sterile: no patches, no names, no unit, no rank, but it was Cooper just the same. Size gave it away.

He'd lain dead on his right side all morning long. The remaining arm was black and blue, and knobby knuckles glowed waxy dark with puddled blood. "B-40 rocket," Dodge guessed.

Saturday, after signing over to Team Kentucky, they left Dak To and landed at CCC in time for morning formation. It's not that they had to, but it was Awards and Decorations, and Garner got his CIB, Combat Infantryman's Badge, for the action on his first mission. Afterwards, they cleaned equipment, lounged, enjoyed steaks in the afternoon, and were drunk in the club by eight o'clock that night.

"Well, that's it for me," slurred Larsen. "The team is yours, Phil. I got three weeks. I quit. And thank you, Ted, you saved my ass. My mother and my father thank you too. I been thinking about it a lot. Thanks." He slurped Scotch, while murmuring incoherently. Then he caught Canada's attention.

"Hey, Canada, *lai day, co*, come here."

She floated over to take the order.

"Canada, will you marry me for the night?" All the others laughed.

"Why you be so mean *Trung Uy* Larsen?"

"I love you, Canada."

"Oh, bull, GI, I know you. You be nice. You be nice like Garnah here. He good man. He no lie to me."

"Ah, Canada," said Dodge. "You don't know our Garner. He's working miracles. After these VN ladies are with him for the night, he gets their hormones so pumped up, they just pop out from an A cup to a C cup." He motioned out with his hands. "It's magic."

She tried not to giggle. "You GIs. You think big is good. I tell you small is better." Then she turned, and walked away, smiling as they laughed.

They sat with Jim Harmon and Danny Dravos from Team Texas, which had come out the second day of Bright Light from a road watch. Two tables over, Tony sat alone, drinking quiet, blinking tears for Cooper.

"Well, I've got to admit I'm scared. I don't know what I'll do when I get reassigned," Dravos said.

"Yah, you always prefer the devil you know, to the one you don't," said Dodge.

"And it's all because you snore?" Garner asked.

"Snore? No," said Harmon. "Bellow is more like it. Danny didn't start off like this, but something changed. Lay him on his back, his front, his side, no difference. We can't shut the SOB up. We were on a road watch sleeping twenty meters back in the trees. This guy sounds like a Russian tank coming down the trail. Every night the Yards were pounding on him five, six times to shut him up."

"Yah, I can't help it. I don't want to quit, but I'll get someone killed."

"It's not like you mean to do it," Harmon said.

"Yah, the Yards have been real good, but they're getting scared. I've got to go, and there's nothing open in camp. I just can't sleep quiet in the bush anymore."

They talked of Bright Light, of Miller and of Cooper. Quiet toasts clinked, with sidelong glances at Tony by the bar. The room was full, and conversations varied only slightly. Deaths were talked out full.

Garner's money wasn't any good while Larsen bought beers, talking about the action. Embarrassment and pride caught him off guard, and again a tinge of shame came creeping in as he accepted subtle elation going hand in hand with killing other men, other armed men. He'd saved a life and taken two, maybe more. As usual they had their chance. He wiped the slate and took another sip.

Dodge said. "Well, Ted, here's a toast to your breaking your cherries."

He raised his glass while Garner stabbed him with looks.

"Your cherry. You got your CIB. What do you think I meant? Here's to it." They raised drinks around the table, and Dodge grinned suspiciously.

"And to show you the measure of my esteem, I brought you this." He pulled a paper bag from underneath the table. "Here."

Garner looked around, wiping lips and moustache. "What is it, a bag of dried elephant dung?"

"You don't trust me? I'm wounded. Look."

He reached in, pulling out the banner with the star in the center. It was the Viet Cong flag.

"What? Wow! Phil, I thought you sold it?" He scooted back, spreading it across his lap as everyone smiled. It was different though, not quite as faded as the first, with holes in other places and not as many rusty spots of blood.

"What is this?" he finally asked.

"That's what it looks like, a VC flag!" Dodge answered. Larsen laughed.

"What's going on here?"

"You've got one of Phil's flags," Larsen said. "They make great souvenirs. I sent mine home four months ago. It gave the folks the willies, till I wrote and told them it was a fake."

"What a dummy I am," Garner said, and slumped back as the others doubled over, hooting and laughing.

Harmon said, "The guys on Kentucky brought a real one back what, five months ago? Phil bought it and took it to a seamstress in Kontum. She's turned out fifty or sixty since then for you hasn't she?"

Garner felt Dodge study him. "More," he said. "I shoot holes in them, sprinkle chicken blood, rinse them in a weak solution of bleach and weather them out on the roof of the team room for a while. The Legs love them. I make sure to take a couple along whenever I leave the compound. Good pocket change, Ted. See, I told you it wasn't worth fifty bucks."

"Damn." Garner shook his head and laughed. "I should have known. I should have known."

After finishing up the beer, he caught Canada's eye and ordered another. Then he went wobbling to the latrine and stood before the urinal. His eyes grew wider and his face lost all expression as he felt the first trickling, tingling pulses of pain.

THINK
RECON COMPANY
SOA (CCC) 5TH SFG (ABN) 1ST SF
APO San Francisco, Calif 96499

SUBJECT: Policy & Information

TO: All Recon Personnel

WHAT DID YOU ACCOMPLISH TODAY???

1. a. The monthly promotion board will be held in B Company, Pleiku, on the 20th of the month. Personnel to attend, are listed below and will depart this location at 1400 hours on the 19th.

To: E-7	To: E-6	To: SGT
SSG Williams	SGT Stamp	Sp4 Backburn
SSG Kaden	SGT Buckman	Sp4 Cane
SSG Dodge	SGT Anderson	Sp4 Sardo
SGT Samuels	Sp4 Garner	
SGT Harmon	Sp4 Garcia	
SGT Buker		

   b. If your name does not appear on this list, and you feel that you have been overlooked, or slighted, then see your 10, who in turn can see me. If necessary I will see the SSM.

IS YOUR JOB WORTH DOING: THEN DO IT RIGHT!

2. Ten 10s attended yesterday's "Exchange of Ideas" session. Subject presented was: "Trail, Road, and Stream Crossings." Tomorrow the subject will be "POW Snatch." All 10s be there, and be on time.

WHEN DID YOUR STATE ENTER THE UNION?

3. Washington got out with help from Iowa. Good job. Welcome home.

YOU CAN NOT AFFORD NOT TO

4. SSG Miller and SGT Cooper were KIA. Also SCU Diet, Phong, Kayme and Tho. Date and time of Memorial Services will be announced.

DO YOU HAVE TIME NOT TO TRAIN?

5. Yesterday morning, NW of Kontum City, a jeep hit a mine. Results: 1 US KIA, 1 US and 1 ARVN WIA. A sweep of the road turned up six Soviet anti-tank mines.

WHY?

6. This publication will be printed as a supplement to the unit bulletin board. You are STILL required to read the bulletin board twice daily.

#1 SHEPPARD OR GLENN?

7. SGT Keats arrived today from Okie as SSG Johnson's replacement on RT New Mexico. Introduce yourselves.

S.A.L.U.T.E.

8. When sending in a spot report, send all information in the clear except coordinates or any other information that may give your position away. All such potentially dangerous information should be coded with your kak cards. No exceptions.

SEND: WHO, WHAT, WHERE, WHEN.

9. Fourth Armored Division received mortar fire last night from the vicinity of Kontum City. Don't think it can't happen here. Think quick.

WILLIAM DONNALLY
1SG Recon Co.

10

"I can't believe it. I can not fucking believe it!" Garner winced as the medic injected his right buttocks with putty.

"Well, you got it, partner," the medic said. "One good-sized dose of clap. Streptococcus, gonococcus, you got it. Better steer clear of the ladies for a while."

"Oh Jeez, you sure that's not a ten penny nail you're using?" He popped on his toes and went to buttoning, while the medic put together a packet of pills.

The twenty-bed dispensary was on the western half of camp, south of the dining hall and club. He refused to go at first, but heard gleeful stories about soldiers screaming in latrines, twisting and bending water pipes above the urinals. He was a believer after just one day.

Outside, in the ward, were VNs, Yards and Americans. They had worms, dysentery, malaria, and minor wounds, needing mostly time for healing right. He'd looked for Jackson, the black staff sergeant, but major trauma cases flew to Pleiku hospital right away. The man lucked out, and was going home alive.

Garner shifted back and forth, deeply mortified, while waiting for the doctors. Three seats over was an ARVN sergeant wearing just a shirt. He was hunkered down and quiet, constantly referring to the black bush hat covering his lap. Garner tried, but couldn't keep from glancing over time to time.

The man sat pressed against the wall, as if wanting to disappear. Then after looking around he lifted the hat to study himself in disbelief. It was a mass of purple cauliflower, and Garner's pressure shot up with the sight of it.

"Oh, just venereal warts he let go too long," the medic later said haphazardly.

"My God. That won't happen to me will it? Doc?"

"No, no. You just follow directions and take the tetracycline like you should, and you'll clear up fast. Just don't make a habit of this. Be a little more careful where you dip your wick. You can build up resistance to this stuff you know."

"Yah, I've heard. I won't. I swear."

"Well, at least you're lucky. I treat five and more cases a week. At least your symptoms hit you here and not in the field. How do you think the Old Man would like it if you had to be extracted 'cause you got the clap? Huh? It's happened, and it ain't a pretty sight. Watch it. Next!"

Stand down was over. They went into training, and a new man came in. Larsen went to supply for his final two weeks, Dodge became One Zero, and Garner rejoiced, moving out from under the radio and turning it over to the new member just assigned, Jim Reynolds.

He was a lanky boy from Dallas, or there about. He had a swimmer's chest and narrow hips, and an Adam's apple that bobbed up and down with his Texas twang. Garner imagined him in boots, kicking dung, riding horses, drinking beer, but he was a city boy. His father was a banker. It didn't show.

They went back to the range, working fast-action drills. In combat, most teams were hit head on. It made sense. It was expected they would wander head first into trouble. The team zippered open, firing and moving. They also practiced truck ambush, working timing and placement. Next, they rappelled and climbed the ropes and ladders. Drills with wounded were important. They practiced with saddle back carries, fireman's carries, improvised slings and stretchers. Dodge worked from different points, yelling, "Ambush to the side!" and they went leapfrogging backwards and away, one half moving, one half firing.

They wanted immediate timing and response, like a halfback skimming down the field confronting three tacklers. They'd bury him if he analyzed the situation, plotting timing, course and speed. He needed to see and recognize what was happening as it happened. So too, they wanted no slack time, no pause, no fatal, second-guessing judgments. Take the best of bad, go with it and do it fast.

Garner taught them "quick kill," a technique he'd learned in Advanced Infantry Training, back at the little compound outside Fort Gordon, Georgia, called Camp Crockett. It was an immediate aiming technique designed for close jungle combat. Instead of coming up to the shoulder to aim and fire, they locked the butt stock under the arm, keeping the left one straight, as a guide to sight along and fire.

Sights were fine for a hundred meters, but close in, the thing that kept people alive was timing. Quick and dirty. Get it up and be the first to shoot. Lock in the position so it never wavered. Always be exact in the position. Always be the same. Only then could they automatically know where the three-round bursts would land.

Back in the States, they practiced by rolling metal disks and firing pellet rifles, like gunfighters shooting pistols from the hip. In Vietnam, it proved deadly up to fifteen meters. Garner taught repetition, repetition, repetition. Form mattered in that the left arm should be straight. The eye could judge the difference in the angle, but if there was no constant form or framework, the bullets were simply wasted.

The Yards became quite good at hitting targets, but were heavy on the trigger, shooting five to seven rounds by being lazy. He yelled and yelled, showing by example. He could back away, turn and bring the weapon up to nail a chest-sized target twenty meters out.

They trained every day and finally had a chance to take a break when Dodge and Garner both went to Pleiku for promotion boards. They were up for different ranks of course, but everyone had to sit before the B-Team committee of five officers, and answer questions ranging from thoughtful philosophy, to politics, to the inane.

They covered military history, the functions of S-1, S-2, S-3 and S-4, opinions of the war, the protestors and the M-16 versus AK-47. Dodge told the truth the way he saw it, and everyone thought he blew his chance to make E-7.

"Well, Sir. The M-16 is a fine weapon, now that the Pentagon finally stopped messing around with the ammunition, and redesigned the weapon."

"What do you mean, soldier?" The lieutenant colonel sat like a center piece, with other lower ranks spread out to either side. He examined Dodge over glasses, looking like a principal with a heavy ruler tucked behind his back.

"Sir. I believe the first M-16s over here were designed for civilian manufactured ammunition. It's cleaner than Mathieson gunpowder used in the old M-14s and M-1s. Well, from what I've heard, the Pentagon said it didn't matter, and simply used that standard powder, refusing to redesign the weapon for more tolerance, so it kind of jammed on rapid fire. You've got to figure a GI is gonna have second thoughts if he finds his buddies dead with cleaning rods in their hands.

"Now you can almost shove sticks and leaves in an AK-47 and it will still fire, but you've—" They cut him off, not wanting to hear the rest.

The boards finished late, so they stayed a second night. Others there were from A-Teams, the foundation of Special Forces front line work. They were small camps dotting the high country, forging villages into fighting hamlets that protected property and secured the military area. B-Teams were more middle management locations. They had limited combat duties of course, but most people assigned there had more support oriented jobs.

The club was a hodgepodge of ranks and units. Promotion boards pulled people in from all over the Kontum valley area, and they sat, drinking in clumps, secure within their own tight circles. However, Special Forces was a career, and time and again Garner heard uproars of laughter and greeting, as those who'd served together in prior assignments spotted one another across the smoky room.

Others got pulled in, as introductions went from one unit to another. Within an hour, the unique fraternal bond of Special Forces brought them all together, mingling, joking, laughing, drinking. It was a process Garner marveled at, while its warmth spread around the room.

He roamed with others, talking to members of the A-Teams. They swapped war stories, and one glaring thing was no one ever made reference to operations across the fence, just long-range recon. They were brothers of sorts, but every unit was responsible for secrets, even those that were not especially well kept within their private circles.

Late in the evening the club began filtering down, and he sat with Dodge. The team leader seemed depressed, and Garner sensed something behind the eyes, wanting out. It finally broke when the conversation turned to women, as it eventually always did.

"Now you take Canada for instance. She's a pretty little willowy kinda thing. Reminds me a little of my old lady."

"What? You're married, Phil?"

"Was once. Long time back. We split. Today's our anniversary."

"Oh, I'm sorry."

"No, no. Not to be sorry. It was best. But, like I say, Canada kind of reminds me of her."

"She was Oriental?"

"No. Eskimo."

"Oh, bullshit. I should have known."

"No, no. She was."

Garner started laughing until he saw a flint of feelings behind the eyes that turned him quiet.

"See, I was born and raised outside of Phoenix, and the wilderness down there is wide and beautiful. But as big as it is down there it's too open for me. I love the trees. I love the jungle over here too. When you get high up and deep into Prairie Fire, you can find pines and such, not at all like southern swamp jungles. More like old Appalachia.

"Anyway, I was craving for the trees, so when I got out of high school I headed north. I bounced through British Columbia and ended up in Alaska, working gofer work with mining companies and oil wildcatters.

"I'd come into Anchorage kind of like on R&R, and I met her at a beer drinking contest, believe it or not. It was the twenty-sixth annual Rendezvous. The 'Rondy.' It's an old-time kinda festival in February, where trappers bring in winter furs and do their trading. They've got contests and sports, and the whole place kind of goes nuts for a week or so. Jane was something."

"Jane?"

"Yah, Jane Nageak. She was Inupiat Eskimo. What'd you think they name them all, Nanook?"

"No, Phil. I didn't mean anything by it."

"Her folks ran commercial fishing boats. Pretty well fixed by Eskimo-Aleut standards. Well we got it on pretty good. Those were salad days. I guess we made love every chance we could find a dark corner and half an hour's time. She was fun."

He coughed a laugh. "You know that Airborne marching cadence? 'I don't know, but I've been told, Eskimo pussy's mighty cold. Honey oh baby mine. Go to your left your right, your left,' and so on? Well, not so."

He smiled drunkenly from somewhere far away.

"It's warm and full of laughs and love. I miss her sometimes. Canada's kind of like her, but she was more of a cross between an Oriental girl and the Yards. Wide face, high cheekbones and just a hint of Asian in her eyes. She was thin and pretty. Yard girls remind me of her too, 'cause they smile quick and laugh so much. Round-eyed women seem too uptight to me anymore. Like they mentally go through life with their legs crossed."

"What happened?"

"Well," he took another sip. "It didn't work out. I got to feeling tied down. Man, you want a comfortable life, don't be a commercial fisherman in water that has ice floating in it. It's hard and it stinks. If you don't get washed overboard, you break your back with a falling boom or drown in a tangled net.

"Anyway, I split after about a year and a half. Went back to wildcatting for awhile, but the fun was out of it. I drifted around and then went down to the lower forty-eight. Finally said to hell with it and joined the Army."

"I just don't understand, Phil. You're so damned wild, undisciplined. How can you stand the Army? It's so restricting."

"Nah, Ted. It's all how you look at it. The Army's not bad, at least not Special Forces. Every couple years, duty station changes. You climb a couple ranks and get out of chicken shit details. You travel, meet God knows what kind of people. It's not bad. Besides, like I said, it's attitude. Take it too serious, and you'll end up letting these officers scare you. Then you're totally screwed. Stay loose."

Garner considered his friend, and studied the pause as Dodge stared down at puddled condensation ringed around his glass. He took a sip and fingered tracks in the water, spelling out CCC as Garner pushed the conversation on.

"Well, have you considered Officer's Candidate School? You'd make more money, and climb above a lot of garbage that flows down hill on enlisted ranks."

"Climb above it? An officer steps and rolls right in it. I said attitude, Ted. If you don't care, they can't take anything away from you. An officer has to care. Christ. I wouldn't be an officer for five times the pay, let alone double.

"If I was an officer I'd be so uptight I'd be a complete jerk. They go through life terrified, politicking for this assignment or that assignment. They're scared they'll get a lousy post and get passed over for promotion by mistake. Or worse, they're scared they'll screw up and get passed over just the same. It's all over if they tick off some guy on top and get a bad Officer Efficiency Rating.

"You ever seen a Navy destroyer hit a dock? Or turn starboard instead of port and jam another ship? I have. There's one or two careers down the tubes every time it happens. Army's no different.

"I'll pull my time. I won't make the money, but I'll live it the way I want. The day I can't, I'll pack it in."

The next morning they roared back north in the CCC deuce and a half, old number sixty-nine: weapons ready, hanging over the edge. Tanks and armored personnel carriers were parked far out to either side, and occasional Rome plows ripped the earth, fighting constant regrowth of the jungle.

Dodge hung around outside the B-Team gate, talking with the grunts for half an hour before finally boarding. On the way back, he laughed while riffling notes and confessing, "Best thing about this trip is that I sold three flags."

Two days later, he was proven right on his prediction of the coming change in MPC. It was an experience Garner would forever remember with a sense of shame and heartfelt pity for the people.

They first noticed the gates were locked at morning formation. Both sides of the compound were sealed off from the open road. Guards were being posted while Donnally made regular announcements to the motley crew standing at parade rest. He hit them with it at the end.

"Gentlemen, no one will be leaving the compound today. After formation I want you to check my detail list and report to your normal assignment areas for sandbag filling duties and bunker improvement. Be sure to check your claymore wires coming out of firing ports. Several were found cut again yesterday, on the north wall.

"There will be another formation at eleven-hundred hours. Be sure you bring all your script. A Mister Baxter from Saigon will be here, exchanging old script for new."

Murmurs grew and heads twisted. Dodge looked back, cupping his mouth with the left hand. "Hey, Ted, now you know why we seal it up in envelopes and turn it in, whenever we go to the field or out on R&R." A small bandage was glowing dull white near his thumb.

"Quiet in the ranks," Donnally said, without glancing up from the clipboard. The first sergeant was over six feet tall, with a medium build, high forehead and an angular face. He stood ramrod stiff, but his penetrating look was often softened by a quick and sometimes patronizing smile.

"One final item. It has come to my attention, gentlemen, that someone at promotion boards took the liberty of carving a message on a table in the B-Team club. It read, I quote, 'CCC, Recon. B-Team sucks Mo Jo'."

Everyone broke out laughing, glancing back and forth with exaggerated "Who me?" looks.

"Gentlemen, I realize we are not attached to the Fifth Group right now and that B-Team duty is not necessarily front-line duty. However, your promotions do come through the Group, and we are all in Special Forces together, no matter what our temporary duty assignments might be.

"Please, I don't want to have to go through this again. I had to tell the colonel down there that Mo Jo is Montagnard for 'stupid,' and that it happens to be the name of the camp dog up here." He shot Dodge a glance, but he stood fast at parade rest, locking his eyes straight to the front. "I guarantee you, that was not fun."

A few other minor items followed before they were dismissed. Meanwhile, news of the MPC change was spreading, as Vietnamese tried reporting for work. They were not let in, and shouts of panic increased as some started racing back to Kontum to try and unload the money on those not yet aware.

Teams were at assigned bunkers all morning, replacing torn sandbags, improving drainage, checking wires. They couldn't see the gates on the other side of perimeter buildings, but they heard the increased panic of the local population as word passed along.

Garner went to the latrine closer in, and saw them hanging on the gates, screaming for someone to take their money. He watched armed guards protect the barbed wire, and realized this was going on all across the country.

It didn't matter how they got the money. Tips, bribes, prostitution, legal or illegal. The point was that they weren't supposed to have it, and as he watched, he knew he was seeing poor people's wealth being destroyed before his eyes.

Women were crying and begging, and some of the hooch maids who washed clothes and cleaned team rooms threw wadded-up rolls of blue money over the wire, hoping they could see and recognize whoever might pick it up. If a soldier did pick it up, she'd come later, begging, hoping he'd give her some portion of value in return. It was sordid, and higher ranks were watching and the guards knew it, and did their duty. They threw the money back across the ten-foot-high wire, yelling. "*Di di mao. Di di mao.* Go away. Go away." But they couldn't go away.

Teams worked on the bunkers, weeding out between the rows of barbed wire, out to the edges of the mine field. Noise grew in the background, and several went inside the team rooms, working on busy work to get away.

As eleven o'clock neared, many more started drifting off with the excuse of cleaning up for formation. Garner had a rotted wooden frame around one of the firing slots, and was replacing wood and bags. Then he finished, checking around one last time and heard his name from far away.

"Garnah! Garnah!"

It was Canada, ninety feet outside the wire. She wore a full white blouse, and black pants went fluttering as she took long strides, prowling like a cat trying to get into the canary cage. She paced back and forth, arms rising and falling in exaggerated swings of frustration.

"Garnah, Please help. Please help."

He looked around, hesitating. The fact that she was caught with money was her own damned fault, not his.

"Please, Garnah. Please, Garnah." Her voice keened at him. She was crying, screaming.

The trap was there. A sense of guilt was there, and then it overwhelmed him. He finally raised his hands, loosely pointing toward the road. Her face lit up, and as she started jumping with excitement, he watched her change from the cat into a bounding puppy, tripping and prancing outside the wire.

He crouched and ran down the trench behind the bunkers, to where the wire narrowed at the junction of the road, the fence and the second armored car. He was behind the motor pool, looking around. Then he motioned to her as she ran up only twenty feet away on the road.

She jumped, throwing the canister; it sailed over the wire clattering behind him. Then he raced along, scooping it up, heading for the team room, never looking back.

It was like he thought, small change. The cork top was off the coke can, and spread before him on the bunk, were hundreds of smaller-sized MPC, twenty-five cents, fifty cents. Only a few were of the larger dollar size. One was five dollars. Altogether $157.75.

He separated each denomination and got to formation as roll was being called. The exchange was a typical military maneuver of Hurry Up and Wait. It lasted several hours as they stood in line outside the TOC, entering in groups of five.

Inside it was bitter cold, and they each stood, in turn, before the little man behind the desk. He wore civilian clothes, looking bloodless as his delicate hands counted out the money taken in. Garner grated his teeth as the question was asked.

"These are a lot of small bills, aren't they Specialist? Where do you get so many small bills?"

The little man was cold, with a dark coat draped around his shoulders. Garner thought of the badly made propaganda movies made during World War II, and muffled a smile at the little Nazi-like figure before him. "Ve Vill get ze invormacion out of you von vay or ze ozer, Garnah. Now tell uz everyzing you know."

"Well, Sir. I, ah. I play a lot of poker, and like to keep a reasonable pile of chips. I've ah, I've got a kind of special box I just throw my winnings in, and it kind of builds up you see."

"Oh, I understand," the man said slyly. "But given your rank, you haven't been in country all that long, have you?"

Garner studied him: officious jerk, long hair, civilian, a clerkish bully. He got his back up and leaned forward, placing hands flat, halfway across the desk, and said. "I guess I'm just a lucky kinda guy!"

That broke it.

"Well, let's see." The delicate fingers started counting.

Everyone was still restricted to base, but by two o'clock Mr. Baxter was gone to his next assignment and the gates opened to camp workers. The men, motor pool workers, kitchen help and drivers, were sullen, broken, mad. The women, hooch maids, bar maids and dining room helpers wept softly, and swollen eyes blazed messages not to be denied. Hurt and anger were everywhere, and Americans caught the backlash, even though they had no part in it.

That night they drank in the club as usual.

"Ya know, Ted. I didn't know you played that much poker." Dodge said across the table.

"I play a little."

"Well, that was quite a roll you pulled out wasn't it? I mean I was right behind. You should have seen it, Bill." He motioned a double-handed doughnut, showing Day sitting across.

"And you know what got my attention? Although I never would of had bad manners to say anything in front of that jerk Baxter. It's just that most poker games around here have a minimum bet and raise of a buck even." He finished his drink while grinning wide.

"Phil, do me a favor."

"What, Ted?"

"Go tell Donnally how you got that cut on your hand down at Pleiku."

Dodge looked at the left palm where the knife slipped.

"Touché, touché. I've been struck by a barb from your quiver of stinging insults. Ha. Ha. Hey, Canada!"

She came over, smiling and sidling up to where Garner's left shoulder almost touched her lower belly. "Yes, *Trung Si* Dodge, you want bourbon?"

They gave their orders, and when she returned, Garner paid and gave her a twenty-five dong tip. Then he said,

"Oh, Canada. I brought that copy of *Life* magazine you wanted to practice reading English with." He handed her the folded magazine. "I suggest you read it carefully and learn the meaning of the words."

"Thank you, *Trung Si* Garnah."

"I'm still Spec. Four Garner."

"Yes, *Trung Si* Garnah." She hurried away with the tray and magazine. He knew she'd go to the ladies' room, and find far more than what she'd hoped for. Tucked within the magazine was an envelope with $160.00 in crisp bright red bills. The note was printed large. "Never again!"

11

THINK

RECON COMPANY
SOA (CCC) 5TH SFG (ABN) 1ST SF
APO San Francisco, Calif 96499

SUBJECT: Policy & Information

TO: All Recon Personnel

ARE YOU PRACTICING ANY NEW PROCEDURES OR METHODS

1. It has come to my attention that last Christmas, Eastman Kodak refused a request by Recon members at our sister compound, CCS, to have cards manufactured. Evidently pictures were sent showing members brandishing weapons and standing on top of enemy bodies. The caption was to be "Peace on Earth, Good Ill toward Men." Gentlemen, this is unprofessional conduct and I don't want to hear of things like this from our compound. Although Eastman Kodak refused this order, the cards were evidently manufactured in Bangkok.

TOMORROW MAY BE TOO LATE

2. Brown and green ground sheets are available in the Recon orderly room. 10s can pick them up if desired. They are hard to come by and are expensive, so be conservative.

TRAINING PAYS OFF

3. All Recon 10s turn in to me a roster of your Montagnard personnel by Ethnic Group (Tribe) as soon as possible.

"SPARE TIME FOR 10S?????"

4. Congratulations to all those whose promotion orders came in today. Listings are behind the Recon orderly desk. Check and see. Good news all the way around.

SCU AIRBORNE CERTIFICATES???

5. A letter from SGT William Jackson from stateside is posted on the bulletin board. Take note of the return address and drop him a line. I'm sure he will appreciate it.

#1 LZ FOR EXTRACTION IS A SITDOWN

6. Sample weather report: WX Vix. 3 mi, clouds sctd, brkn, 3000.

#2 LZ FOR EXTRACTION IS A LADDER

7. Special Combat Unit Combat pay: Explain to your SCU personnel that combat pay in the amount of 150 dong a day will only be paid for time on actual operations and time on Bright Light. No combat pay will be paid for convoy duty, ambush, or for local sweeps, unless enemy contact is made. This information comes straight from Finance Section.

#3 LZ FOR EXTRACTION IS MCGUIRE RIG

8. The S-4 sent in an emergency re-supply request for insect and leech repellant. Lt. Glass went to Pleiku today to try and get some from his friends in the meantime. Conserve what you have.

HAVE YOU HEARD ABOUT "PARTICIPATION DAY?"

9. A&D Ceremony will be held at 0830 hours Saturday on the basketball court.

WHO ARE THE SENATORS FROM YOUR STATE?

10. SFC Billings departs CCC on the 12th. He desires to say farewell to all Recon personnel at the 0730 formation. Be there!

WHO IS YOUR GOVERNOR?

11. Spot reports are still coming into S-2/3 from RTs with insufficient information. Recommend each 10 get together with his team and explain what is required in a spot report.

CAN YOU IMPROVE?

William Donnally
1SG Recon Co.

12

All during the next ten days in the club, Garner could not shift in his chair without Canada coming right over, checking on his drink or asking if he needed cigarettes from behind the bar. The other bar maids questioned her, but she said nothing. The Americans asked him if it was some kind of new cologne, or if there were spells or magic involved, but he said nothing.

Finally, one night, embarrassment forced him to whisper a request to have her meet him outside behind the mess hall. He left first, working his way between shadows and the lights flooding out over the perimeter wire. He went to the large Conex containers used as walk-in vegetable vaults, where the dark was deep and cool.

Three minutes later, soft scuffling came down the gravel path. A small figure rounded the mess hall's corner, peering into the shadows. She looked pensive, and backed away until he whispered.

"Canada."

She stopped, hesitated, and then walked into the dark.

"Canada, you've got to stop treating me special. It's embarrassing. Do you understand?"

She came in close, and he smelled her, feminine, sweet, something he couldn't trace. It certainly wasn't *nuoc mam*, the sun-baked fish oil the hooch maids and other Vietnamese ladled on their food. No, this was a western, soapy, aroma, catching him off guard. It was hidden by beer and stale air in the club, but out in the open, up close, it hit him hard, and a flashing thought of washing her with soap and water brought him to full and immediate arousal.

"You've got to stop treating me different than the others. Do you understand?"

"I understand, Sergeant Garnah." She moved in, palping her hands against his chest. "But you help me out of very big trouble. That money. It may not be much money to Americans. All Americans are rich. But to Vietnamese in this countryside it is much, very much. You gave it back to me. You gave me back more than what I had. You did not take any for yourself. I have been waiting. You have not asked anything of me. Why? Why? I think you like me? I think I like you. I want to show you. I like you much."

She moved in, brushing against him, feeling the erection against her stomach. She giggled. "Yes, I think you like me too, very much, Garnah."

He whispered. "Canada, don't do this because of the money. I won't do it again. If you get tips or whatever, you'd better change it over into dongs quick. Next time you'll lose it all. I will not help again. I cannot help again. My orders tell me not to. It's bad for me. I broke my orders. Do you understand?"

"I hear you, Sergeant Garnah. I hear you. It's not the money. I promise I will do as you say. Whatever you say. I do not want this for the money. I say thank you, but I do this for you. I do this for me."

Then she interlaced her fingers behind his neck, pulling herself to his mouth. Her tongue was hard and searching, and his hands roved beneath the elastic band of her satin trousers. Her round bottom undulated as he rubbed and probed her body. Gate guards talked off in the distance somewhere by the road, and as his hands made her wince and roll, he cursed the lack of a bed or even a clean floor.

Instead, she led him to grassy shadows, away from the perimeter's glare. She backed off toward the dim lights, and he watched her twist, bringing her blouse up over her head. Then she stepped out of the pants and stood before him, blue starlight glinting off her hair and shoulders. Her face was in shadow, and the sight of her silhouette made him tremble: small waist, flared hips, and shapely legs that bordered a small triangle of light high up and in between.

She came closer, and his hands circled her waist. He cradled her, and started kissing as his right hand moved up the hollow of her spine. Then the other dropped down to cup and squeeze her bottom. Both were panting, kissing deep and breaking loose for air. Then she dropped her right hand and stroked him, feeling his length and breadth. Garner groaned so loud he thought he'd summon up the sentries. He caught his breath, and lowered them both to the chilly grass as he kept control through sheer hard force of will.

Next mission was a simple trail watch. Instead of roving over the mountains for nine days, they would insert, find a suitable trail, and watch it all day and early evening, for a week.

As usual, false landings were conducted to hopefully confuse trackers and listeners on the ground. There were not many breaks in the canopy far north, and landing unopposed grew more difficult over the years as Charlie increased guards along the road. In fact growing successes made their jobs all the more dangerous. Intelligence estimated 50,000 troops were tied up across the fence, guarding the roads, searching for teams, protecting the convoys. SOG teams were bait that kept 50,000 North Vietnamese soldiers from ever fighting in South Vietnam.

The lack of open landing sites made northern targets difficult from the start. Of course B-52 Arc Light bombings were conducted all along the valleys where the road ran. Craters opened many square miles of jungle floor. However, since they were directed on the main road systems, insertion by using these open craters was difficult at best. It would be like Charlie landing in the plowed areas either side of highway QL-14. He would be on the ground, but there would be no surprise, and he'd be immediately surrounded.

Rumor control talked about the use of daisy cutters, 10,000-pound bombs rolled out the backs of C-130s. They had a fifteen-foot rod extension added to the nose tip firing pin. Coming down, the tip hit and the bomb exploded above ground, blowing a football field-sized hole in the jungle with very little crater.

After the second false insertion, they got off on a clean LZ east of the road, and disappeared north. They moved for two days, looking for a reasonable trail. It had to be large, and used enough to make the watch worthwhile; it also had to be open, where they could see along its length in both directions. Garner never met McDaniels, but he knew the memory of his death haunted Dodge. He wanted a view giving Team Iowa all the advantages of surprise.

Further north was just such a trail, he said. He'd seen it on a Visual Reconnaissance with Covey, Triple Nickel. It was wide and open, running for a klick or two down the middle of a pasture-like field.

It was a wild field, no crops, just knee-length grass running across the valley floor. Off on the western edge, down in the woods, was a stream, and several ponds dotted the northern half. Isolated trees were splattered around, and some of them looked like pines from the air. Dodge said it reminded him of Cades Cove, in the Smokies back home.

It was a unique pasture, wild and beautiful. Coveys and the helicopters used it as a quick reference point to figure distance and direction to northern targets. They called it the "Golf Course."

As they moved through the woods, it looked more and more like that would have to be their goal. Trails they crossed were large enough, but they wound around, twisting, so that if they were spotted or tried to grab someone, they wouldn't know if the soldier was alone or point man for a regiment. They'd find the trails, consult, reject, and stop just long enough to leave surprises, and then move on.

Sometimes they planted a toe popper on a trail. It was a small anti-personnel mine, Garner believed was dreamed up by some especially sadistic soul deep inside the Pentagon.

It was round, the size of a can of snuff, but thicker. Once the hole was dug, the mine was placed and armed with a twist of the lid. Then it was covered with an inch of dirt. When it was stepped on, the C-4 inside blew off the offending foot. Trails were peppered with them, and they made cripples out of both NVA and innocent Laotian tribesmen.

Their purpose was to maim not kill. If Charlie died, his friends blinked tears and dug him deep. However, if just his foot blew off, then new vistas of problems appeared. First was the panic. Screaming soldiers were unnerving, spreading fear throughout the ranks. Then there was the use of men and material. Soldiers had to carry the screaming cripple, and scant, hard-pressed medical attention had to be expended on him. The war could be won if 40,000 North Vietnamese soldiers lost a foot.

Other surprises were called Italian Green, or Pole Bean, or Armed Propaganda, depending on the person, time and place. It was booby-trapped enemy ammunition, and each team carried something in and dropped it off: 7.62 rifle ammunition, B-40 rockets, or mortar shells.

The munitions were taken from captured supply depots and flown to special factories in Okinawa. Technicians pulled casings apart and replaced the powder or propellant with C-4 explosive. Then everything was resealed, shipped back and left out on a trail or in a base camp, so Charlie would pick it up and reincorporate it with supply. SOG bought all its AK-47 ammunition from factories in Finland.

The doctored ammunition blew rifle bolts back through soldiers' faces. Mortars and rockets exploded. The intent was more than death. The intent was to breed suspicion and fear of the quality of Charlie's weapons. Like Dodge said, the AK-47 was a good rifle, but having them blow apart could make a soldier think and maybe even hesitate a little, maybe just enough.

They forded the stream Dodge was looking for by the third morning, and stood on a rocky outcrop at the south-west edge of the Golf Course, looking out from under trees, across long grass that rippled with a frigid wind. They'd crossed five trails and dropped off one B-40 rocket, one case of ammunition, and two toe poppers. Now they examined the sixth, tracking it north with binoculars, as it wandered over several swells and disappeared into the wood line over two kilometers away.

"Phil, are there many places like this out here? God this is some view."

"No, not that I know of, Ted. There are a lot of open areas down in Salem House, but it's flat, dry and dusty, timbered out, single canopy scrub. When I spotted this on the VR with Broken Bottle, I asked him about it. He said the only other areas like this are way west, over by Attopeu in the Mekong river basin; nothing else in our area of operations."

"Feel that wind coming across. I see what you mean about the pines." He reached over, pulling scaly bark off the tree next to him. Needles carpeted the rocks jutting from thin soil.

"Yah, after I leave you'll have to get back out here in December and cut yourselves a Christmas tree. Looks like some kind of spruce. Well, let's go."

They pulled back in the trees and moved north along the wood line, finally stopping at a slight rise. They were on the west edge near the middle of the oblong field. The trail ran down the center, and the view stretched for more than half a mile in either direction.

They were blind directly to the front, however. The rise swelled out of the woods, running up into the field, and the trail passed on the downhill side away from them.

"This is perfect," Dodge said as he gathered the team together to talk.

"We'll set up here and count heads. If we see just one or two people, we can diddy bop out on the other side of this slope and set up an ambush in the grass before they get to where they can see us. It looks like we can work it from either direction. The trail's on the other side, only two hundred meters out, so we ought to have plenty of time.

"Now, Dominique, tell everyone to look sharp to the sides. If I was Charlie, crossing a big open place like this would scare me to death. I don't care if it's in his backyard or not. Keep a look out to the sides. God knows, they could be scared about being spotted from the air and skirt the wood line like we did. I mean it. No smoking and joking. Tell them to look sharp."

They couldn't see both ends clearly from one location, so Dodge sat with Dominique, monitoring the south, and Garner sat with Djuit fifteen meters away, watching the north. As usual, they set claymores in a fan behind them, and up along the wood line. Reynolds and the rest of the team rested back in the middle.

Dodge changed people off from time to time, but always kept an American at each position. "The Yards are brave, Ted, but they're dangerous children. They play grab ass and bullshit with each other. They get bored easy. Pay attention to it. You've got to kick them in the butt once in awhile to get them to do things right.

"If we didn't monitor the trail, or show them by example, they'd get lazy and not pay attention to what they're doing. They could let a whole company walk right up on us. You're going to take over this team. Pay attention to it now."

Two hours later, first movement, north.

"We got something!" Garner whispered and motioned.

There was movement in the grass far north, where the trail climbed the tree-dappled rise. People were coming. There was a point man twenty meters out. Nine others strung along behind at three-meter intervals, looking like swinging baubles on a chain. All had packs and weapons. The AKs were slung low at a cautious, but not a ready angle. Dodge and Reynolds came crawling over, and the leader studied the squad with binoculars.

"See those rifles, Ted? They're not back slung over the shoulder. They're forward slung. That means word is out we're in town. No need for Charlie to be paranoid over here unless he knows we're in the area. Damn, we may not get a chance to grab someone."

Reynolds whispered. "I thought this was just a trail watch. No one said a thing about a prisoner snatch."

"Well, hell," said Dodge, "We get paid cash out of club profits and get a week's worth of lying around in Taipei for every prisoner we bring back. Hell, I might try to nab a whole platoon and just sit out the rest of this damned war."

Garner knew he was only halfway joking, but smiled, saying nothing to Reynolds, who looked decidedly uneasy.

They let them pass. They let the others pass too. Eight groups in all came down the trail, north to south. The largest was fourteen men, the smallest, four. That was the only one without a man on point, but it didn't really matter.

Prisoners were targets of opportunity, unless a specific man was wanted for specific information, such as a truck driver. Otherwise, anyone alive and walking was fair game. However, risking getting killed by attacking four armed men in the middle of an open field, for no other reason than a trip to Taipei, did not seem reasonable even to Dodge. They let them pass.

For two days they let them pass. It wasn't a steady stream but a trickle of men and material coming south. One larger group of twenty-five on the second day had three carts with boxes and packs. Sticking out the back of each were the long folded tripod legs and the flat snout of a .51 caliber antiaircraft machine-gun, three weapons capable of killing helicopter crews and fighter pilots. No air crews were close enough to call in for a strafing. They watched in frustrated silence, and let them pass.

Each night, after moving down into the woods to RON, they discussed strategy and expressed opinions. The stream to the west added a soothing counterpoint as it riffled over rocks and snags.

Garner whispered, "Phil, I don't know about you, but I'm getting tired as hell of this. It's one thing to watch the trail. That's easy, even though it's frustrating to see all these people and not be able to do anything about it. What's getting to me is this wood line. I keep seeing movement that isn't there. I keep straining my eyes, and every time the wind picks up across the prairie, the leaves get blown around and I imagine I see a hundred NVA coming straight at us from back in the woods."

"I know what you mean, Ted," whispered Reynolds. "Last night at dusk, when we just made out that last group, I swore I saw movement along the trees, but when I really looked close? There was nothing there."

"Well what do you want from me?" Dodge said. "You want me to call Leghorn and have them tell Dusty we're going to drop back in the woods for a day or so and rest our eyes? They'd think we were smoking junk and take back those new stripes you and I just got, Ted. I can't do that? We're scheduled for another four days at least.

"I don't know what I hate the most, the leeches or the rain we catch every day, or the lousy C-rations. All I know is this. Look, my old man was a plumber, a hard workin' guy. When I was a kid I used to ask him what I ought to do in life. Well, he says, 'Son? Every job has problems that go hand in hand with it. I don't care who you are, there are bad things to accept in any job. The day you can't stand them any more, get out.'

"'Now for me as a plumber?' he says. 'I've got to squeeze into tight places, deal with drippy faucets and rusty pipes, and live most of my working life in musty basements. That's the job. The day I can't stand musty basements any more, is the day I better go to school and learn to be a math teacher, or a jet engine mechanic, or something else. But it doesn't really matter, 'cause every job has got its own kind of musty basement.'

"And you know, that old man was right. Everything has got something that you hate about it. Out here, we got all kinds of 'musty basements', and I'm not even talking about getting our asses shot off for people who don't care, either here or in the States.

"The job is cold, wet, hungry, tired, scared, leech bitten, thankless, dangerous, and probably unfrickin' necessary, but it's the job you signed up for. I'm not mad. Don't get me wrong. It's just that every time I sit in the rain and feel a trickle of water run down my crotch, I see my old man and his musty basements.

"You've got to keep sharp on the wood line. Besides, Recon gets to run from a firefight."

At dusk, the jungle came alive. Army ants tracked inch-wide ribbons, changing bivouacs, moving up trees, down fallen branches, around trunks and over rocks. The mini river of thousands of ants was on the move, and when Garner studied and blew puffs at them, they chirped and whirred loudly. Guards with huge mandibles stood to the sides, wavering, snapping at the air, trying to kill the unknown presence. They clattered with every puff, but would not be swayed from whatever route the collective mind had chosen. The line tracked over twenty meters, coming into the RON from one side and disappearing into the woods on the other.

At night, lizards came out in force, calling for their own. "Auk ooo, auk ooooo, auk ooooooo." The calls started high, slowly trickling down to a last croaking "Awuak ooooooooo." They were fondly known by all GIs as "fuck you" lizards.

Of course snakes were out too, but they were seldom seen. Some were green, some brown, some gray. Some were cobras, some were not. Garner heard the Cambods down at CCS called bright green ones "Hanuman." They lived in trees. Americans called them all "Charlie two step": bite, two steps, you're dead. All were killed in equal fear whenever found.

For Garner the worst thing was the leeches, his musty basement of sorts. They were almost two inches long, hanging on branches, wavering, looking for a scent or movement. They dropped down from above, or if to the side they came lumping along like a crippled inch worm, dragging the sticky foot behind, trying to find a space, an opening to muzzle in and bite in painless silence.

The tops of boots were bad. Sometimes fatigues pulled out, and they came in up the leg. Pulling them off made him gag, and he used the insect repellant in revenge. It made them melt into a mucous puddle.

By late the next day another six groups passed, and they reported each in their sit-reps to Dusty through Leghorn, the stationary radio relay site on a Laotian mountain top. They gave size, direction of travel, uniforms, weapons and so on. Added all together according to Dodge's notes, a total of 168 soldiers came filing past.

The sun was cooling, backing off to late afternoon, and shadows grew long and thin on the prairie. Again, off to the north came movement.

"Dodge. Dodge," Reynolds called, motioning. "Look!"

The three Americans gathered together in a clump.

"Good God! Look at that," Garner said.

A solid line of men came walking south along the trail. There was no point element. They walked easily, as the sinuous line of green uniforms unraveled from the wood line. It was over two hundred meters long, and it kept on coming. There were rolling carts with boxes, and behind were bicycles loaded down with bulbous packs. Over three hundred men walked in file along the track.

They were stunned, watching it unravel, and Garner used binoculars to look beyond the serpent line, to the far distant edge of trees and brush. There was movement far off along the eastern woods, where the setting sun still lit the prairie in a golden glow. It hit him.

"Oh, my God," he muttered, swinging the glasses left to the northwest woods. He found what he was looking for. There, no more than sixty meters away, was a twelve-man squad of soldiers cutting through the grass on the outer edge of trees, in the shadows, heading right toward them.

"Jesus, no wonder no point element. Look! They've got them skirting the edges of the prairie. They're coming right at us. Get back. Get back. Get back," he whispered.

The others twisted, confirming the truth, then motioned to the Yards, and all of them started backing down the wooded hillside. They made no more than seven meters before stopping for fear of noise. The enemy patrol came up along the edge of woods, passing in blackened silhouette.

Trash was always repacked, but all the signs of three days' presence were there to see: crushed grass and broken sticks showed faint paths winding down the hill. They were obvious signs, but the shadows saved them. The sun was nearly spent, and the western edge was almost black, even though the center of the prairie glowed with fading colors of the day. The silhouettes passed without a pause, and Dodge motioned to stay low as he wormed back up the hill. Then he motioned for Garner to join him.

"What do you think, Phil?" Garner whispered.

"This is too big to let pass. We've got to hit this. We've got to have the guns at Ben Het hit these suckers, if they'll reach this far. Get Jim, and then code up the coordinates for a point on the trail about three hundred meters before it enters the southern woods. Hurry up, they'll be there pretty quick."

Reynolds and the rest came up to the edge, and Dodge set half the team guarding the north as he watched the point perimeter squad meander south. Garner got on the radio.

"Roger Rattler One, this is Leghorn. You have a what? Over?"

"Leghorn, this is Rattler One. I say again, we have a Fire Mission for Kansas City. Here are the coordinates. Don't mess this up. Over."

Garner tried giving the coded numbers, but saw the delay and stopped to start again, giving them in the clear instead. There wasn't time. The line of soldiers was on the blind side of the hill, and Garner saw them reemerge, continuing their slow march south.

"Roger, Rattler One, I'll pass the numbers on to Kansas City and see if they can hit it. Leghorn. Out." They waited.

"Rattler One, this is Leghorn. Over?"

Dodge took the mike and hit the talk button. "Go ahead Leghorn. Hurry up! Over."

"Rattler One, Kansas City is jumping around and says they can do it, but they asked for a clear confirmation of position. Kansas City's looking at his map and wants to know if your numbers put him square on the dotted black line, and if the map is correct as to its location? Over."

Dodge looked down at the map. Contours were brown lines, rivers and streams were blue. The trails and roads were black dots, and their locations could only be guessed at in the woods, but here out in the open the trails were exactly plotted. He gave a whispered shout.

"Leghorn you tell him to get the shots in the air. My numbers put it square on the black dotted line. Who the fuck is running the guns? Use the damned coordinates we gave you. Don't Mickey Mouse around about dotted lines and crap. Shoot the shot. He lets this get away I'll fly up there and kick his ass, whoever he is! Over."

"Roger Rattler One, passing on, wait one. Shots in the air, Rattler One. Please provide adjustment. Over."

They waited an eternity. Two eight-inch and several 175mm guns at Ben Het faced primarily westward, and the chance to use them came so very seldom that the crews jumped up and down whenever they were called out. The huge shells traveled many miles, and since the team was west of the prairie, they never heard them coming in.

Almost half a mile away, the trail erupted in two blinding blasts of light. Men and bicycles disappeared in the flashes, turning immediately black and gray with earth and smoke and bodies. The chattering thunder of the simultaneous shots hit them, "Kawhaammm," as Dodge screamed into the mike.

"Fire, fire, fire for effect! You're right on 'em! Over. Everybody get down!"

Shrapnel skimmed the grass like a swarm of locusts. The metal flew above, passing overhead, peppering the trees behind, cutting branches, shredding leaves. More shots rained down in an ever-growing circle, and they tried watching the carnage, timing shots and ducking heads. They synchronized, but shots roared in unevenly, until the deadly swish and patter of hot metal shards surrounded them. They huddled down, listening to the screams between the hits. "Kawhaammm, kawhaammm, kawahaammm." It came closer and closer, rippling their shirts. Then it stopped. They shivered for twenty seconds, then stood and looked around.

The southern field was transformed from golden grass to a spotted, cratered landscape. Small fires picked up at different points, but progress was slow. Stubble was blown down, and winds of the day died with coming darkness. Craters, spewing radiating lines like blackened daisies, were everywhere in a circle a quarter-mile wide.

All around was movement. In between the craters, there were unrecognizable lumps. Some twisted, rolling in slow undulation, like lazy sleepers in bed, but they were few. Most of the lumps were quiet. Off to the sides, the movement was more active, and forms went stumbling, running, crawling in all directions.

Garner's ears deadened with the fire, but now started clearing, and he heard wails of butchery that would linger for years in his sleep.

"Ah, Leghorn, this is Rattler One. You, ahh, you can tell the guys at Kansas City they did a hell of a job. We got KIA and WIA all around out here. Over."

Dodge looked down at the ground, handing the mike to Garner.

"Rattler One, that's great. Can you give me any numbers I can pass on? These guys never get to really hear if they help out much. They're asking me for something. Over."

Garner said, "Leghorn, we see movement and survivors, but it can't be any more than fifty or so out of over three hundred. We're in the middle of trying to count, and I shouldn't be talking in the clear like this anyway. Tell them they can get the rest from Dusty. Tell them thanks. I never thought I'd ever see anything like this. Rattler One. Out."

They counted movement in the darkening twilight, and Garner took notes. Then up over the rise in front came a stumbling silhouette. They stood in the dark wood line, and Dodge motioned "No," as Djuit raised his rifle. The figure came closer. No weapon was in sight. It stumbled, hitting the downhill side, rolling in the grass, where it finally lay quiet, sobbing. They came up cautiously, staring down into the face of a teenage boy.

His eyes went wide, and he tried moving, but couldn't. His right side was peppered red, and he clutched his upper pelvis, where a silver-dollar-sized piece of bone showed dull white through holes in the green uniform.

They picked him up, bringing him back and down into the woods. Then they packed up the claymores and moved west, across the stream, setting up in the dark, waiting for morning. They were lucky that Reynolds was a medic. It was the one SF training specialty there never seemed to be enough of. Their training was the longest and most intense, and any team with one had a leg up on survival.

He patched the kid, saying he should make it through the night easy. They tied him up, put claymores out ten meters, like the spokes of a wheel, and for a change posted guards all night.

Two hours after daybreak they came out. The helicopters took scattered fire while circling the impact area looking for bodies. Cobras strafed the southern woods as the Hueys dipped toward their red smoke, and in just a minute they were flying home. A mask of abject terror warped the young boy's face.

13

THINK

RECON COMPANY
SOA (CCC) 5TH SFG (ABN), 1ST SF
APO San Francisco, Calif 96499

SUBJECT: Policy & Information

TO: All Recon Personnel

DID YOU CHECK?

1. VRs: When you return from your VR, you must report to both the launch site from LZ reporting and the S-2 for Intel briefing.

JOHN Q. ADAMS

2. Ensure that all equipment drawn on a "mission only" basis, has been cleaned prior for turn in. This applies to all silenced weapons as well as the Green Bata boots.

DID YOU CHECK YOUR HANDSET?

3. In light of the recent activity, some confusion as to proper radio procedures evidently exists. All coordinates will be coded over radio transmissions. Also, artillery classes start on the fifth of the month. RT Arkansas will

attend first. You will be notified, one day prior, when your RT is scheduled to participate.

USAFI

4. Training area projects still pending:
   A. 1,000 inch range
   B. New Huey body from Pleiku
   C. H-34 body from Kontum AFB
   D. Stands/towers for chopper bodies
   E. Rebuilt repelling tower. Old one becoming unsafe

BURSTING RADIUS OF A WP (WHITE PHOSPHOROUS) GRENADE

5. SSG Barnes was KIA today. Illinois is out. Date and time of memorial service will be announced.

WHERE ARE YOUR MEN RIGHT NOW?

6. S-4 received a limited quantity, today of the following items:
   Jungle boots   Indigenous ponchos   Face paint   Hats
   Insect repellant   Fatigues

WHEN POSSIBLE, PUT THE ODDS IN YOUR FAVOR

7. Commencing Monday morning, police call will be from 0730 to 0800 and PT/DD from 0800 to 0830. This change is being made at the request of many 1Os.

THROW SMOKE ON LZ WHEN TEAM IS ALL OUT AND TELL COVEY RIDER

8. The below named individuals must have paperwork re-submitted, by their 1Os, to receive their Combat Infantryman's Badges. Somewhere along the line it's disappeared.
   Abrams, Sardo, Williams.

ARE YOU PHYSICALLY QUALIFIED?

9. Lt. Wilcox has been assigned to RT Wyoming. He is a former enlisted member of CCC, Recon. Introduce yourself.

STAY ALERT

10. Forth Armored Division again got shelled last night from somewhere in the Kontum area.

WILLIAM RANDOLPH WHO?

11. Eight claymore wires were cut inside the compound on the north side again. Check yours. Do not let hooch maids hang clothing on the concertina wire to dry in the sun. Wires are being cut. If you see this taking place, stop it. Your life is at stake. Take responsibility for it.

HOW MANY PULLUPS CAN YOU DO?

WILLIAM DONNALLY
1SG Recon Co.

14

She rolled over on her back, sniffling in her sleep as his left hand pulled back the sheet covered with yellow flowers. His shoulder blades touched the wall, and he leaned on his right elbow while looking out the window. Then his vision drew in, and he studied a rectangle of moonlight stretching out across the lumbered floor. He'd been listening to crickets and the dark snuffling noises of Kontum, when the first thin wedge of light crept over the windowsill. He watched the sliver grow, until it squared and then became oblong, taking control of the night.

He couldn't sleep. She was too much to leave alone, even though it had only been two hours since they'd collapsed the third time, spent and glistening wet. He tracked her curves in the pale moon glow, and began caressing again with his lips and his hand.

She stirred as fingers found the folds, stroking deep within her cleft. He entered, and she stirred again, arching as he brought up lubrication for the task. He rolled her clitoris, and studied the small nipple of her right breast. It stood pert in the moonlight, like a candy kiss on top of a shallow scoop of peach ice cream. He chuckled at the silly image, and as she stirred again, spreading her legs a little further, he nuzzled in and suckled.

It was like this now for three weeks. Every Saturday he crept downtown. Twice, during the middle of the week, he missed morning formation, but Dodge covered for him. Sunday was the only day without them and the head count that could get him into trouble. He had to content himself with staying over once a week and missing steak. He enjoyed candy instead.

There was little secret to it now. She catered to him in the club, and others saw the glances or the light brush of her hand across his shoulders as she passed. His initial embarrassment passed, and he preened, strutting to the stares of others. She was not a whore. She was beautiful and freely given. They could say no such thing about women they bedded.

Dodge gave warnings that there were many prices to pay for women, and that money was only one, but Garner didn't listen. He couldn't listen. Canada was both teacher and student. They learned from each other as she broke from the self-imposed restrictions she'd lived under for so long.

She was vibrant and alive, and many times her hunger exceeded his own. The mewling arches of sleep hinted at her physical capacity for making love. She was active and aggressive, showing him what she wanted. They explored together, and she tried so very hard pleasing him. She was open, willing, very vocal and totally wonderful.

"Hmmmnn." She stirred again, as he continued rolling her clitoris like a marble in oil. Skin puckered back and forth to goose flesh as his lips wandered over different parts of her. She was coming out of sleep now, quickening with awareness. He marveled at the power of his hands, and she groped with hers, finding him in the dark. He was hard, but he stopped her from stroking back and forth. This was her time. He would make her squirm with wanting.

She groaned louder, and arched up while opening and closing her legs time and again. He knew it was a slow type of torture, but couldn't stop. The power in his hands was just too strong. She rolled, and the tension in her built until she was a tightly wound coil. The power in his hands made him giddy with the knowledge that such control was his to wield, that he could do this to a woman, make her dance and turn in helpless supplication.

He felt like a conductor, directing the music of her body. His lips tracked down across her stomach, and as she cried out, arching up to greet him, he triumphed in the knowledge he could make this woman's body sing.

"Well, what do you think, Phil? Did Donnally give you a better idea about when we'll be able to go to Taipei?"

"No, Jim, he really didn't. Flights are filled up for a month or so. He just says, 'Soon.' He'll try to get one where a lot of CCC people go together. Have a better time that way, you know." Dodge was twirling ice in his drink, shrugging his shoulders at Reynolds.

"Well, I hope it's soon," said Day. "They owe me one for my extension. I don't want to go someplace all by myself."

Team Iowa sat in the club. They'd been given mission orders that day, and as usual once the word was out and the uncertainty was over, the nerves became more frazzled. They sat with Morrison, Day and Samuels, waiting for the movie to start in half an hour.

Beetle Nut Mary came over checking drinks, and they ordered. She was hunched and far from young, with hazel brown teeth. Reynolds teased that she was stooped because of all the Chi-Com mortar shells she carried on the back roads late at night.

"Hey, Ted. Haven't you told Mary that only Canada can serve your table?" asked Day. "What are you gonna do if you come back from Taipei and give her the clap or something. She'll wring your nuts, my man. We've all seen her mad before?"

Garner's left hand was down along the chair's edge, scratching Mo Jo behind the ears. "Come on, Bill, lighten up a little. I don't talk about it. Whatever's going on is between the two of us. Okay?"

"Okay. Okay. Don't get sore. Just commenting that's all."

Garner shifted, scratching the dog along the back. He was proud of his relationship with Canada, but refused to boast, even though the others sometimes carried on a running conversation.

"Well, I'll tell you. I'm like Dodge here," said Morrison. "He's said before he prefers Asian girls to round-eyes, and I have to agree. I've grown kind of partial to them myself. Hell, they're not bad looking, they keep their shape, they're sexy, and they don't run their mouth at you.

"Anytime I get up behind a round-eye girl, I think back to something I saw as a kid. A couple of praying mantis were mating in the brush by our barn? I was watching them, and the female just swivels around and starts munching on the head of the poor fellow that's servicing her. Christ, she ate his head right off. Gave me the shivers. Still does, never forget it. White women are like that sometimes."

Dodge started laughing. "Hey, you want women who'll chew you up and spit you out? How about the WACs. White, black, Oriental, I don't care. I've never run across a crustier bunch of women in all my life. They make our swearing seem tame.

"I remember back near Smoke Bomb Hill at Bragg, there was a Women's Army Corps detachment I passed on the way to the PX. The Women First Shirts were out there blistering their troops worse than ours ever did to us. One was yelling at the top of her lungs how terrible their barracks were. She yelled, 'Ladies this is the weekend coming up and there's twenty miles of dick out there on that fort and you aren't gonna get any of it unless you get in there and clean those barracks.' Man I never knew women could swear so bad."

The others clapped and hooted around the table.

"I heard one once like that," Samuels said laughing. "They must bust top sergeants out of the same molds or something, 'cause this one was at Fort Leonard Wood when I was in Basic. She was yelling at her troops out on the parade ground, and a bunch of us were watching on break.

"They were doing 'Right Face' and 'Left Face', and these girls were getting flustered by being yelled at. Plus, they saw us watching. The top sergeant knew it too, but didn't give a damn. She yelled, 'You are the sorriest bunch of bitches I have ever seen. Now when I tell you to do a right face, I want you to turn so sharp and so fast that I can hear those lips slap together.'"

Day fell off his chair, laughing, spilling his drink.

The conversation roared around the table about the women. All soldiers were the same, any army, any country, any war. The ladies could be white or tan or brown, young or old, but the stories held the same plot line of sex. Then the conversation took a twist when Garner mentioned Yards and Dodge's claims.

"What? You've been with Yard girls, Dodge?" Morrison asked. "I didn't think they played around. Sure, maybe there are individual hookers in the whore houses who've been separated or thrown out of their tribes, but going in and tapping one in a village? I wouldn't do that for a thousand bucks. They'd string you up if you screw with their women."

"Maybe. Maybe," said Dodge. "Most of the tribes are kind of run by women. Did you guys know that? They own the property, and a man marries into his wife's family, and not the other way around. I don't know if it's all like that, but a lot of the tribes are run that way. The ladies might look subservient, but they carry a big stick in the tribe."

"I can tell you this, from what I've heard. If someone supports the FULRO in a village backing that organization big time? Then the ladies like to show their gratitude."

"FULRO? I've heard of that from a medic I know down south, but I really don't know what it is. How about it, Dodge?" asked Reynolds.

Dodge was silent, but Morrison answered. "It's an independence movement in the Yard tribes. It stands for a French phrase. The title of it, ah hell, '*Front Unifie Pour La Liberation Des Races Opprimees.*' Something like that. The 'Unified Front For The Liberation Of The Oppressed Peoples'."

"It sounds Commie to me," Reynolds replied with suspicion.

"It sounds like our motto on the Special Forces Crest," said Garner. "'De Oppresso Liber,' To Liberate the Oppressed. What's the deal with this FULRO anyway, Phil?"

"It's a secret organization spread among the tribes, promoting the creation of a separate Montagnard nation up here in the mountains. Self autonomy, that kind of thing," replied Dodge. "Everyone in the higher levels figures it's riddled with Commies. I don't know, maybe it is, but what the heck, they've got to hope for something."

CHAPTER 14 • 121

"I heard the rebellion back in sixty-four was sponsored by the FULRO," added Morrison.

"I don't know," said Dodge. "But a full-blown rebellion almost got going back then."

Garner's curiosity spiked when he saw the change in Dodge that the others missed. "What happened, Phil?"

"Well, I was just coming into SF then, but a couple thousand Yards revolted, took a couple camps over and they made SF detachments hostage. Then they lined up all the VN counterpart advisors and killed them. They grabbed radio stations or relay sites, and tried to get the rest of the Yard CIDG camps to revolt with them, but the SF advisors protected the VNs and successfully kept the rest of the camps in line. It must have been hairy for a while."

"Well it sure as hell must not be over," said Reynolds. "I've got a buddy I knew at Fort Sam Houston, he's the medic down at Loc Ninh, and he's told me that they've got to keep a close eye on munitions, C-4, radios, mortars, you name it. The Yards are lifting it. They must be big into FULRO down there, 'cause he says they're stealing it to store up so they can revolt again some day."

"Man that's all we need, is two wars in one country going on at the same time. Right, Phil?"

Dodge looked over his drink at Garner, then brought it down and said, "It's time for the movie. Let's go. I haven't seen this thing yet."

The movie for the night was a big event. Some had seen it, others had not, but everyone heard it was full of an unbelievable amount of fiction.

They sidled to seats, and just before the lights dimmed, Canada checked Garner's row for drinks, making sure to brush him like a cat as she passed. Things went relatively quiet. There were giggles, someone threw a beer can, and off toward the front three or four tried singing; "Fighting soldiers from the sky, ba dump bump bump, Fearless men who jump and die, ba dump bump bump. Men who mean ju—" They were pummeled into quiet.

Credits rolled, and up came John Wayne and *The Green Berets*. Things went wild, with whistles, stamping feet, and more airborne beer cans. The Duke was a hero that even lifers grew up with. They watched credits roll and the movie begin. There were familiar scenes of Fort Bragg: the PX, Smoke Bomb Hill, the new barracks, and even the colonel in charge of Training Group got a bit part. Although things were reasonably quiet, there were running commentaries being made all through the theatre.

"You ever notice how the Duke has gained rank over the years?" asked Dodge of no one in particular. "Back on Guadalcanal he was just an old puke sergeant, like the rest of us. Now he's a full-blown colonel running around in the woods doing crazy stuff his own troops ought to shoot him for. You see that?"

The film showed the movie star lying on his stomach, intentionally setting off a trip wire with the barrel of his rifle. They laughed and yelled at the thought that someone might really do that.

"Look out, John! There's a dud two hundred and fifty pound bomb at the other end of that trip wire. You're gonna set it off, you dummy!" People were yelling all over. Up on the screen, a huge Malayan Gate booby trap swung around, driving a mass of bamboo spikes into a tree above the movie star's head. "What a lucky stud!"

"Look at that guy! They got sixty-year-old colonels out there running missions. What the hell do they need with us young guys?" Dodge was really enjoying the show. Chaos reigned.

"Look at this. See him pointing?" yelled Samuels. "He's wearing a Yard bracelet. A friendship bracelet. I heard he claimed he'd never take it off. He's a hell of a hawk on the war you know."

"Sixty-year-olds can afford to be," Dodge yelled back, and as he slurped his third drink, the brass ring on his right wrist flashed in the dim light.

It was all downhill as things got progressively rowdier. Finally, at the end was the coup de grace. Those who saw it before, yelled a warning to the others.

The star was in Da Nang near the beach, and all the loose strings of the movie were tied up. Deaths were mourned and the final call for freedom was given. The Duke put his arm around the little Vietnamese kid, who signified hope for the future, and they walked out on the beach together watching the sun set over the ocean, tingeing everything in a golden glow.

"What's this?" Dodge howled, and all the others threw beer cans and cups. They were all laughing and yelling as up on the screen the sun set slowly in the *east*. Final credits rolled. THE END.

Four days later, just before going in on the next mission, Garner got a package from home. He ran to the team room and opened it on his bunk, as Dodge and Reynolds looked on.

Each American Recon barracks was comprised of four rooms housing two teams. The One Zero took one by right, and the One One and One Two bunked together in the adjoining room. Outside doors were locked at night by order. Any attack could always be preceded by sabotage and satchel charges.

Garner glanced at the enclosed letter from his mother, and put it to the side. Then he pulled the final bit of packing away, and started handing items to the others.

"Good. Good. Good," he said. "No more leech bites for me. I'll bet we're the only ones in all of Vietnam with things like this."

What he handed out were brand new, tan-colored, World War II leggings. They were canvas, and wrapped around the calf and ankle. A thick strap ran under the instep, and eyelets and buttonhooks came up either side of the split edge.

Once a lace was looped through the eyelets, it was simply pulled over the corresponding button hook and tightened up. They were easy to put on, and would keep pants tucked in the boots. They also added ankle support when cinched up tight, and as Garner laced he could see they reduced chances of a sprained or broken foot in the mountains.

"I can't believe this, Ted. These are brand new. They've never been worn. Where did you get these?" asked Reynolds.

"I asked my folks to look around for them. My dad bought some for me when I was ten, out playing Army with neighbor kids. See, back in Rock Island, Illinois there's a military compound out in the middle of the Mississippi river. It's called the Rock Island Arsenal, what else. Anyway, it's been a government installation since the French and Indian wars. They make all kinds of stuff there. Back in the forties they manufactured equipment and uniforms.

"Well, all up and down the river are army surplus stores loaded with this kind of stuff. This isn't junk called army surplus. It's the real thing. There's one place in the next town, Moline, that must be a couple of acres in size, with nothing but OD material in it. You go in, and it smells musty and full of moth balls, kind of like your grandmother's attic."

The other two were trying theirs on, lacing up the sides as Garner scanned the letter. "My mother says the guys in the store went nuts when she came in. She told them we wanted them because of the leeches, and the guys went to tearing around looking through all the crates. I guess it really got them going to be able to help us out over here." He looked at the others in the box. "Jesus, look at this." He pulled out the other pairs for the Yards.

Here were items of war from another time, another world, another generation. Would anything ever change? The leggings were tangible reminders that made them queasy. The thought was not one to bear, and it swept away with idle chatter.

The next mission was an area recon down in Salem House. Six days of wandering flat land: open, hot and growing wetter as the year progressed. They were ten klicks west of the road, and the difference in terrain was substantial. It was nothing like Prairie Fire up north. Jungle was thin, scrubby and only double canopied at most, reminding Garner of clear-cut lands he'd seen in Alabama.

Without dense forest the mulch was thin, never having a chance to build. Large patches of red clay baked with the sun or ran like thickened tar in the rain. Heavier growth sprouted along the streams, but overall the land was open, and therefore dangerous.

The monsoon season was upon them, and showers grew from scattered drizzles to leaden skies dumping sheets of water by the day and not the hour. The transition was subtle but steady. When he came over, it was the dry season, and he knew no better. Now came the meaning of misery. It was one thing to be scared, but another to be wet and scared.

Dangers were twofold. First, there was the danger of extraction. Monsoons meant clouds were scudding low across the hills, and helicopters couldn't fly. No team wanted to hear they couldn't be pulled out no matter what the reason. It meant they were totally alone: no jets, no helicopters. All they had was Covey flying high above the clouds, passing on the daily bitch and moan.

The second danger was the wet itself. Some teams were stranded for weeks in the field, and he heard a term never dreamed of before. It was from another age, another time, another war. Like others on Recon he was prepared for many things, but not for trench foot.

They dropped off two Italian Green mortar shells the first day, and then on the third, shot and ran from a patrol they'd stumbled over. It took a day and a half of hard moving to shake the hunt. Then they settled back into a quiet Recon. Rains increased, and Dusty's advice was, "Break contact and continue mission." By day five it changed to, "Hold up. Nothing's flying in the rain. Don't get in trouble you can't get out of."

The sixth afternoon, they ran across a truck park. Phe had point, and saw the cab of a US Army truck as he rounded a clump of bramble. He stopped, then backed away. Dodge motioned for them to low crawl through the dripping brush to get a better view. It was like the movies. Garner saw half a dozen trucks painted olive drab. They were US Army trucks, and even had faded white stars on the doors, but they didn't belong in this war.

They had steeply slanted hoods and rounded fenders. The metal sides of the flatbeds were long gone, and wooden stakes poked up every foot or so. These belonged on Normandy beaches, and all the other places of all the newsreel footage he'd ever seen of World War II. They were antiques running with the proddings of good mechanics. They ran on bailing wire and cannibalized parts of more unfortunate brethren. Metal crumbled in quarter-sized chunks of rust, but they ran, by God. He realized the achievement, and mentally congratulated the North Vietnamese.

"Phil, it's drizzling," he whispered. "We've got no chance for extraction. Reynolds and I don't want you writing our folks about how you got us blown away. Let's just back on out of here."

Dodge grinned, but didn't nod. He motioned for Dominique and then Kui, the M-79 man. "Dominique, ask if he can hit the big black bubble under the truck. The one facing away from us."

Dominique whispered in Bahnar to the smaller man. He grinned wide, nodding yes. "Ted, remember the stream with better cover? The one we passed through earlier this morning? Well, go ahead and plot an azimuth back to it. No sense us being out here unless we're having fun."

They were sixty meters away. All the vehicles were loaded with packs and boxes wedged behind the wooden spikes along the sides. Dodge waited till Garner finished with his map and nodded ready. Then, Dodge braced the team, patting Kui on the shoulder, signaling go. The Yard swung the slide sights up, adjusting them as he steadied on a pack in the mud. He fired. The M-79 gave off its hollow "Punk!" and sent the forty-millimeter grenade hurling toward the target.

Some of the Yards were amazingly good with the M-79. It was a single-shot weapon everyone wanted along, but no one wanted to carry. Single shots of any kind scared people.

Inside the canister, wrapped around the explosive head, was a coil of wire with notches cut every quarter inch; the same design as the M-26 grenade. On detonation the notches broke, and slivered metal flew in all directions. In heavy brush the small shards were easily deflected, but out in the open, it decimated troops.

The gold-colored round arched up and then bent back down, skimming just under the tailgate, impacting on the gasoline tank's backside. Two explosions were like a double clap of thunder: "Whoom-kawhoom!" The truck exploded. They had to stay and see it. Then they turned and ran as people started screaming. A second truck exploded. "Kawhoom!" Flaming gas splattered other trucks and cargos. Behind, in the growing distance, came distinctive popcorns of cooking ammunition.

They moved south, but the area was up and active now. Phe stopped in scattered brush, listening to voices. He crouched. Djuit was just behind and to the left. Whean was next, looking to Dodge, who motioned right. He took two crab-like steps, settling down just as the first four enemy soldiers broke through the brush in front. They were startled by the crouching figures, which were the last things seen in this life.

The Yards were always wasteful when scared, and each enemy soldier caught at least seven rounds, reeling backwards, spinning, jerking. Phe and the others turned, running backwards through the team, dropping spent magazines, grappling to reload. Enemy fire from at least a dozen weapons came in response. Few were seen beyond the first four, but AKs had a special "clack, clack, clack." Dodge was firing and moving, then Reynolds, then Dominique, then Garner, Kui and Kehn. They were heading back to the trucks on a run. Dodge motioned to the right, turning east toward the road. Rain was coming down as a solid torrent now, and they left a deepening track in the mud as they ran. Dodge gave Garner a "Sorry" kind of look.

They trotted through the rain until sunset, taking small breaks every half an hour. Garner figured the chase was off until the next morning, but they couldn't stop until they found thicker brush. Besides, the longer they ran, the better the chance was that their tracks were washed away behind.

Rubber ponchos were rolled and stored away; they were no good on the run. They sparkled with every movement, standing out in the jungle like a flashlight in the dark. They had to find shelter. Only then could they stop and cover up. It was the only way.

Brush thickened. They moved and crawled, and soon found a mud-red stream twenty feet across. Wind rippled the water, and Garner motioned, "First." He was tallest.

He moved to the edge and promptly lost footing, landing on his knee, spattering dung-like mud for six feet. Curses came fast, but the drumming rain soaked up the sounds. He entered, and his boots went seductively deep. Up north, in the mountains, streams were fast and the beds were hard, but here they were slow, letting silt and clay settle layer on sifted layer.

He pulled out, wallowing further in. Red water swirled around his legs, then hips, then stomach. It stopped. He struggled on, coming up the far bank while swishing back and forth to wash the canvas leggings. Others followed, fighting the pull of the clay and the push of water.

Finally, all were across and moving north along the stream, staying in the deeper cover. A place to pull into could not be near the crossing. Too many signs would mark it. They had to get away and lose the track again. Water overflowed the banks in many spots, and they trudged on ankle deep, looking for a refuge. It was almost dark now. They found a scrubby hillock squatting three feet or so above the standing water. It was enough. They nuzzled in, quickly taking care of necessary chores.

Rain continued as they threw off packs and hovered over, protecting contents with their bodies while digging deep. Plastic ground cloths lined the insides.

Garner stood in the downpour, stripping web gear, harness and pistol belt. Then he cursed, shucked the shirt and dropped his pants. No one wore underwear in the field. The body needed breathing. He checked for leeches and washed away red mud cakes swirling down inside. Then they were up again, cold and clammy, and he pulled out the poncho, making it ready. The extra shirt was next, and he threw it on, not bothering to button. Then he ripped on the web gear, pack, and covering poncho, pulling up the cowl. He buttoned the dry shirt in leisure and studied for a proper place to settle, but there were final chores before blackness overtook them, and he hurried with the others.

They dug out claymores, and checked perimeter positions while considering brush and openings in areas of responsibility. Then they spread out from the RON, unraveling wires, placing mines ten meters out. When all was ready, they moved back to the circle and placed the charging handles near their designated sleeping spots.

The rain continued, as Garner stripped his leggings and boots. All their feet were swollen, and six days' worth of constant immersion made them peel and hurt. They tried keeping them dry, but it was impossible. Garner patted his with a cloth, then put on new socks, and shoved the whole painful mess back into the wet boots. They couldn't air dry overnight. No one had the luxury of having boots off more than five minutes.

Finally, all was rainy quiet, and the circle huddled down, as Dodge talked to Broken Bottle high above the clouds. He motioned "Three more days," and Garner settled back, drifting with the patter of the rain. Rivulets slalomed from neck to groin; he cursed, pulling the strings tighter, bowing, dreaming dreams of women, far-off beaches, and sun. He slept.

First light jolted him awake; everything was truly quiet, no rain. A bird called for its mate, and "fuck you" lizards challenged duels: Auk oooo, auk oooo, auk oooo. Dominique nodded good morning. Some stretched and worked out kinks while removing the ponchos. Others removed the round in the chamber of their rifles, and dried it with a cloth. Several ate C-rations. Then Phe stopped, looked over his shoulder and dropped his can.

He scuttled behind a clump of brush and faced south. Garner heard nothing. Then Dominique and others rolled behind the nearest cover. He still heard nothing. Wait, there was a slight brush noise somewhere southeast. No, it was southwest along the stream, the way they came. No, it was straight south. No! It was all three. A fifty-man sweep was coming in. They found the crossing, and hiding places were too few further east. Mud tracks headed north. They were only three feet apart, coming on, looking, listening. North Vietnamese soldiers filled the southern bramble.

Dodge motioned to Dominique, Whean and Kehn. The line closed on their claymores. When he touched his off the others followed suit, and a wash of metal pellets fanned out through the closest fifteen men on line. They went down, shooting and screaming as the sides of the sweep closed round, firing in.

Grenades punctuated the rifle fire, and Garner saw Dodge roll into a depression created by the root ball of a fallen tree. He popped out like a jack-in-the-box, firing short bursts. Kehn and Kui hid behind the tree itself and fired over the top. Two claymores went off on the east side, hitting troops as they wrapped around the RON.

Then there was movement to Garner's front, and he looked to Djuit. They watched the line firing as they advanced, and then blew them backwards with the claymores. "Kawhoom!" Garner aimed, when he saw grenades fly over his head. He ducked. One went into Dodge's depression, and he yelled a word of warning through the chaos as it went off with a muffled "Whoom!" Mud flew out, and the depression turned quiet.

He yelled, "Dodge, Dodge, Dodge. Dominique, can you see him?"

The interpreter turned from firing east and looked. "No Garnah. I can not see him. *Trung Si* Dodge, *Trung Si* Dodge! We must go, Garnah. We must run, Garnah!" He turned and fired another magazine. Garner tapped Djuit. "Shoot, shoot, shoot," pointing west along their side. Another grenade came in, and he shriveled. "Whoom." He turned, scrambling to the hole, falling down the shallow side.

Dodge was on the bottom digging in his pack for more grenades. "Phil, are you all right?" Dodge didn't turn until he saw the movement. He jumped and then settled back to digging. "Are you all right?"

"What? I can't hear you. The grenade!" Garner finally saw the blackened hole from a root that pulled out when the tree fell over. Dodge kicked the grenade in the natural sump, so the explosion funneled up, but he was temporarily deaf.

Three NVA got to within five yards of them, as Dodge pulled out grenades. Garner looked over the rim of the hole, brought his rifle up on automatic, and fired one round. The first man went down. The other two came on, and Garner looked in disbelief at the spent casing jamming the chamber of his weapon. He was unarmed, and began twisting and wiggling as the enemy took aim.

He screamed, as Dodge and Dominique fired the rounds that saved his life. The NVA fired short, kicking dirt around his legs as they tumbled. Then more grenades came in, "Whoom, whoom, whoom."

He screamed, rolling toward Djuit and Kui near his pack. They were all firing and grappling with equipment, preparing to run on signal. He reached his pack and tore it open, finding the bundle, screwing the pieces together as the others around him watched and fired.

He shook, barely getting the cleaning rod in the muzzle. Then he yanked out the magazine and drove the rod downward, pushing out the jammed casing. The magazine was quickly locked in place with another round stripped in the chamber. He rolled and fired at movement. Three rounds, three rounds, three rounds, three rounds, three rounds and more, then out. He was satisfied and ripped the rod apart as others readied for the run.

He loaded up. They blew the last two claymores facing north, then threw grenades southward in a fan. It would be the direction Charlie least expected. They were up and running behind the explosions, filing through bodies and dripping bits of matter in the brush. They were up and out, firing to the sides when Kui and Kehn were hit. They fell together, and Garner sensed the shock waves of passing rounds.

He yelled and laid down covering fire, then threw his last two grenades. The Yards were policed up, as he and Djuit covered the rear, using ammunition from the other packs.

They ran, calling Covey for extraction. Garner vowed to kick Gable's butt when he questioned them on having wounded. "Break contact, my ass," he said.

It was morning, and clouds were usually thinner than in the sullen afternoons. Broken Bottle saw enough holes to justify a launch. Fifty minutes later the helicopters found their way below the veil and finally brought them out.

15

THINK

RECON COMPANY
SOA (CCC) 5TH SFG (ABN), 1ST SF
APO San Francisco, Calif. 96499

SUBJECT:	Policy & Information

TO:	All Recon Personnel

WHEN YOU KNOW IT ALL, LEAVE

1. All personnel departing on the Taipei Flight, report to S-1 NLT 0900 hours. When you arrive at your destination have a good time, but above all keep out of trouble. These flights are a bonus for work well done. Don't foul it up for others who may want to go next.

ARE YOU A GOOD GUY OR A LEADER?

2. (S-2) The recent slow down in enemy activity is reportedly over and the NVA are on the move again.

DID YOU CHECK YOUR CLAYMORES?

3. (S-2) This morning, 12 Kms south on the Kontum, Pleiku road, 3 AT mines were removed by a mine sweeping detail.

'WHAT'S IN IT FOR ME?'

4. We have a new shipment of 1,500 lbs of C-4. This will be distributed on an as needed basis. Please be conservative. Munitions, grenades, explosives are not to be taken lightly. These are mission materials and the only reason for any of it to go out the gate is for training or road protection on a trip to Pleiku or Kontum. SCU will not take ammunition cans to their villages.

ARE YOU REALLY TRYING?

5. VC agents contacted our local food supplier two days ago, wanting to know how many people were in this compound. (He told them all he knew.) Info also received was that VC are trying to infiltrate this compound as laborers and SCU.

ARE YOU PHYSICALLY QUALIFIED TO LEAD?

6. A two man 4.2 mortar crew, will be on stand-by each evening, and will sleep at the launch site in the compound. The detail will come from each section.

KNOW AND HAVE THE FACTS BEFORE YOU TALK

7. Iowa is out but Illinois is still in. They're fine, just wet and hungry. Still trying.

WELL DONE=DONE WELL

8. Sp4 Harmon, RT Florida departed today to attend 10 school.

IT IS WORTH THE ATTEMPT

9. SSG Allen, RT New Hampshire departed today to replace SGT Morgan as CCC instructor at the 10 school. Morgan will be 11 on New Hampshire. Introduce yourselves.

CHECK YOUR TEAM MEMBERS' MEDICAL RECORDS

10. To stop the rumors. Yes it is true that CCN lost two teams the last three weeks. No indications of trouble were ever given over the radio. The second team didn't even have a chance to give a "Good Day" signal immediately after insertion. Names of US personnel involved are posted on the Recon BB.

TRY ALL KNOWN FREQUENCIES FOR ARTILLERY TARGETS AT NIGHT

11. No, I am not disbanding Florida.

FIFTH PRESIDENT?

12. Blood expander should be turned into the dispensary. Most of the cans issued have been found to be defective.

WHY? WHY NOT!

13. "10" medical kits are to be drawn from the dispensary on a mission only basis. Return them upon your return from operation

WILLIAM DONNALLY
1SG Recon Co.

16

Talking was impossible as the C-130 picked up runway speed. Garner thought the noise was just too totally compelling to try screaming above. It always surprised him that something that made so much noise could possibly hold together. He closed his eyes, and the acceleration had all eight of them straining in their seats. They slipped fractions of inches, with hips touching hips as they pushed against the building acceleration.

Finally, at 3,500 feet the forward thrust slackened. The plane angled to a gentler climb and they rearranged themselves, spreading out again, getting away from unwanted physical nearness. These were occasions when crude jokes and laughs helped break tensions among men forced unwillingly too close together.

"Hey, Ted," said Day. "Did the medics figure out if the Yards were hit by grenade or AK rounds?"

"It was just one round. It hit Kehn on the inside thigh, then went on and hit Kui. They pulled it out of the right cheek of his butt. They'll both be out for a month or so. Maybe longer if they don't keep the wounds clean. They both went home.

"The only reason I even knew they were hit, is that I felt the shock of a couple other bullets pass by; then Kui spun forward, into me. We could have been a full five to ten meters up before we noticed it, if he hadn't caught my attention."

"Well, that's something you're gonna have to save for Donnally's 'Tips of the Trade, Lessons Learned' papers. Always look behind you when you're on the run. That and reconfirmation about condensation making the first round jam. When I was on Illinois, the first thing we did at daylight was take the round out of the chamber and wipe it dry. I never got hit that early in the morning though."

Garner considered the circumstance that almost cost him his life. "I've got to admit I was lucky Phil got those other two. I was dead meat. It's not that I was being lazy or anything like that. I've always cleaned the round, every morning, and I had tape over the muzzle to keep out water, and around the sides to where just the back of the flash vents were open, so the barrel could breathe. I guess I still got water down into the chamber though. One thing's sure, I'm never again gonna sit on my ass and eat a can of Cs before I change out that round."

There were eight of them going to Taipei. Dodge, Reynolds, Garner, Sardo, Day, Samuels, Danner and Adams. Both Danner and Adams were with the A-Company, bunking with Sardo and Jenkins since Cooper was killed and Fazio went home. Danner was the bigger of the two, and was known as the Duke, because of his incessant John Wayne imitations. He swaggered across the club with his left shoulder canted down and in, like a drunk walking into a stiff breeze, his arms swinging wide with every step. Then he'd rear back, plant his feet and say, "Well listen here Pilgrim, this here bar's too small for the both a us. I suggest you shoot outa here." It was like the Olympics, but instead of flashing score cards, they rated his impersonation by granting applause or throwing heavy objects. Sometimes they said he sounded more like Henry Fonda, and it was easy to see that hurt.

Adams was from New York, like Sardo, but from Staten Island instead of the Bronx. It was all New York to Garner, and Adams tried telling him there was a world of difference between the two. Staten Island wasn't like "Long Gyland" any more than Kansas was, he said.

They were flying into Tan Son Nhut, and would spend the night in Saigon before leaving for Taipei in the morning. Special Forces had a safe house there, called House Ten, and it was clandestine home for any SF wandering in and out of town. It had beds and a bar. Like Dodge said, what more could they want?

Sardo motioned to the .45 automatic next to Dodge, asking, "You gonna sell that thing down in Saigon like all those flags you've got stuck in your duffel?"

"I don't know, Tony. Donnally says I can keep it, but I can't send it home as a war souvenir."

"Did you just get it the last time out?" asked Danner.

"Yah. When we started to run, I saw it laying in the palm of this guy's hand. We just offed a bunch of them with claymores and ran through the opening. He must have been an officer directing the sweep. Probably nothing but a lieutenant or something. If he was a major he'd have one of those Chi-Com pistols with the red star inlaid in the grip. At least I could take that home. I can't do anything with this except keep it here."

"Is it stolen US?"

"Yep. They checked serial numbers, and it was lost in some operation back in sixty-five. I guess I'll keep it and sell it to someone when I leave in three months. Not in bad shape. It rattles, but hell they all do."

"You know, Croaker Herold, plays chicken with his," said Day.

"How so?" asked Dodge.

"Well, he keeps the pistol in his right hand and at the same time he pulls the trigger he jams the muzzle into his left palm. The slide pushes back a quarter inch or so and won't let the hammer fall on the pin. I heard once a guy almost got killed that way. The position was being overrun and he grabs the forty-five as a dink comes right in on top, fighting him. He shoves the pistol in Charlie's gut, pulls the trigger and nothing happens. The hammer falls, but the slide's pushed back and won't let it hit the pin. So he nails Charlie on the head, cocks it again with the thumb and blows him away from six inches out."

"You say Croaker plays with it?"

"Yah, I've seen him do it. He says it's not loaded, but I think sometimes it is."

"Jesus."

Croaker Herold was Luther Herold and was relatively new, but had a wild reputation with those who knew him back in training. He was from Virginia along the West Virginia border. Hill country is what he called it, and his accent was genuine red-neck. They heard he got in trouble once and stood before the judge claiming innocence by reason of insanity. Then he looked up past his left shoulder, talking to empty space, saying, "Ain't that right, Harvey?" The story was the judge started laughing and couldn't stop. He croaked like a frog and scared everyone he ran with.

By early afternoon, Garner glimpsed Saigon through the side door window. Then they banked to starboard and the Loadmaster made them buckle into their seats. The city spread to the horizon. It was much bigger than Garner expected. Over two million, Dodge said. Canals and rivers webbed below where barges and sampans hugged the edges two and three deep, leaving narrow trails for navigation.

A smoky pall hung low, like a coroner's sheet; it was stark testament to a hundred thousand charcoal fires scattered everywhere. Roads choked with dust, and the last thing he saw before sitting down, was the first of many rows of fighter planes lined up on the side runways. They dipped, and dropped like a rock into Tan Son Nhut.

Things were squared away, and a three-quarter-ton truck was waiting for them when they landed. They drove into town on Vo Di Nguy Street, and Garner's first impression proved correct. It was busy and dirty, and the SOG driver finessed his way through swarms of bicycles and motorbikes jamming traffic. Three-wheeled motor cabs and cars added to the crush.

Most of the men on the street wore green fatigues. The women had conical straw hats and wore white *ao dais*, cut far up the sides, showing off black satin trousers. They were practical and surprisingly feminine, loose and flowing down below, but tailored tight around the waist, showing breasts to good advantage. Choker collars gave a distinctly virginal feeling to the outfit. Not many wore them in Kontum, but in Saigon they were all around.

The city had wide contrasts and disturbing disparities. Like many third-world nations, the rich and powerful preyed upon the poor. They existed side by side, and he guessed those in higher station looked upon the others with no emotion other than fear that they should one day join their ranks.

Thi Nghe Canal had multi-storied hotels of major worldwide chains on both sides. On the edges were rows of sanpans and rafts where families lived in filth. Children swam naked in the turgid water, and Garner saw a cat bobbing to the side among floating papers, chunks of wood and plastic bottles.

They passed jewelry stores where beggars sat on curbs with rice bowls to the side. Cripples and the maimed of war were everywhere with hands out. One without a leg fought children ten years old. They stole money from his bowl, and he tried rising as they ran away. He settled back down, lost within the swirling crowd.

Other children ran alongside any vehicle with Americans or Europeans, screaming for money. The whites were easy pickings. Their guilts welled up and overflowed. The Vietnamese, however, knew the system. It was theirs. They ignored all but those they dealt with when it came to doing business. One corner had drainage pipes stacked in three layered piles. Well-dressed men and women strolled the sides, paying no attention to refugees living in the pipes.

The truck bullied down past the American Embassy and the Presidential Palace. There was no remaining evidence of the violence of Tet '68. Avenues were broad and lined with trees. The Colonial French laid it out with a characteristic sense of balance and openness. Parks were everywhere, and people jammed wide walkways and outdoor cafes, hawking things to sell or examining things to buy. Every twenty feet, people haggled with transactions. They stopped in the flow like boulders in the middle of a busy stream. Humanity simply washed around the edges and continued on in both directions. Garner sensed the pulse of this dangerous, exciting city.

After pulling up to House Ten, the SOG driver said he'd see them in the morning. They climbed up ten broad steps, entered, and were alone together.

CHAPTER 16 • 139

House Ten was communal property. It was a spacious, white-brick, two-storied house, with a windowed mansard roof and small yard, walled and wired. Five blocks away was the main boulevard and the Presidential Palace. Architecture was French, and Garner guessed it once belonged to some colonial administrator. He knew from rumor it didn't belong to SOG, but to the Fifth Group in Nah Trang. If SOG owned it, no one else would be allowed, but Fifth Group was the papa of them all, and everyone was welcomed home.

They all signed in for rooms, and Garner chuckled at the term "safe house." It was a term in Special Warfare designating a safe haven deep behind enemy lines, a hidden place. It meant a house where inserted guerrillas ran to for help. That was the nature of their training. The legacy and lore went back to the OSS in World War II, and guerrilla networks and safe houses in France, and sabotage and the use of locals, and all the stories of long ago with girls called Frenchy and men named Jacques.

A safe house in Saigon was descriptive of a war where no one knew exactly who the enemy was. The bureaucratic American command was just as worthwhile evading as the Cong. Special Forces went its own direction. Few people knew about House Ten, and they kept it that way.

After checking in, they hit the streets and walked and walked, finally stopping at one of the many sidewalk cafes down near Tu Do street. They eyed heavy clouds and sat drinking Bau Muy Bau beer, Number 33 beer. It was bitter horse piss, said Garner.

Dodge sold two flags while drifting through the afternoon, watching one of the city policemen direct traffic from his little stand in the intersection. Cars stopped at command, and a swarm of mopeds and bicycles worked up between, filling all the cracks and openings, no doubt scratching paint as they crowded in. The cop turned, signaling "Go!", and the hive moved en masse across the open space.

It looked coordinated, but was really just the opposite. Each driver dodged, weaving for position and personal advantage. Garner watched the aggressive mopeds as they jockeyed back and forth, and he had the flashing image of driving a '59 Cadillac through them at highway speed.

The policeman stood straight, waving arms. Other cops strolled the streets in pairs. They wore white shirts, light gray trousers and policemen's hats. Pistols strapped their sides, and they strutted and swaggered while stopping to chat with call girls on their beat. GIs called them all "White Mice."

Just around the corner was Tu Do Street, where bars and women clustered in uncounted numbers. Call girls did not wear *ao dais*. They were western in their colored blouses, tight mini skirts and high heels.

Coursing in and out, on moped or on foot, were groups of watchful boys, seeking advantage wherever. They were cowboys, and although most were young and small, they were as agile as feral cats living by their wits. Some pimped, some picked pockets, others used extortion and the threat of violence, all exchanged money and dealt with other aspects of the black market.

At dusk the town got mean. M.P.s patrolled everywhere, checking for drunks, weapons, trouble. Shootings happened all the time. Little kids hid under their sisters' or their mothers' beds picking cash out of GIs' wallets as they dropped their pants on the floor. Drunken soldiers fought outside bars over women. Shortchanged pimps cut their girls.

He'd heard that after dark the town was called Dodge City. They didn't want a run-in, so when the sun went down and the craziness started, they packed it up to sit and drink in the House Ten bar.

"Man, this is my kind of town," said Dodge. "You see those girls over on Tu Do Street? It would take a year to work yourself through that crowd."

The barkeep, an E-6 who was in Training Group with Day, passed drinks and said, "I wouldn't go down there looking for girls. You guys are on your way to Taipei aren't you?"

"Yah," said Dodge.

"Well, over there the girls are regulated by law. They're clean and have to be inspected and have doctor certifications. All you're going to get down on Tu Do is a lot of lice-infested hookers, carrying just about every disease known to mankind. They're for the grunts in for a day or two from the boonies. If you stay in Saigon long enough, you get yourself a girlfriend. Set her up so she's not walking the streets behind your back, and you've got a pretty good deal."

"We won't have time for anything like that," said Garner. "We're like the grunts. We fly out of here tomorrow at eleven, come back in after a week or so, spend the night again and then head back to Kontum."

There were seven or eight others in the bar, but this wasn't Pleiku, and introductions and back slaps seemed out of place. The atmosphere was quiet, hunkered down, reminding Garner of old Bogart movies.

"Hey, Jimmy," Day called to the barkeep. "Do you know any of these other guys in here?"

"Sure. See those three at the table to the right? They're from the Group in Nah Trang. They come down here once a month working out supply hassles for the CIDG camps. I think most of the camps live off the local food vendors and such. They'd probably starve if they had to depend on everything from Group, but some things Group can help with.

"The two in the corner are in for the week from An Loc. I think it's business of some kind, but they always seem to be drinking or out on the street playing around."

"Any MACV-SOG types?"

"Yah, those other two are, but I don't know what project they're with. We got some guys from Earth Angel and Phoenix living over at the Americana Hotel. They come in sometimes just to shoot the bull. They don't stay over though."

There was pounding on the front door down the hallway to the right, and one of the House Ten custodians turned, leaving the room. Thirty seconds later, two other men came in from the front hall. They wore civilian clothes and sported crew cuts. One was big and beefy, with a ready smile. The other was smaller, with a pinched face and straight nose. His hairline came down to a pointed widow's peak.

Garner watched the ferret's unblinking eyes as they swept the room. Their vision locked for half a second, and moved on. The small man stood at the bar with an air of nervousness, but Garner sensed it was his natural stance. He also sensed there wasn't a shred of humor in the man.

"Kidwell's not here tonight?" The man addressed the barkeep, but it was more of a commanded acknowledgement than a question.

"No, Mr. Riggs. I haven't seen him today."

The barkeep moved a step back from where he was leaning. His eyes were bright and aware, like someone expecting trouble.

"I'll wait. Give me a vodka tonic. Warner will have a beer."

"Yes, Sir. Coming right up."

Garner sat on stools with Dodge and Day. The others were off at a table. He looked over, motioned with his drink, saying, "Hey, how's it going?"

The ferret turned from checking out the rest of the room and nodded, "Fine." Then to Jim the Keep: "How about those drinks?"

"Coming up, Sir." He turned from the back work area, bringing them to the men by the door.

"Are you fellows civilians or something?" Garner asked.

The ferret looked him over with command superiority, asking, "Who the hell are you?"

Dodge spoke up. "We're from up at Kontum, CCC, Team Iowa, Recon. How about you guys?"

"Iowa? Kontum?" He looked at the other bigger man and gave a rasping laugh. "Well, Warner, these must be the heroes who brought in that kid that didn't know anything. Is that right? Are you the heroes who caught that kid they sent us last month?"

"Who the hell are you?" Dodge asked.

"It doesn't matter, and watch your mouth. It'll get you into trouble. I asked are you the guys that caught that kid?"

Dodge bridled. "I pretty much let my mouth run where it wants. I don't see the need for your being snotty to strangers, but to answer your question, yah, we sent a prisoner down to Saigon last month. What of it?"

"Hear that, Warner? They're the guys."

"Yah, I hear." The big man chuckled, bringing the beer back up to his mouth.

"Your kid wasn't worth the cost of aviation fuel to fly his ass down here. He was fifteen, coming south with a bunch of other babies. He'd been in NVA service three months and didn't know anything. Christ, send us truck drivers or something." The ferret drained the glass.

"Well next time we'll pass a questionnaire around three hundred NVA troops, finding out who knows the most. Then we'll make sure to blow everyone away except him. That okay with you guys? Or would you like to step off the choppers and find them yourselves?" asked Dodge.

The ferret eyes narrowed. "You the team leader of that screw up?"

"I'm the One Zero, what of it?" Dodge said.

"Nothing. Ain't worth going into right now. I'll see if I can help you out a little, that's all. Maybe show you it's not so smart mouthing off to people you don't know. Never know what can come of it. Eh, Warner?"

"Don't sweat it, Riggs," the big man said. "We've got other things to do. These guys are just drinking. Don't sweat it."

"Warner, shut the hell up." The big man stopped with shock, then turned red. He choked it down, draining the beer, crushing the empty can on the bar top. The smaller man took no apparent notice, finished the drink, and said to the keep, "You see Kidwell, you tell him I'm looking for him. He dodges me one more day and I'll get even with him. You tell him that."

"All right, Mister Riggs. I'll tell him that."

The two men left the bar.

"What was that all about?" asked Dodge.

The keep looked embarrassed. "Those guys are with Intel or somebody. No one here really knows who they are. Maybe CIA. I don't know. They go around stirring up trouble. The big one's okay. I got into a poker game with him once, but the little one's a screw. Don't mess with him. He's hurt some people before. I heard he was able to get a guy busted one time."

"You figure they're civilians?" asked Dodge.

"Don't know. If they are, they're the strackest civilians I've ever seen. They've never pulled a rank, but they act like they've got all the power in the world.

I saw a major saying 'Yes, Sir' to the smaller one once, but he might have just been scared 'cause he couldn't get a handle on whether they could hurt him or not. It's always smart to say 'Sir' to someone who can mess you up, and I believe those two can."

They tried to let it pass, but Dodge was testy for the next hour until the memory faded. He never pulled rank on anyone, but it was easy to spot when something ate at him. Finally, about nine-thirty, another group came in after pounding on the door, singing dirty songs outside. The four men, also in civilian clothes, came around the corner and entered the bar.

"Hey, Jimmy. Draw me a tall cool one!" The drunk had his right arm around the shoulder of one of the others. They trundled toward the bar looking for familiar faces. When the light got better as they approached, Garner's face lit up.

"Dravos. Danny Dravos. How the devil are you!"

The drunk looked startled, then his face came alive with recognition as he scanned the clutch of old friends.

"Garner, Day, Dodge, Sardo. Hey, you guys, what are you doing down in this piss tube?"

They all shook hands, laughing and talking while further introductions were being made. Dravos said he was with the Earth Angel project, MACV-SOG, 36-Alpha. He worked with Road Runners, NVA soldiers who were sick of fighting and used one of the government amnesty passes to surrender. Planes dropped millions of the passes all around the country and across the fence. They promised safety and a new life for defectors. The Cheu Hoi program brought thousands to the government's side.

However, it was well known that many Charlies considered it a form of R&R. Guerrillas came out of the jungle half starved and emotionally drained by the constant pressures of the fight. They'd Cheu Hoi and sit back for three months, eating good food, putting on weight and listening to long and boring propaganda talks, trying to reinforce their decision to give up.

At some point the guerrilla would dodge his keepers and make his way back to his old unit, refreshed and strengthened at government expense. It was understood not to trust a Cheu Hoi. They might work for the government, but they couldn't be put in a position to hurt someone. Dravos had plenty of stories about them.

"When I first got here I went around with a trainer, showing me the ropes. Guy's name was Menendes, Carlos Menendes. Big broad Mexican Indian features. We'd go around bumming rides for our troops, and people sat up taking notice of him. They thought he was mean. He was one of the nicest guys you'd ever want to meet.

"Anyway, what we do is take these Cheu Hois up to the border and bum rides with armored units making sweeps. First time out we were up by Loc Ninh, dropping off two NVA about a klick from Cambodia. See these guys have two uniforms on, a sterile green on top and a lighter NVA uniform underneath. Once they drop off the APCs, they diddy bop in the woods, take off the outer uniform and just start walking the trails and roads, talking to NVA and Cong they meet. Hell, they've got North Vietnamese accents and forged paperwork accounting for them being in the area, so it's a pretty good way to pick up information across the border.

"They got a little radio with them, so we sit back at Loc Ninh monitoring calls with a VN counterpart taking down the information. After ten days or so, they come out of the bush and Cheu Hoi all over again. At least that's the way it's supposed to work.

"Well, this time we drop them off and by the second day we get a weak call begging for help. It's the team leader. The other guy's dead. They got stopped and questioned on the road, and had a firefight. He says he's wounded and can't move, but he's got all his equipment and the radio and his maps. He knows right exactly where he is, and asks us to come and get him with a helicopter.

"Now this VN counterpart is a pudgy guy called Captain Peters. Some silly fake name for a VN spook, ain't it? He talks to this guy on the radio and what the hell, I'm all for packing up and going and getting him, but Peters smells a rat. They must have some kind of question, answer code with these guys, checking if everything's all right. Anyway, Peters smells something and won't go in. The guy broadcasts calls for help for three days, and then the air goes dead. We hung around another two days, but nothing else came in.

"That was two months back. Three weeks ago he comes staggering into Loc Ninh. He's all busted up, no pack, no weapon, almost dead. We get him back down here and he admits that they were captured the second day out. Charlie hurried up and got everything ready and gave him the radio to make the call, and just to show him how serious they were that he didn't screw it up they took his partner to the side and blew his brains out with a pistol. But he played it square with us. He didn't give the right answers to Peters, and gave a warning without Charlie catching on. Why they didn't shoot him afterwards, I don't know. He got away.

"They had a company of soldiers scattered around the LZ, and two .51 caliber antiaircraft machine guns set up. What's more? They had a camera and a film crew ready to take movies of them shooting down American helicopters. What a screw up that would have been."

CHAPTER 16 • 145

They talked and shook their heads, and Jimmy the barkeep huddled with one of the others who came in with Dravos.

"He just said you'd better stop dodging him. He wants to see you about something."

"That little pinch-faced snake," the other man said.

Dodge asked, "You're Kidwell?"

"Yah."

"You got some nice friends. Who the devil is that little jerk? He came on like Attila the Hun."

"The name's Riggs. Roger Riggs, and he's a royal pain."

"He was in here?" asked Dravos.

"Yah," said Dodge. "Got his spiny back up real quick and started bullying around. He can't be SF. Who is he?"

Kidwell slumped. "He's with one of the government agencies, I guess. I don't know for sure. I've seen him escorting political hotshots around Saigon, and I know he's somewhere in the pipeline for information. He knows about our Earth Angel projects and what comes in."

"He knew about a prisoner we brought in last month," added Dodge. "Why's he looking for you? He seemed pretty mad."

"He wants me to pimp for him. See I'm trying to angle for a government job when I get out in six months. I love SF and clandestine work, so I thought I'd use contacts here and join Air America. I heard they were hiring, and hell, even if you just start out kicking door bundles out of the airplanes you get pretty good pay. Everyone knows that it's a CIA front. I figured it was a good way to get my foot in the door.

"This Riggs, he sees me with this round-eye nurse over at the hospital, and he starts bugging me about her. Get him a date. Set him up so he can pop her, that type of thing. She's my second cousin! I wouldn't even know her on the street, but my mom writes and says she's here in Saigon and wants me to look her up.

"Now I get Riggs on my ass. He says he can help me get on with Air America if I introduce him to her and throw out some cock-and-bull story that he's a good buddy and a great guy. Of course he leaves it just thin underneath that if I don't help him, he'll nail me so I don't get hired."

Garner asked, "What are you going to do?"

"I figure I'll cave in and introduce them, but before he gets anywhere with her, I'll pig stick him and tell her what's going on. She's a big girl and can look to herself. If she wants to take him on after she knows what he's up to, then that's her business. He makes me feel like a pimp."

They commiserated, talking and joking till midnight. Dravos said he still had to hitch a ride back to Kontum and get his plaque they owed him. He wasn't a One Zero so he didn't get a jacket, but he ran missions long enough to justify a plaque.

It was hardwood based with a painted inlay of brass. It had the skull and beret, and the background of exploding light from the MACV-SOG emblem, but beneath it was a banner with CCC. Further below were crossed weapons, an AK-47 and a CAR-15. They were out of plaques when he left, but he would not leave country without one.

Finally, they kicked in and hit the sack. The next morning they had to board the plane and keep appointments with all those waiting Taiwanese women. Dodge checked his pistol in the House Ten safe, and they loaded up and were gone.

17

THINK

RECON COMPANY
SOA (CCC) 5TH SFG (ABN) 1ST SF
APO San Francisco, Calif 96499

SUBJECT: Policy & Information

TO: All Recon Personnel

WELL

1. The following information and policies were put out at the Commanders' conference on Thursday.

   A. This morning NW of Pleiku, a truck hit a mine. Results 2 US KIA, 1 ARVN KIA and 3 Civilian WIA.

   B. Also this morning, B-40 rockets were fired into the NW bunker line surrounding Kontum City.

   C. Last night 4th Armored again received mortar fire from somewhere in down town Kontum area. Flashes of light could be seen.

   D. No US personnel will accompany, or attend, the funerals of foreign national deceased, outside the Kontum area.

   E. Personnel must be in full military uniform when leaving the C&C compound unless going to or coming from an operation or training area.

F. The areas between the bunkers and barbed wire need the trash picked up. The communication trench on the east wall needs policing.

G. When leaving the C&C compound for any location other than Kontum or Pleiku, you must sign out in the S-1 office. If there is any doubt about your status then ask your 1st Sergeant.

CAN YOU PRODUCE?

2. All operation RTs doing okay. WX is bad or Illinois would be out. They are wet, wet, wet, but okay. Trying for tomorrow. Wyoming reports many civilians in area but no invites to dinner.

NINTH PRESIDENT?

3. 10s, I expect you to set the example. This applies to unit and company policies plus down-to-earth soldiering.

SPRAY CS IN CHARLIE'S BUNKERS

4. "Tips of the Trade, Lessons Learned" sheets are being assembled. Will be putting something out in the next week or so. Any other suggestions you feel are important will be considered for inclusion. THINK!

STROBE LIGHTS NOW AVAILABLE AGAIN FOR US AND ARVN PERSONNEL

5. (S-1) A. All outgoing mail must have your SSN, Unit, and APO number on it or it will be returned to you.

B. When purchasing money orders, you must have a pre-addressed envelope with you. The clerk will put the money order in the envelope, seal it and drop it in the mail bag. In addition, to buy a money order, you need your ID card, Social Security Card, and your white MACV currency control plate.

C. R&Rs for the month of June will be posted today.

WILLIAM DONNALLY
1SG Recon Co.

18

They flew in low across the water, coming into Taipei from the northwest, over the river. It was smaller than Saigon and looked more businesslike. Off to the south were mountains.

After passing through the airport, they exchanged money at the rate of 40 NT, New Taiwan dollars, for one American dollar. Then they shared cabs, and rode off toward the Continental hotel, where most SF usually stayed. It was near the action, and was relatively clean and modern.

Garner saw this city was much more westernized than Saigon. There were urban industries, like steel and automotive plants, but even more noticeable was the way the streets laid out. They were narrower with fewer trees, like ones back home, much more businesslike than Saigon.

The people were like the city too. There was nothing Oriental or ethnic in their dress. Women wore western clothes, not the *ao dais* or any other kind of Chinese equivalent. Whereas Saigon was eclectic, open, agrarian and cluttered, Taipei was streamlined like a bullet, and just about as charming. There was dirt and there were slums, but everything about it screamed out business, money, commerce, and anyone standing in the way was ruthlessly blown aside and left behind.

All during the flight there were animated conversations about the better R&R centers: Sydney, CCK, Bangkok, Taipei, and Tokyo. Garner admitted putting in for Sydney later in the year, but others were adamant about Taipei and Bangkok. Where else could GIs get such sexual services, so much for so very little.

Australia would never wink at prostitution, bringing it to such high levels of big business and artifice. Oriental countries were masters of it though, and to prove the point, after meeting in the lobby, they started cruising streets together.

They walked through the district, fighting off advances of the pitchmen outside bars on the sidewalk. They were all around, yelling like carnival barkers, with sleeves of their starched white shirts rolled up. "Many girls. Cheap drinks. You come in. Many girls to choose from. Number one girls. You come, you come."

The laughing Americans walked on, feeling smoldering stares trace their backs. Rumor Control said most of the better girls were only in a few spots. It was hard to judge the truth, but finally they found the place they wanted, and went inside. Neon flashed, "Eros Bar." Garner flushed with embarrassment.

He judged maybe Dodge and Sardo had the brass to go in such a place by themselves, but he was sure the others needed the courage of a crowd. At least he did.

Lights were indirect and low of course, hiding dirt and cracks, and things that crawled. Formica tables wobbled out towards the middle, but they sidled along the edge, settling into booths with their backs against the pale pink wall.

They no sooner sat down, when the hustler came prancing over. His name was Billie, and after mincing, and winking, and taking orders, he promptly disappeared.

Across the room, forty feet away, were the girls. Over thirty of them were standing with hands on hips or crossed in front, milling, mingling and chewing gum while boldly studying the soldiers. They were an intimidating mass of meat on the hoof, and he was waiting for the auction to begin, but they held back behind some invisible cattle guard. It was like some kind of perverted YMCA dance, with the hookers on one side and the shameless GIs on the other. No one had the guts to be the first to cross the line, but that didn't figure. If anyone had guts he knew it had to be these girls.

Then he saw the pattern and smiled at the thought of all the girls fighting over customers. What a catfight. No, they stood across the room eying the soldiers, probably wondering what they'd have to do for the money, but their names were no doubt on a list, and they had to wait their turns like ladies.

He wasn't surprised when Billie brought the first four over with the drinks. The hustler was unctuous, with a smile as thin as wet rice paper, and Garner was sure he'd just as likely cut their hearts out for the money, but he stood there bowing, making introductions. The game was played in full. Girls were waitresses offering conversation over drinks. Contracts came later.

They were stamped from molds: petite, black hair, and mostly pretty, but the eyes were cattle like, listless, large and dark, and they went nodding dully to the yes or no of acceptance or rejection. It was brutal.

He sensed he and Reynolds said "Yes" just to get it over with. Dodge said yes because he obviously liked the one they offered. They nuzzled in the corner of the booth. But Sardo sat on the outside edge, turning down one after another.

"No, Billie, let me see some more please." He brought them on, and rejects crossed the floor, mentally going to the end of the line. He sat like a USDA inspector grading slabs passing on a hook. He looked up and down, making some pirouette before rejecting them. "No, Billie, sorry. Can I see some more?" The Americans reddened at the display, and finally started complaining.

"Get off your lead ass."

"Pick one, dammit."

"You're gonna keep us here all night."

"Sardo, you animal."

"What are you waiting for? They're running out of girls."

That might have given Billie an idea. He broke it by asking, "You want boy? I know very, very, nice boy. I can get him here in ten minutes. You want boy?"

Sardo snatched the next girl offered.

They sat talking and drinking. The girls spoke good English, and were visibly relaxing, once their own parade of meat was over. They were out of the rush for at least one night, and now the soldiers had to buy enough watered drinks so they could leave. If they kept the young men happy, they could stretch the date out for a full week, but if not, they'd be back on line the next evening.

They had simple western names, and the Americans glanced back and forth at the sad joke, names like Linda, Susan, Kay and Betty. Garner's was Margaret, but he insisted on using her real name, Kie Chu Ling. She had high cheekbones and deep dimples that flashed with every smile. As with the others, she was petite, and he guessed most of what was stuffed inside her sweater was either foam or implants.

They sat drinking for several hours as the bar was filling up with more Americans. The charade was playing out on either side, as girls came sliding across the floor. Finally, the ones they were with asked if the soldiers liked them enough to leave on a date. All eight said immediately they would. They motioned, and Billie brought the contracts.

The joke was that the girls waited tables, and if they left with a man, the bar was losing a waitress for the night. Therefore, the bar should be paid for business losses suffered. They counted out the $15.00 in exchanged NT, and left. It was another $15.00 every day the contract was extended. Sardo asked about a discount, like a baker's dozen, but the Chinese found no humor in the joke.

It was almost dark. They wandered aimlessly, as final flickers of pink disappeared westward. The young men were enjoying walking with the girls in the lights of the shops, talking and joking, forgetting the violence and war they'd soon return to. Garner stretched, breathing deep with the immediacy of the "now."

Children think little of the past and nothing of the future. Existence is wrapped in what is happening at the moment. For a child, the past holds no remorse for poorly considered actions or words that came out wrong. Likewise, the future cannot exist beyond the "now" of living. There can be no fear of what's to come if awareness of the future's never there. The boy represents clean and pure experience, with none of the man's mental baggage.

But, somewhere it starts building, innocuous and subtle, with all the tendrils of a cancer choking a happy life. Fears of the future are the first to sprout. It's a short-lived inequity, however. Regrets for actions taken creep in, until a whole framework of worry about the past and future is built. By the late teens the child is gone, and the shining immediacy of the "now" is dimmed.

Only rarely can that light shine through, quickening the senses. The shortest and most intense power was the threat of death. Firefights offered that.

After the run, every sense screamed with the awareness of life. The colors of leaves, the touch of the rain, the smell of cordite or napalm, or even ozone after lightning strikes. All was fresh, alive, and tingling, but like the ozone, the memory of it was short-lived, wafting away and evaporating as half-forgotten memories. It was a mental high dissipating with fears of what was to come, and the knowledge they lived life on the edge of violent death.

Nothing surpassed the heightened sense of living after almost dying, but other things gave the flavor, if not the seductive sustenance of it. That's why there was such a thing as R&R. It let soldiers sense the "now," and forget the future. It gave the body rest, and the mind a chance to heal. It gave men the right to laugh and cry, and cut the fool and later not regret their acts.

It offered intrigue and safe danger. Then of course there was the sex, open and available, without a shred of regret. However, when compared to cheating death, all other guiltless thrills were shadows of imitation, the way a roller coaster imitates a plunging airplane crash.

They didn't tingle with overloads of heightened senses, but the young men breathed collective sighs while walking hand in hand with the girls. No regrets, no fears, no guilts. Just the physical awareness of the "now," and the knowledge they didn't have to think beyond the night.

"Boom! Boom! Boom!"

"Wake the hell up in there, we're going out to breakfast. Want to come along?" Dodge was pounding on the door.

"Boom! Boom! Boom!"

"Wake up!"

"I'm coming. I'm coming." Garner opened it as she rolled and covered parts of herself with the sheet. The right breast was pale, with the nipple pointing toward the ceiling. Dodge thrust his head through the doorway, ogling it. Then he whispered, "Implants huh? Like we thought?"

"Yah, implants." Garner scratched his head and yawned.

"Mine too. Come on, let's get something to eat. After pounding nails all night I get hungry!"

"Okay, okay. I'll meet you in the lobby in ten minutes. Are the girls coming?"

"No. Are you going to keep her for a while?"

"Yah, I think so. She's nice, and I don't want to go back down to that cattle auction again. I'll keep her."

"Good, tell her that and tell her to sleep in, you'll be back. If you don't, she'll figure you're done with her and *di di mao* back to the club. See you downstairs."

Ten minutes later, seven of them were walking down the street, looking for a place to eat. Sardo's appetites were seemingly insatiable, and he yelled through the door that he was eating in. They left him.

They wandered north, in the opposite direction of the district. Finally they found a place with pictures of ham and eggs on the menu in the window, and went inside. After ten minutes of fighting to make themselves understood and twenty minutes of waiting, they were served at two tables. Conversations carried on between bites of runny eggs and buttered toast.

Reynolds said. "I've decided to come back here for R&R when I qualify for one later in the year. You can't beat good food, good sex, good booze, and a clean bed. To hell with Sydney. Those round-eye girls down there probably have soldiers standing fifteen deep trying to get at them. What kind of shot does a regular kinda guy have with only a week to kill? They're probably like those Doughnut Dolly volunteers, who serve the troops and talk prattle all the time. I like this. Off the boat and in the sack."

"You know, I talked to one of those Doughnut Dollies once down in Nah Trang at Group Headquarters," Danner said. "She was thick as a stump. Thought she was God's gift to the GIs, and that all they wanted to do was sit and talk over a cup of coffee, look moon-eyed and dream of home. She couldn't even get a handle that all the guys were doing was making time and figuring a way to get her in the sack. I don't think the oriental girls are born that naive. How about you, Ted? Did you enjoy last night, Pilgrim?"

Garner laughed. "Yah, she was nice, but it's kind of fake, knowing that you're paying for it and all."

"You're just used to getting Canada for free," said Dodge. "You think she's not fake? You think she loves your young ass or something? I told you before there's lots of prices to pay. You better wake up, Ted. That woman's getting her hooks in and wants you to take her to the States."

"No, Phil. I'm not gonna marry anyone. There's too much ahead. Besides, who says I'll even make it out of here? She's not angling for marriage, but even if she was she's sure not going to get it."

"Oh? What if you knock her up? You think she'll sit back and keep the kid, an outcast for Christ's sake? She'll dump on you in a heartbeat. She'll angle to get you to marry her somehow, and if you're killed? So what? She's a war bride. She'll get insurance and a ticket to the States, and then ping on your folks. 'Garnah, he love me too much, too much.'"

Garner was getting a headache. He rubbed his eyes and stopped listening. "Look, Phil, Please, let it be. If we're friends then let it be. I came over here to have a good time like the rest. I don't want to think about it. I don't want to worry. I don't want to stay awake at night and sweat about going back. Okay? The last thing I ever expected when I came to Vietnam was to have woman problems. Let it be. Okay?"

"What's the matter, Ted? You never had woman problems in the States? Back at Stone Island?" asked Adams.

"That's Rock Island. Yah. I had woman problems, in a way. I spent two years at a small college where girls thought birth control pills were things they held between their knees. I've got more problems over here than I ever did back there, so just lighten up, okay? Let me enjoy the trip. Screw with me back at Kontum, but not here. Understand?"

They understood of course, but that didn't stop the hassle. It continued for a while, until dying a natural death by being all talked out. Then the spotlight of attention turned to other subjects, and he was left in relative peace.

That night, Sardo, Day, Samuels and Reynolds took their girls dancing, while the others went to a movie. Danner saw posters while walking in the afternoon. His hero traded in his Green Beret for an eye patch. It was *True Grit*, and John Wayne rode across the screen with all the power of a thunderstorm, just as relentless and unstoppable.

Chinese sat in awed silence, chewing popcorn and staring apprehensively at the big man. Garner looked around, and saw he was a very popular movie star. Subtitles flashed at the bottom of the screen, and the Americans marveled at the incomprehensible writing. The symbols were a mystery, and the boys wondered if they carried specific meanings, or general concepts.

The Chinese characters flashed across the screen and were immediately read, and many times the audience laughed a full four seconds before the actors said anything remotely funny. Time and time again it happened, making Garner realize just how much a foreigner he was. They watched their own reactions, because each time they had an urge to laugh, the audience had already quieted back down.

"We've got to let Samuels know the Duke is still wearing his Montagnard bracelet," he said, as they filed out on the street.

The night wind was brisk, and they wandered three blocks away, hand in hand, looking in shop windows, when suddenly they were surrounded by teenage boys. There were twelve of them with white shirts, rolled-up sleeves, and black stovepipe pants.

Dodge said, "What the fuck is this? Taiwan's version of the Vienna Boys' Choir?"

Then they started screaming.

The one Garner took to be the leader broke out of the surrounding circle, stepping in. Dodge, Garner, Danner and Adams formed a box with the girls behind. The leader stood there, screaming Chinese insults at the whites who had the gall to buy their women. It needed no translation. Others shifted uneasy, and Garner thought he saw a blade.

Dodge said, "You know I was in a bar once up in Fairbanks, and this huge lumberjack gets drunk and yells out, 'Come on you suckers, fight. Big men, two at a time. Little men just as fast as you can get here!'" Dodge was working up, getting ready to spring when the girls broke out from behind.

They stood in front, screaming back at the youths and taking their taunts. They shook fingers, and the leader's neck bulged with a fury that made it look like it would burst, but a crowd was growing, and the girls were taking the edge off their madness. They screamed some final epithets and finally broke it off before police arrived. Americans were good tourists, and the girls were legal tarts. They finally left in peace, and went to dinner.

That night he gave Kie Chu Ling a bath. They talked and sipped wine as he sat on the edge, washing her from top to bottom, feeling the power building in his hands. She writhed, and sloshed, and groaned as he worked her up to slippery tension. Her toes strained white against the porcelain, and she arched back while crying out. Breasts shivered, and he leaned in to suckle as she came to full release.

He nuzzled deeper as she moaned in his right ear. Her breast was large, with the nipple well defined and hard, like most Oriental women. He buried his face and kept her groaning with the pulses. Two inches beneath was the implant making her larger and supposedly more alluring. He knew women were doing such things in the States, and shook his head at the thought. These went bad and were turning hard.

It made him mad women should mutilate themselves for men. There was no need. He thought of Canada and the things Dodge said. Maybe she was right. Small was better. Small was real, and suddenly he realized he missed her.

They toweled each other and slipped between the sheets. She was a hooker, and he liked her. She'd fought the boys like a tigress. They called her names, like the big white man she slept with, but she spit it back, telling them to go to hell. Her life was her own to do with as she pleased. They had no right to comment. She told him all these things, and he found common ground on which to understand her and her way of life. She didn't see herself as a victim, and he was glad to finally learn it. They slept.

All during the week, the well-practiced girls took them to different tourist spots. The tradesmen laughed and joked, calling each by name. They went to a zoo, then to a park by the river where lazy boat rides filled the afternoons. Tourist hustlers took pictures, and he was sure she'd later get a cut of the price. They went to dinners at off-street kitchens where sounds of life were real, with dogs snuffling at the sides, babies crying and cats meowing, where the smells of sauces, meats and spices assaulted them half a block before the lighted door. It was a week of fun, gone all too soon.

The last night they were on their own, walking hand in hand back to the Continental after dinner. It was dark, and the attack came just two blocks away. There was a scuffling off to the right, in the alley next to the last restaurant they'd passed. Garner sensed a flicker from the corner, and came up with a rowing punch that caught the first boy flush in the face with the back of his right fist. It broke his nose and he screamed, dropping the knife, clutching his face. Blood spurted around the alleyway while others piled in.

Garner shoved the girl out in the street, where she stood screaming for help as he began kicking and backing away. He got knocked into a spin, and the eight boys surrounded him. The leader and his bullies were going to beat and cut an American to prove a point. He started backing into the alley, pressing against the brick wall of the restaurant, between garbage cans and empty vegetable crates.

They came in, and the leader showed martial skills with a high roundhouse kick, shattering the crate Garner grabbed as a shield. Slats splintered, held together by wire. He shook it loose, keeping two wooden spikes, throwing the rest at the approaching boys.

He kicked out at swinging fists, connecting two times, sending the first one reeling. The leader came around again, kicking the spike away and numbing Garner's right hand. Then he tried a frontal kick, and Garner blocked it with his foot. The next one came in toward his face and he ducked left, driving his left fist into the boy's unprotected groin. The leader's face went white with shock, then he bobbled, shrieking and tumbling down the alleyway before collapsing.

They came in and overwhelmed Garner. He fell. A knife appeared, and he dodged it as his second wooden spike found the other's mark instead, going deep to the vitals. Another shrieked and fell, but the rest had him now. They knocked the second spike of wood away, and pummeled his face and groin. He thought he saw another knife, but couldn't stop it. It was looping low, and he knew they'd start up between the legs.

Then he was the center of a small explosion, and all the white-shirted boys jerked backwards and away. They fell like tumblers. Further out in the dark were other moving forms. Then he understood. They weren't blown away; they were pulled away by meaty hands, heavy hands, angry hands.

There were blurs of actions he couldn't register. Across the alley was a rippled back, with piston-like arms that destroyed a man pinned against the wall. When the body fell, Dodge turned, attacking another. Then other hands came in, lifting him, until Garner stood and watched his rescuers finish off the last three attackers, sending them gimping down the alleyway. He caught a glimpse of Kie Chu Ling coming towards him, as he heard the Duke say, "Yah better watch yerselves around these parts, Pilgrim. There's injins afoot."

He saw Danner, Adams, Dodge and Sardo in the alley with at least six others he didn't know. Kie Chu Ling helped him forward, and he realized she'd probably saved his life. She'd yelled at Danner as he left the hotel, and he in turn ran back, calling for others. Americans boiled out of the Continental like a fraternity house, running down the street to her screams, doing the quick and dirty job. The last thing he'd ever recall about the evening was the stupid grin on Danner's face, and his patting it, saying, "You dumb fucking Cowboy. Thanks."

It was all a dream by noon the next day. He was busted, but not broken or cut. Bruises were building in different places, and there was some trouble walking as his testicles shot slivers of glass through his body. He boarded the plane, realizing he'd never been hit there before, and he guessed the all-consuming male protective urge came from some evolutionary blueprint rather than first-hand knowledge. Never was there contemplated pain of such magnitude. To walk was punishment enough; to run would be masochistic self-abuse.

The girls were gone, and the city disappeared in a fuzzy haze. Saigon reality was coming, and he slept with the others, feeling surprisingly better when they finally circled around Tan Son Nhut.

They caught some cabs into town and again passed jewelry shops, canals and stacked sewer pipes overflowing with humanity. A kid stuck his head out of one on top and ducked back in, reminding Garner of a goldfish he had as a boy. It hid in the small ceramic castle, poking out to look out for danger and search for food. The fish didn't know it was safe in the bowl. Garner understood that the boy was smart in realizing that he wasn't.

At House Ten he took off civilian clothes bought on R&R, changing back into a clean uniform and jungle boots. The beret was back on top, flash over the left eye, flap down and to the right, not like some pie plate!

Then, he gathered with the rest in the bar, trying to decide where to eat. It was a long damned day, they said, and crackers and a bit of juice on the plane was hardly more than food for rodents. They decided on going out, and since his crotch was tied up tight and feeling pretty good, Garner decided to go too. House Ten had drinks, but little food. They'd make a night of it before the return to Kontum.

Right away they splintered into groups. Sardo, Danner, Adams and Samuels wanted to stay in Saigon proper. It was raining again, and the thought of going far held no appeal. Besides, they said, there were plenty of eating places on the northern side of town.

Garner got pulled along with the rest. They wanted to go to Cholon, the Chinese section, half the consolidated city to the south. They caught a cab, and all four clambered in: Garner, Dodge, Reynolds and Day. Fifteen minutes later they crossed into another world.

Garner felt like he stepped into a Charlie Chan movie. It was so Chinese. They drove down Dong Khanh Boulevard and eyed the narrow side streets dripping with rain. Mandarin wings topped the buildings. Wood carvings and perforated screens decorated windows of the stores. There was nothing western in appearance, and he felt much more foreign than he ever did in Taipei.

Cholon was a traditional Chinese city, founded in the eighteenth century by Chinese businessmen. There was little reminiscent of Saigon or Taipei. The other two were far different. Taipei was western, businesslike and modern. Saigon was more French in layout, and it showed in the wide and liberal use of trees and parks. Cholon was, however, transplanted from another time, and it vibrated with a life force all its own. It was cloistered in and dark, and privately sinister.

Driving through the city at night was an act of desperation for a westerner, he guessed. He kicked himself for coming. Vietnamese tolerated the strong and preyed upon the weak. Several times he swore he saw scuffling figures, and he remembered the stranded beggar and his rifled bowl. Like the black market, this culture fed with a cannibalistic excess.

They finally stopped the cab, climbing out on a narrow street where night life and signs pointed out they were foreign and generally unwelcomed. Dodge of course paid no attention to the complaints. He searched for a meal of subtle tastes and generous helpings he'd heard about. When they found the place, he reprimanded them for lacking faith.

The blood-red door gave way. Entry walls throbbed with the color of the door, and black brush strokes depicting wild horses ran along mountain sides of ink. The crisp drawings were mastered with just a few lines, however, all the grace and power was there to see. Garner admired the graceful lines as the hostess came through the beaded curtain.

She was full Chinese, wearing a satin gown as red as the surrounding walls. It fit her like a latex glove, from top to bottom. Its choker collar was like an *ao dai*, but the slit on the side showed shapely legs instead of black satin trousers. More black designs rippled around the gown. She smiled seductively, motioning them to follow.

As they parted the beaded curtain, Dodge whispered, "I think we just fell into an episode of *Terry and the Pirates*, and this sweet thing must be the Dragon Lady."

Heads swiveled at five other tables, and the four green-clad soldiers felt the vacant stares. She ushered them to the far right corner and left menus behind. Then a kitchen helper in an apron took the orders, since her English was best. The hostess looked decidedly put out, but it was business.

They sat for over an hour, taking course on course of food: soups, egg rolls, sweet and sour, shrimps, pork and chicken. Rice, vegetables and spices were to the side. Unknown sauces, glazed and sticky sweet, were ladled over everything. It was a meal he'd long remember, both for taste and texture. They wolfed at first, then settled in, savoring different subtleties. Finally, they were at the end of the wine, cracking the last of the fortune cookies, laughing at the Chinese symbols and their own naiveté. They thanked the hostess, generously settled up, and left.

The wet streets reflected red and yellow lights in their shiny puddles. They walked along for ten minutes, and in front of an open basket shop, two young Vietnamese called to them from the shadows.

"GI. Hey, GI. You want to exchange MPC? Give good exchange. No bullshit, GI."

Dodge stopped and studied them. They were young, wiry, cowboys, like a hundred thousand feral others in the streets. "How much?" He said.

The boys stepped out from the shadows. "We give best exchange. Two hundred dong for MPC. Okay?"

Dodge nodded, moving closer. Reynolds and Day looked decidedly nervous, and finally Reynolds said, "Look, Phil. There're MPs around, and if it's all the same to you, I don't want any trouble. We're gonna walk down the block a little. Catch up to us when you're done. Okay?"

Dodge nodded, and entered the shadows of the basket shop entrance. The old man sitting inside watched the puddles, totally ignoring the transaction taking place ten feet away. Garner couldn't leave Dodge on his own, so he came in behind.

The first boy was pulling out a wad of bills rolled up with a tightly wrapped rubber band. He took a while undoing it, and Garner wondered why they wrapped it up so tight, but the thought didn't register a warning.

He peeled off bills as Dodge pulled out MPC, counting eighty dollars out of several hundred. Then the boy showed the corresponding handful of piasters and twisted them up into a separate roll of bills. He wound them tight with another rubber band, and as the money went to change hands, the second boy standing to the side whispered. "Shush. MPs."

The Americans turned, examining the few people in the street, but saw nothing. Then they twisted back, and the boy said. "I wrong. I see white hat. It look like MP helmet." He smiled through a pock-marked face, showing bad teeth. They exchanged rolls of money, and the Americans walked to the sidewalk as the others dissolved into the shadows behind.

Dodge worked the tightly wrapped roll of five-hundred-piaster bills, finally breaking the band with his teeth. Then he unraveled it and saw the outer note was wrapped around a core of smaller bills of fifty and twenty piasters. It hit him right away, while Garner stood confused.

"They palmed the roll on me. They palmed it!" He flew into a rage, and before Garner could grab him or yell to stop, he bounded off the sidewalk, disappearing into the dark, yelling, "You little bastards!"

Garner stood bouncing on his toes, not knowing what to do. Shadows were full of knives. He wavered, looking for help, afraid to yell. Finally, he swallowed hard and plunged in, following the screaming voice of Dodge.

He ran through the shop, and his groin said, "Slow down." He stumbled on overturned baskets, feeling wicker and bamboo give way with brittle crunches. Then he hit the back door, throwing it open, entering a steel blue alley. Dodge screamed off to the left, and he ran, following the best he could.

The alley backed on cluttered tenements and small businesses, where boxes and trash piled high, and people huddled in the dark. Charcoal fires dotted the edges of the alley, and between the buildings where families ate their nightly meals. He came to a T intersection, and stopped to get his bearings. A baby was crying somewhere near; barking dogs were further out. To the left, the T section ran back to the street. He turned right, plunging in deeper.

People huddling on the sides were cowering from the running figures and screams of rage. He stopped a hundred meters further in at a gap in the side buildings, where Dodge yelled off to the left. Then he turned, walking into deeper shadows of the path, moving along, feeling with his hands outstretched. There were rattling garbage cans and thumping scuffles up ahead. The walkway opened on a courtyard, where the backs of two-storied buildings formed a dirty moonlit doughnut hole. Stairwells crawled up surrounding walls.

There was a cluster of men toward the middle. Dodge was beyond them, against the bricks, yelling.

"Give me that money back right now you slimy little dink, or I'll blow your ass away." He stood, with the pistol glinting in the moonlight. Garner caught movement to the left, as one of six young men threw a brick, knocking the pistol off aim as he fired. The pistol clanged around the courtyard, and the boy to the right of the leader crumpled, holding his knee, screaming in pain.

The leader was in the air, coming around. Dodge tried to adjust, but the kick was good, knocking the pistol far to Dodge's right. Dodge caught one man with a square left to the jaw, then went down with the others swinging on top.

"You give us money now, or we cut your balls off GI."

The cowboys had their backs to the courtyard while facing Dodge, hitting him repeatedly against the far wall. Garner heard Dodge fight back, but they used a club or something early on, and his attempts were feeble at best. He crossed to the right, and the boy writhing on the ground was the first to see him as he reached the weapon. The others turned as he brought it up on line.

"Back off! Back off, right now! *Di di mao!*"

They straightened, shifting side to side, showing knives. He was fifteen feet away, moving in, as they finally stood still next to the slumped figure.

"Back off. Move away from him. Keep the money. Go. Leave him be."

The leader saw a chance, and grabbed for Dodge to use him as a shield. Halfway through his side step the pistol roared, "Klanggg!" The boy snapped in the moonlight, and for an instant all his hair stood out, like he'd been hammered with a bolt of electricity. Shock waves passed, and his hair fell back, almost covering the baseball-sized hole in the back of his skull. He looked out with three eyes; then his legs let loose and his bowels dumped into his trousers as he crumpled backwards in a bloody tangle. The others fled down the path as Garner skidded over.

He propped Dodge, taking inventory. He wasn't cut, and finally stood like a wobbly egg in the dark. He staggered to the body, pushing it over with his foot, kneeling and fishing in the pockets, until he came up with the roll. Then, he stood again, and Garner got under his right side, making sure to keep the pistol free. They looked from the body to the boy with the smashed knee, whimpering in pain. Then they made it out to the alley, as sirens neared.

Reynolds and Day were close, calling out, and Garner headed straight at the alley intersection, hitting the street half a block down to the right. He whistled, and the others came running.

There was building activity, and as they tumbled in a cab, Garner thought he saw some White Mice running. They pulled away, and two blocks later passed the first of three MP jeeps with flashing lights. They made it back to House Ten, locking the door behind. Then they sat in the bar, drinking quiet. The next day each held his breath until the Blackbird lifted off, and they were safely on their way back to Kontum. Garner finally relaxed, sleeping and rolling in ugly dreams.

19

THINK

RECON COMPANY
SOA (CCC) 5TH SFG (ABN) 1ST SF
APO San Francisco, Calif 96499

SUBJECT: Company alert SOP

TO: All Recon Personnel

1. In the event of an alert, incoming rounds, or ground attack, the below listed RTs will take up position behind the sandbags on the east side of building #20 (Sergeant Major's Quarters):

    NEW MEXICO—THIFT LOI—TENNESSEE—OHIO

2. The information in paragraph one applies to the RTs listed below with the exception that they will take up positions behind the sandbags on the north side of building #26:

    WASHINGTON—ARKANSAS—NEW HAMPSHIRE

3. Reference paragraphs #1 and #2, the main purpose, mission, of these RTs will be to act as a second line of defense in case of an enemy penetration of the outer perimeter and line of bunkers. The ranking 10 in each of the two sections will take command in the event of an alert, practice or actual, and the other 10s will act as assistants.

4. In the event of a ground attack, all personnel will refrain from shifting positions as much as possible.

5. All RTs not previously mentioned will move to their assigned bunkers in the event of an alert, unless the alert is called while the RT is on Wall Security. In the event this happens, the RT will remain in the positions already being manned.

6. Once an alert has been called, no RT or individual will leave their alert positions until the Company CO, First SGT, or a member of the CCC staff gives the all clear, in person.

7. Weapons, web gear and protective masks are mandatory items of equipment to be taken on guard duty and alert.

8. Casualties will be moved by an assigned CCC medic only if the individual's life is further endangered if left in position

Patrick J. Henderson
CPT INF

THINK

RECON COMPANY
SOA (CCC) 5TH SFG (ABN) 1ST SF
APO San Francisco Calif, 96499

SUBJECT: Policy & Information

TO: All Recon Personnel

DO YOU LOCK YOUR DOORS AT NIGHT?

1. Illinois is out after sixteen days of rain. SSG Kilmer is in the dispensary because of his feet. Say hello.

KNOW AND HAVE THE FACTS BEFORE YOU TALK

2. If you have any suggestions for improvements, gripes or complaints, then come and see me. That is all a part of my job, and the orderly room is open during all daylight hours, and sometimes longer!!

BE IT EVER SO HUMBLE

3. There will be no more cartons of cigarettes sold by the carton in the club. Orders from Hqs.

4. Bulk sale of liquor will only be made to personnel residing on the CCC compound. Orders from Hqs.

5. Keep a record of all DZ and LZs you come across while out on operations. Report them to S-2 upon return to base. The format for reporting is in your SF handbook.

6. CCS and CCN received STABO rigs. No further comment.

7. Again, the Fourth Armored Division was shelled last night from some place in Kontum area. If you are out on a local training mission and see flashes or indications of enemy activity be sure to call in artillery support. Procedures are on Recon Bulletin board. Make yourself acquainted with it before going out on local operations.

8. SCU and CIDG are authorized to receive US awards for valor. Those that I presently have, that are completed, will be turned into the A&D section. Some names of deserving individuals were turned into me but I will now need a complete statement of the actions that took place.

WILLIAM DONNALLY
1SG Recon Co.

21

"Snake doesn't look all right to me. Does he look all right to you?"

Danner considered Garner's question and studied the small man sitting alone across the room by the bar. He was motionless, with his right hand wrapped tight around a glass.

"He looks the usual, Ted. Drunk maybe. Maybe a little too drunk, but usual. Why not, he's going home. It's his privilege.

"Yah," said Garner. "But he looks a little drunker than I've seen him. I think he's sad about leaving. He's been over here so long I'll bet he's forgotten how to act stateside. What, three tours and two extensions?"

Samuels said. "I've heard he gets the DTs in the field. Goes to shaking and all that."

They all looked over now, considering the huddled figure. The only motion for thirty minutes had been mechanical lifting of the glass and the increased bobbing of his Adam's apple as his head tipped progressively backwards. Then he'd give a nod or wave to Canada, or Beetle Nut Mary, for a refill. Garner saw liquor run down the edge of every new glass.

Snake Martin was lost inside the blousy uniform. His forehead was high, with a central widow's peak. His eyes were set wide apart and the nose, which could have been described as pug when he was a boy, was broken and crushed against the backdrop of his face. He got his name because of his looks and his thin smile, but also because he never telegraphed a punch when he decided it was time. He was like a rattler, coiled and ready.

Snake was the Old Man on Recon now, a lifer at thirty-one, with more field time than any other three members put together, with the exception of Billings. He wasn't mean spirited. It's just that he was unreadable and therefore unpredictable.

"I heard he had over fifty missions. Maybe even sixty, but of course that includes one-day shootouts too," said Danner.

Garner stirred bourbon with his finger. "I can't imagine why a guy would do that. I came over here to prove something to myself I guess, and I suppose if I make it out of here I'll be satisfied. I better be. But fifty, sixty missions. I'd be having twice as many nightmares.

"I don't understand guys like that. Most of us are living scared out, but then you see the ones who need an adrenaline pump like a shot of coffee in the morning. I just don't understand. I guess all this sitting around makes us all edgy." He finished the drink, sucking on the one remaining cube of ice as he raised the glass, ordering another from Canada who was never far away.

It was the end of summer, and the rains slowed things down. The killing of the cowboy in Saigon was three months past, and Garner sweated when he first got back. The wounded boy was caught of course, and told the White Mice about the American soldiers and their berets. That narrowed the search, and inquiries were made as to who was where and when. It got close enough that Donnally and the colonel called them in, asking questions about their trip.

"Sergeant Dodge, you were the ranking NCO on this last trip to Taipei. Why don't you tell us what happened?" the colonel asked.

"Well, Sir, first of all, let me tell you the women were great."

"I don't mean what happened in Taipei, Sergeant. I mean what happened in Saigon."

"Sorry, Sir. I don't know what you mean!"

The colonel studied the disingenuous smile and skipped down faces that were intently staring at walls, and boots, and crawling bugs.

"Gentlemen, in case you didn't know it, there was a shooting of a Vietnamese national down in Saigon by someone supposedly wearing a green beret during the time you were gone. We've been requested to check upon your whereabouts on the evening in question. Now, do you men know anything about this?"

They stood mute, then Garner stiffened as he asked, "Sir? What ah. What ah, will happen if they catch the guy?"

The colonel locked on him. "There will be an inquiry and no doubt a convened court martial, or the Vietnamese government may choose to try the man in its own courts."

"Either way, he's screwed," offered Dodge.

"That's enough, Sergeant. Is there anything you wanted to say, Sergeant Garner?"

"Well, Sir, what if this soldier shot someone kind of in self-defense? Or in defense of others?"

"Then he'd be acquitted I'm sure," said the colonel.

"Well Sir I—"

"I agree with Garner, Sir," said Dodge. The colonel snapped back with the interruption.

"You agree what, Sergeant?"

"Well, Sir, he was gonna say that a lot of Legs wear phony berets when they're out on the town trying to pick up women or just look bad assed. It could have been anyone. Besides, late at night who can see the color. It could have been one of those bogus blue Air Force berets for all we know. Some Airborne units are wearing unauthorized black berets too. Right, guys?" The others on line murmured assent as the colonel squared himself in front of Dodge.

"Who said anything about the shooting happening at night, Sergeant Dodge?"

He squirmed.

"Sir?" said Reynolds. "Everyone knows Saigon goes nuts at night. Like they say, it's Dodge City. I'm sure Phil just assumed it happened at night. I know I did. How about you other guys?" All but Garner started nodding heads and talking at once.

"All right. All right," said the colonel. "So no one knows anything about this killing?"

Dodge asked innocently, "The fucker died, Sir?"

The colonel ignored him. "First Sergeant Donnally, unless you can think of anything else I'll contact Saigon and tell them we had no part in it."

"Very good, Sir." The colonel left the briefing room and the first sergeant looked them over. "All right men, you're dismissed." They turned to go. "Oh, Sergeant Dodge, do you still have that recaptured US Army Colt automatic pistol?"

"No, Sergeant. I sold that this week to some Engineers on the road. It rattled and couldn't shoot straight. I didn't want to keep something that couldn't hit a wall at ten feet."

"Good, Sergeant. Pistols like that can be dangerous. Dismissed."

The killing was a low priority in a city where over five hundred lost their lives in similar fashion every year. The matter dropped as quietly as a folder in the bottom of a filing cabinet.

When they first got back they found Team Illinois out of the field with trench foot and infected leech bites. They ran out of food on the thirteenth day and insect repellant on the sixteenth. Walker, the One Zero, was medevacked and Yards went home on leave. The other two Americans walked the compound for six weeks without duties or training. Their pants were rolled up, and they wore sandals, letting their feet breathe. They moved like they were old and broken, hunched forward, as if to lighten themselves and reduce the pain. They said it was like walking on shards of glass.

Every other week Team Iowa went to the village, fishing with grenades and drinking rice wine. They blew the stupefied fish to the surface, and younger boys swam through the ruddy current, retrieving them. Then the crowd headed back up the hillside, holding hands, laughing and smoking, as clouds scudded low overhead, dumping several inches of water every afternoon.

Clay was greasy red and they swished their boots in pans of water before entering the long house to drink sticks of rice wine. By the late afternoon, when all sense of time and reality blurred, they climbed aboard and drove back along dangerous roads to the safety of the compound.

Every visit began by off-loading goods and presents. Reynolds didn't seem to notice, but each time, several green laundry bags loaded with unknown materials were taken without fanfare to the main Long House. Dominique or Djuit disappeared beneath the stilted house, between carved log coffins, stacked for future use, and the wall of piled kindling. Dodge ignored it, but Garner felt eyes studying him for a reaction.

Rumor said the rains slowed down Charlie too, that troops were backing up along infiltration routes across the fence, filling up corridors of movement like water trickling into a glass. More people meant more chances for teams to be discovered. It meant more soldiers on the chase, and on the sweeps, and on the flanks of runs. It meant more deaths.

Rumor Control also said CCN lost two whole teams without a trace. One gave radio contact they were hit, but after that all was silent. Someone said a team up north had seen a round-eyed woman with the NVA: blonde, Nordic type, an advisor perhaps from a Communist Bloc East European country, Russian? She didn't wear a uniform, just khaki shirt and pants. Who she was they didn't know, but many nights were filled with dreams of capture.

Hamilton got it on a Visual Reconnaissance. He sat behind Broken Bottle in the little plane looking for a good LZ. Clouds were low and so were they. He took one stray round up through the ear and out the canopy. Washington, New Hampshire, Kentucky and Hawaii were hit: three Yards dead, seven wounded, two Americans dead, four wounded, two of which were medevacked.

Buckman took a lucky one while coming out on strings with Minnesota. Morrison had gone stateside and Lieutenant Glass had taken over. They had wounded and were chased; the helicopters hovered, dropping tied-off ropes with loops. They strapped in as Cobras gunned around. Then they were lifted up and out, and as they climbed, Buckman looked up, screaming in pleasure, and a round came through his left cheek and out his open mouth, leaving tongue and teeth alone. One Yard died.

CCS lost several teams complete. One went down in a Huey, and the crew was added to the list of MIAs. B-40 rockets did that. One man was swept away while crossing a bloated stream. Heavy packs and sucking mud could do that easy. Rumor said they also lost some men downtown in Ban Me Thout, in a gunfight with some ARVN over a girl. The same thing happened in Kontum two years before.

The wet could do that. It drove people inside. They drank, and brooded, and forgot the "now," and feared the future. It made them mean with no chance to work it off. The sodden basketball court was seldom used.

There were rumors of many different sightings, and the round-eyed girl was only one. At different times they heard of Chinese advisors, or Russian advisors, or sightings of American POWs being led away. Someone said a Russian KGB agent was offed somewhere up north. A brilliant red lacquered badge with a golden sword circulated as a trophy. Wyoming woke to sounds of chanting far away. They packed up, working north a quarter mile, and found two hundred NVA doing morning calisthenics in a clearing. They called in artillery, and ran as fast and as far as they could.

Garner sat with his bourbon, watching Canada bring Snake another drink. It was Friday, and he let himself get an erection as he followed her. They'd take care of it the next night.

The Snake's hand twitched, and liquor slipped the edges. That morning at formation they presented Snake with something special. Everyone stood at attention while the colonel gave a speech on duty, honor and the like. Then he motioned to Donnally, holding the award.

It wasn't a medal for bravery in combat or some such thing. Many times those were granted or refused simply on basis of the writing. The more verbose, the better chance and the higher the award. Such things needed witnesses too. A-Company suffered set-piece battles, but on Recon many acts of heroism passed unnoticed in the shadows.

This was an award that truly meant something, because it came from peers and not some arbitrary review board. Donnally held out the rosewood case, lifting the lid. Inside was a chromed 9mm Browning High Power automatic pistol, twinkling in the gray light of morning. The red velvet set it off, and Donnally read the brass plaque on the inside lid. "To William Martin, from officers and men of Command and Control Central. In recognition of dedicated service. Vietnam 1969."

Snake said very little, but his thin smile stretched across his face while showing off the weapon with obvious pleasure. Then, as people drifted away during the day, he began brooding in the club. His last extension was denied, and he was going home at last. Garner considered the man, wondering why he looked like he was going on the most dangerous insertion of his life. Garner took a drink from Canada, and she brushed his shoulder.

They were a regular item now. She cooked for him, and whenever he could get Dodge and Reynolds out of the team room for a night, she'd stay over. There were others in similar circumstances so he didn't feel too selfish or too lucky. Many hooch maids slept with those they cleaned for, and girls from down the road came sneaking in from time to time.

The wet slowed down missions, and the last four Iowa went on were nothing special, two area recons and two road watches. The watches went without a hitch. They'd sit back in the woods all day, waiting through the rains, huddled and quiet. Ponchos glistened, but as long as they didn't move it didn't pose a danger. Toward dusk rains normally lightened, and after stripping off the rubber covers, they crept toward the road. They'd sit back, listening to signal shots passing down from guard to guard, signaling all clear. Then the trucks started rolling, and two of them crawled, closer under cover of the engine noise. They counted trucks and marching troops.

The first time out, two 37mm antiaircraft guns on flatbeds drove by. The second time a strange rumble came beneath the engine noise, and five tanks rolled past, but there was nothing they could do about it. Clouds grounded all the jets, and they were too far north to use Ben Het's guns. They reported all, and sat in frustrated silence for seven days each time. Even Dodge learned his lesson, and refused to try and grab a driver. Clouds dictated all insertions and extractions. If there was trouble, they were all alone. They came out quietly each time.

Area recons were the worst in the rain. They couldn't wear ponchos on the move, so they walked soaking wet for eight days straight. They moved slow, always looking to the sides and back behind. It was their mission to move around, finding what was there, but Charlie didn't have to move. He was in his own base camps, huddled down, keeping dry. The biggest danger was stumbling right on top of enemy troops and not knowing it.

That's how Jamison got it on Kentucky. They moved up a hill and stopped for a break, not knowing they were on the edge of a bunker complex. NVA opened up from less than ten feet away, hitting him over twenty times. There was no way to get the body, so they ran. Garner wondered how they'd list him, KIA or MIA. Everyone knew he was dead, but the military had its rules. MIA he guessed.

They ran light the first two missions, as Kui and Kehn recuperated from their wounds. All totaled, they ran from three firefights during the wet, once on the first area recon and twice on the other. Two times they had ample warning as the NVA blundered onto their position. The other time, surprise was mutual, but they reacted fast enough with quick kill to get away unscathed. At least they didn't walk into anything set up for them, and they felt lucky. They were.

The first area recon was far north, and the third day out, Leghorn confirmed during the last check in, that the astronauts successfully landed. That evening, after setting out claymores, they tried telling the Yards about the flying machine that took men through space all the way to the moon. They got puzzled looks and smiles in return, indicating they expected some kind of punch line to the joke. When Garner convinced them they were serious, the Yards huddled, whispering to each other.

Suddenly, he guessed the moon was somehow sacred, and the disturbing information threatened to upset their sense of reality. The team smiled, nodding to the Americans condescendingly, and he knew they didn't believe it. Garner convinced Dodge to let it drop.

They also pulled a tour as Bright Light again, but this time things were lucky. Most Bright Light duty was quiet, with teams acting as guards for the launch site, or as extra hands helping resupply the company in the field. This time it was quiet. The company was back at Kontum preparing for insertion in another week, and there were only three teams in the bush.

Rains came every day, and they stayed indoors, playing cards or reading magazines and books they'd brought along. Of course Bright Light had a wish list of extra training they were supposed to conduct. The Army always liked a busy soldier, but the wet changed all that. The idea of doing anything unnecessary in the rain was repulsive.

Garner drained his fifth glass and sat looking around the club. It was filling up. Dinner was over, and troops were cleaning up and coming in. Tonight was a special night. It was the monthly Hail and Farewell, but also outside entertainment night. There was a Korean band and a stripper act setting up in the theatre. He caught Canada's eye and got another drink, while Dodge and Day approached the table. A stranger followed Day, and looked around in apprehension.

"And this is Garner, Jack," Day said. "Ted? This is Jack Randal. New One Two on Kentucky. Just came in."

"Hey, how's it going?" Garner stood up.

"Fine. Fine." The young man said, raising his hand to shake.

"Now, Jack, if you want a pair of leggings this is the guy you'll have to see about it. He's supplied just about the whole compound with these old World War II puttees. They're great for keeping out leeches, and they look neat. Everyone thinks we're Australians or something. Anyway, they keep the pants from being pulled out of the boots by "wait-a-minute" vines. The hooks on the vines can't get a hold of the material. What you selling them for now, Ted?"

"Five bucks a pair, Bill. That pays my folks back and pays for postage and leaves a little profit. Come see me tomorrow sometime if you want some, Randal."

"I sure will, Sergeant Garner. I can't wait to get in the field. I'm really looking forward to it. Thanks a lot."

All the others looked at him in embarrassed silence. Then Garner said. "We'll see how excited you are after your seventh or eighth mission. Don't talk it up too much. It's not good form."

Randal flushed, falling silent as he sat down with Day and Dodge.

"Well, Bill, how's it feel to finally attend your own Hail and Farewell party?" asked Danner.

"It's been a long time coming," said Day, "But now that it's here, I'm gonna get plenty drunk. Nine days and a wake up, then I muster out once I hit Fort Lewis and catch a plane to Colorado. I'll be sure to write you guys, letting you know about all the round-eyed women I'm getting on the ski slopes."

"You start school in September?" asked Garner.

"Yah, about four weeks off. I'll have just enough time to run into Saint Louis, kiss mom and fly out to get registered and set up for transfer orientation. Hot damn, civilian life at last. You ought to check it out when you leave the service, Ted. You said you didn't want to go back to the Midwest. Why not come out to Colorado? You said you were gonna muster out of Fort Lewis too."

"It's worth a thought, Bill. I left college 'cause I couldn't see where I was going. I hated the school I was at: small, uptight, smug, cliquish and cold. With the GI Bill, at least, I'll have some options. I don't know. It's worth a thought. Thanks."

Canada made rounds, and Day whispered a warning to Randal not to mess with her. It was getting loud, and people were ready for the entertainment to begin.

"I found out this afternoon why Croaker Herold didn't want to be medevacked after he blew a hole in his hand with that automatic," Day said. "His folks sent Donnally a letter, and I heard him reading it to the colonel before he flew out to Saigon this afternoon.

"That ridge runner knocked up his first cousin back in Virginia, and he was scared to go back. I guess he was diddling her for some time, but finally got nailed on his leave right before coming over here. His whole family is out for blood. Can you believe it?"

"That's disgusting," said Danner.

"That's probably illegal too," said Dodge. "Jeez, a first cousin? No wonder he was acting so strange this last month. He was drinking his head off. I heard he was doing stupid things in the field too. Well, what goes around, comes around. He should have kept it in his pants."

They talked about the latest SOG rumors. Down south at CCS, someone saw a tiger and tried shooting it. Another team had wild elephants roaming through the RON at night, and they hooted at the thought of dodging kettle drum feet, crushing packs and weapons and claymores into paste. Adams, who was gate guard that night, sat on a snake last time out with the company. They took a break and he crouched down and tipped, falling backwards against his pack. He started wiggling with movement underneath and went boiling to the side as understanding finally hit him. The cobra didn't bite him though. It was deep under leaves out of the rain, and just wanted to escape. People went dodging and dancing as it raced through the circle of men. Finally it was cut to pieces with machetes.

Charlie tried to overrun a camp down by An Loc. The next day they picked two dead camp barbers out of the wire. Americal Division found a Charlie mortar crew on a sweep. The mortar's base plate was driven down a foot, and only a stumpy tube was left. There were radiating lines of a massive explosion and enough pieces to account for six or seven bodies. Guesses shot around the camp on who dropped off that particular round of Italian Green.

Tables were full, and even Martin seemed to pick up as other lifers joined him. Short timers stayed together and mingled well with younger lifers, like Dodge and Samuels, but there was always a stretch when it came to older ones. There was the disparity of rank, two or three stripes normally, but many short timers cut the lead with fast promotions given with waivers of time in grade and time in service. There was the disparity of age, five to ten years normally. There were disparities of goals and experience, hopes and expectations. Short timers were never quite considered equal by older ones, but as the war dragged on they ran more and more teams, and others held their tongues because of it.

Finally, the entertainment began and they all filed out, taking seats in the theatre. The Korean band struck up a chord, going into a medley of recent tunes. They played for an hour while the lead singer mouthed English words with a heavy accent that the soldiers mimicked and laughed at.

Then came the girls, and things got serious. The singer backed away, standing guard with the group's manager. The girls came out in sequined gowns and started strutting as the band played background noise. They gyrated and swirled, and outer garments flared as they turned, showing lots of calf and thigh. Garments were removed and tossed aside one by one, as they preened and strolled. The band played to a heavy beat, and the crowd got edgy.

They stripped seductively, and soldiers mentally licked their lips while leaning forward in their chairs. The girls were good dancers, young, pretty, and small-boned. They maintained an easy sensuality and were gracefully athletic, as they worked the routines.

Garner wondered why Asian women could maintain slender figures with such apparent ease. Their thighs and buttocks were well muscled, with just the right amount of fat beneath. The word 'hips' did not do them justice. These girls had flanks. They were physical thoroughbreds, but such thoughts were chased away as it got down to the nitty gritty.

As they twirled a final time, the last wispy scarves fell off, leaving just G strings. They gyrated, and their small breasts danced and shivered, with nipples standing high and proud. The singer and manager looked apprehensive, as soldiers started scooting chairs closer to the stage. They scraped along the concrete floor, and the eerie sounds of grating wood rose above the vibrant band. The girls kept dancing, but Garner saw glints of fear in their eyes. They did their jobs too well, and now they were on a stage in the corner of a room with no way out, and sixty incredibly aroused men were creeping slowly toward them, barely in control.

The band rose to a crescendo, and the final act was consummated. They reached behind, undid snaps, pulling the G strings off. Two naked women twirled and pirouetted on stage. Wisps of pubic hair were playing peek-a-boo, as their bottoms undulated furiously. It was too much. The band hit a final chord and the girls ran off, but too late.

The first two rows were on them as musicians broke out, tripping over instruments, jumping in front as the manager and singer tried pushing the soldiers back. The girls were to the side, and one made it to the club doorway, running to the ladies' room. The second almost made it, but Sardo caught her with his arm and she sat down splat upon the stage. He rolled her as others grappled, and he tried burrowing in like a tick between her legs. She screamed. They couldn't get a grip on him. His hair was cut too short.

Finally, other Americans got embarrassed and pried him off, and she ran, screaming insults out the door. The band was mad and so were officers, even though they scooted forward with the others. People were screaming "Assault" and making threats. Sardo laughed drunkenly, calling them all names and saying even the sergeant major was making goo goo eyes. Then everyone hit the floor as an automatic weapon erupted nearby.

Everyone tried duck walking into the safety of the club. No one had weapons. Teams rotated wall security, taking turns sleeping on bunkers or guarding the road, but was this an attack? Was it a band member intent on revenge? Weapons were on the other side of the road in team rooms, and Garner cursed the camp's horrible design.

If Charlie sent a company down the road, taking the barricades and French armored cars, then they were all as good as dead. They went scrambling, crawling, squeezing behind the cinder block protection of the club. They were sitting there wondering what to do, when Adams came running in giving an all clear and apologizing.

He was sergeant of the guard, and many times at night there was local traffic on the road. Several families of Montagnards came along requesting permission to pass through to Kontum. He granted it, but took his weapon off safety and ordered Yards to monitor the passage. The families moved along in single file. When they passed through the northern barricades everyone breathed a sigh of relief. It was dark, and Adams didn't think as he pointed the weapon up and checked the safety. He let off seven rounds before getting his finger off the trigger. He'd never live it down, and others began laughing. Then they turned to strangle him for the fear he'd pumped into everyone.

The next day most actions were somewhat forgiven but certainly not forgotten. Sardo, even though he was not successful at what he tried, reached celebrity status, and the band manager swore no one would ever play there again.

It was a well-known rumor that Oriental men were appalled at the thought of oral sex. They tried explaining it to the Yards one time, but all they got were looks of shock and disbelief. When they were finally convinced such things happened, Djuit looked like he was going to be sick, and others spit upon the ground.

"Well, you've got to figure," Dodge said. "When the first SF teams came over here, medics had to teach the Yards hygiene and stuff. Crud, they had to teach the women to wipe themselves from front to rear so they wouldn't get vaginal infections from going to the john. Christ, what a world."

Later that week, Garner was downtown with Canada. Her apartment was the second floor of a small house on the north side of town, and her bedroom window looked out across the valley. He was always careful about going there. No jeep or truck would be available, so he hitched rides or paid a motorcycle cab, always getting out two blocks away, keeping a close watch, making sure he wasn't followed. Of course he kept his M-16 at all times.

It wouldn't do to have it well known she was sleeping with an American. Whores could be bought by the hour during the day, but at night, outside the compound he was totally exposed. It's not that the secret could be kept, but it should not be flaunted. The family downstairs knew about him and so did one across the street. He was sure they did not approve, but as long as they weren't Cong he was all right. Physical need and selfishness made him swallow hard and take the chance.

He'd brought food with him, and after dinner as they lay kissing, preparing to make love, he asked a question that long bothered him. He traced her spine with his tongue, and whispered from behind. "Canada? I've always wanted to ask you something. Where did you get your name? I don't even know what your real name is in Vietnamese. Where did, 'Canada' come from?"

She rolled to her back, checking features of his face one by one, like pieces of a puzzle she was putting together in her mind. He kissed her cheek and she caressed down between his legs.

"When I was a little baby my father died. I never knew him. My momma, she was a good woman. She did laundry for French when they live in Vietnam. One man she liked. One man was lover. I don't remember him much. He was big, strong face, brown hands. He used to throw me in the air and play catch. I think I was three, maybe four. His name was Jacques. My momma loved him. He would bring us food.

"When French lose the war with Viet Minh, Jacques said he must go home. He said he had family in a place called Canada, Quebec. He said he would leave the army and go there someday. He said he would send for us. He said I was pretty, like the country we would go to. I was his pretty little Canada, and he would send for us, and we would go to live with him there someday."

Her eyes welled up, and tears ran down her moonlit cheeks. He kissed the salt away and asked, "What happened?"

"My mother waited so long. She had one letter from him. He said there were problems to fix to be able to send for us. He said he would write again. My momma, she cried and said he would come. I buried my momma with that letter. She loved him very much, like I love you, Garnah."

His left hand was roving between her legs, stroking her inner thighs. It froze in place.

"No, Canada. Don't say that. I'm a soldier. That's all. Don't even think of it, understand?" His voice turned cold. "I'll never lie to get you into bed. I don't love you. I won't love you, Canada. There are too many things ahead of me. I can't get tied down. I won't get tied down. Do you understand? I won't!"

Tears were streaming now. "But, Garnah, I know you care for me. I want to be your woman. I want to be your full-time woman. I want to go to the United States with you. I want to have babies with you. I want to leave this place. Vietnam is poor. I read magazines you give me. I want to go with you. I want—"

He was fully alarmed now, sitting up. Dodge was right. He knew the score far better than Garner did, and he mentally kicked himself for not paying attention.

"Canada, listen to me. When I was a boy I was tempted to lie to girls to go to bed and have sex. It's a very strong temptation. Do you understand?"

"Yes, I understand." She whispered and sniffled.

"I couldn't lie though. I was scared and I wanted a woman so bad, but to lie about love is to use someone like a tool. It's wrong. Sometimes we all use people, but it's wrong." He cradled her head in his hand, stroking her hair with the other.

"I thought we could enjoy each other and let it go at that. If we both enjoy, then there's nothing bad that I can see, but I won't lie to you. I've changed a lot over here, but I won't lie for sex. I'd sooner go without." He came down on his elbow, whispering, "I'm sorry if you thought other things. I should have known. I should have listened. I'm sorry."

"No, Garnah, my problem." Her voice cracked. "I want to leave, but all soldiers are same everywhere. Americans, Vietnamese, French. They come and want to take all and leave nothing behind. My momma, she cried for years. Not for me, though. We take it and enjoy, okay? Like you say. We enjoy each other. Okay?"

She still had her hand down between his legs, but the abrupt turn made him flaccid. She giggled, sniffled again and began stroking as he let himself be carried away. While coming back to full arousal, he realized he never wanted a woman more.

She stroked and arched as he did the same with her. Breathing built to a chorus of groans as each worked the other. Then, when he couldn't stand it any more, he broke off and straddled her. She raised her hips, wrapping thighs around his upper chest, helping guide him in. He was full, and although she was small and never able to accept him without some pain, she started thrusting and straining to do just that.

He plunged, and she cried out. Then they built together, moving in rhythm, building like long-distance runners. They timed themselves, and he used his hands to help bring her to the climax that he himself was working toward. When it came freight-train fast, he rattled as though he'd been hit with an electrical charge. She also flushed with orgasm, and then melted beneath while spreading wider to accept him. Garner slumped, and felt her fingers trace muscles of his back as he relaxed, resting like a child on a mother's breast.

His fading thought was that for all the words, he was a hypocrite, and that he knew it, and that she knew it, and that the sins of wanton use and carnal selfishness were knocking on his door, which he had opened all too gladly. A tinge of shame washed in, and he drifted as she wrapped him in her arms, and he took no notice of her weight until morning.

RECON COMPANY
SOA (CCC) 5TH SFG (ABN) 1ST SF
APO San Francisco, Calif 96499

SUBJECT: Tips of the trade/Lessons Learned, Series #1

TO: All Recon Personnel

I. INTRODUCTION: Keep an open mind when you read these Tips of the Trade/Lessons Learned. You may strongly disagree with some of the statements, but what might not work for one team or individual, when used with his own tactics and plans, may very well work with another. The point is this, "Don't knock it if you haven't tried it." At a later date a Tips of the Trade/Lessons Learned Pamphlet will be published for your use and reference. In the meantime, retain these sheets, which will be numbered, in your reference folder. Remember, you make your own luck through hard work and training.

II. Tips of the Trade/Lessons Learned.

1. Tape the muzzle of your weapon to keep out water and dirt, but leave the lower portion of the slits open for ventilation.

2. Fold paper tape through the rings of grenades and tape to the body of the grenade. The paper tape will tear for fast use, wherein plastic or cloth tape will not. Also, it keeps the ring open for your finger and stops noise and prevents snagging.

3. During breaks throw nothing on the ground, not even cigarette ashes. Put trash in pockets, packs, or bury it immediately after use. Disperse ashes if you absolutely must smoke.

4. If you must cough, then cough in your hat or neckerchief to smother the noise.

5. Put a small pebble in your mouth to cut down on water consumption.

6. Carry a canister round in the M-79 while moving. It is best suited for close-in, immediate action.

7. Tie a string or lanyard to your silenced pistol so that you can drop it after firing and grab your M-16, without losing the pistol.

8. During the dry season do not urinate on rocks or leaves, but rather in a hole or small crevice. The wet spot may be seen plus the odor will carry further.

9. Keep your URC-10 radio secured to your harness or equipment during use. If lost with the beeper on, it will negate all distress signals on the frequency until the battery runs down.

10. Notify an aircraft before firing a pen-flare. They resemble a tracer. Therefore, never fire one directly at an aircraft. A jumpy door-gunner may give you a quick burst.

11. Replace the cartridge in the chamber of your weapon every morning. Condensation may cause a malfunction.

12. Camouflage smoke, CS, and WP grenades with black spray paint. The colors are far too bright.

13. Do not bend the pins on the M-33 grenades, flat. The rings are too hard to pull when needed.

14. Do not carry grenades on the upper portion of your harness. Reason, the enemy will shoot at them, trying to inflict several casualties with one shot.

15. Carry one extra pair of socks plus foot powder with you on Recon, especially during rainy season.

16. When deploying the team for RON, place the point man in a position opposite the most likely avenue of enemy approach, to lead the team out in case of emergency.

17. Each team member should memorize the trees and bushes around his RON position, prior to nightfall.

18. Do not bother retrieving your first expended magazine during contact because it will only slow you down when time is of the essence.

19. Use a reference object when taking photographs, such as a rifle, pistol, or a six-foot rule.

20. Do not fire weapons from helicopters during extractions, once clear of the LZ. Reason: A gun ship may be passing under you without your knowledge.

21. Oil the selector switch on your weapon daily and work the switch back and forth, especially during rainy season. This will prevent the common occurrence of a stuck switch.

22. Sew a long, thin pocket on the side of your rucksack to accommodate the long antenna. Even folded up it is too long for the rucksack and will stick out the top and snag on every vine and branch you pass under.

23. Ensure that all fuse lighters are waterproofed.

24. Carry emergency rations on your person, in fatigue pockets, or in pouches on your harness. You can drop your pack and run if need be. Recommend bouillon cubes due to compactness. One cube in one canteen of water will sustain you for a day.

25. In the RON, uncoil wires to the claymores as you go out to set up the mine. Do not place the blasting cap in the mine until the wire has been fully extended. Coiled wire could build a static charge and set off the blasting cap.

26. Stay alert at all times. You are never 100% safe until you're back home.

27. Only move as fast as the heaviest loaded man can move. Radioman.

28. Never break limbs or branches on trees, bushes or palms, or you will leave a clear trail for the enemy to follow. Push them out of the way.

29. Do not remove the spare PRC-25 battery from its plastic container prior to use or it may lose power.

30. Never do the obvious.

WILLIAM DONNALLY
1SG Recon Co.

23

In just two weeks, Day, Snake Martin, Murphy, Tim Hatton, Billy Jones and Jim Harmon left for the States. New men arrived, and handshakes and quick acknowledgements passed around. Garner saw everything was ephemeral, nothing permanent. Nothing offered support or comfort.

He knew soldiers of other wars, like World War II, trained together and were deployed together. Camaraderie of the buddy system made men commit themselves to unbelievable acts of heroism, saving lives of friends. He knew, however, Vietnam was emotionally a cheap war, no matter what the cost. It was a war comparable to painting by numbers. Men were passed around, expended like ammunition or explosives. There was little thought of loyalties to one another, or the tremendous cohesive power such relationships brought to success on the battlefield. It was after all a little war, and one that didn't merit full concentration of strategies normally accounting for victory. It was a war to be bought, not fought.

Garner considered the differences, realizing one-year rotations were a sad thing for the military man. No one wanted death, but seeing friends go home rather than staying for victory, made him understand the only true loyalty a soldier could give was toward himself and his survival, rather than saving close abiding friends in battle. The key mark was survival, and not the will to win.

He guessed it really didn't matter though. He held few illusions about the war, and after living in Vietnam for more than half a year he cared little about the country. The ARVN Army suffered over 100,000 desertions a year now, and he thought they should be shot for it. If they wouldn't fight for themselves, why should anyone else. He remembered a phrase from history class, stating, "People generally get the kind of government they deserve." He had little doubt how North Vietnam would handle desertions.

Like many voluntary short timers, he wasn't there for Mom and Pop and apple pie. He came for himself, volunteering to find the self he'd never be as a civilian. He considered others running to Canada, or Europe, or the National Guard, and wondered what they learned about themselves.

He thought he knew, but on reflection, he also understood his decisions were only right for him. To pass such beliefs and burdens on to others, simply wasn't fair; but hatred of cowards was temptingly close when he saw pictures of protestors burning the flag he fought under.

Soldiers were of course meant to be expendable. During World War I, hundreds of thousands were sent across the open fields of Verdun, into the teeth of machine-gun cross fire, without a second thought. Dodge was right when he said sixty-year-old men were easy hawks. Only young men died.

But young men died for one another, and not a larger goal or political theory. Two in a foxhole defended each other to the death, never really thinking of reasons for the fight. That's why haphazard one-year rotations bothered him so much. It showed the higher military didn't care. It was a fat man's war, a war to be bought like any other government program. Bundle up money and throw it at the problem, but don't do it with any sense of strategy, commitment or finesse. Buy it off and move along.

Special Forces was a lucky unit though. Tremendous bonds of the beret made up for shuffling numbers back and forth. Friendships built up fast, and a man across the way might be a stranger in name, but a brother by bond, and by experience and training.

Recon took it even further, distilling and crystallizing relationships, tying teams tight together. Every man depended on another, and distrust or doubts were not tolerated even for one mission. It was the nature of the business. There could be no second-guessing as to bravery and fidelity.

Each life depended on others, and a bedrock of faith was that if wounded, any man knew, Yard or American, that he would be taken care of and defended to the death. It simply had to be that way, or men could not trust each other to do the things they had to do. It was a marriage of commitment and action, a chalice of faith.

Garner knew no such bonding existed in the regular grunt lines. They were scattered individuals, many drafted, some lifers, some short-time volunteers. There was little glue holding them together in the crush, and he wondered how many men died unnecessarily because others didn't care enough to make a greater effort to save a new man's life. There was always bonding under fire, but for how many did it come too late? Wars were fought by men together, and the romantic but accurate phrase was "comrades in arms."

It was a sad and hurtful fact that leaders forgot the principles, or never even knew them.

They received operation orders for a linear recon way up north, and considering the mud down south, they took it as a lucky break. Five days before insertion, however, they had the visit from the VIP, and Garner later admitted it was a great example of the Peter Principle, where people rise in rank and stature on ability, only to finally stagnate at their lowest level of incompetence.

At morning roll they noticed broken clouds. The heaviest rains were behind them now, and they looked forward to clearer skies. Within a month it should be back to reasonably brief afternoon showers that were welcomed rather than cursed.

Donnally read off morning notes as usual. Then he said, "I want you to alter your training schedules today and be sure to be back here in formation at ten-hundred hours. We have some people flying in from Saigon this morning, and there will be a Command Muster.

"I want everyone back here with clean uniforms, full insignia and berets. Also, make sure your teams are clean and presentable. We will be setting up in two formations. All SCU will line up according to teams in the assembly area, and we will station ourselves to the side at a ninety-degree angle, creating a corner formation facing the flagpole.

"This does not, however, include Team Hawaii. I want Staff Sergeant Timmons, Sergeant Wilks and Sergeant Harper to meet with me after formation."

He went on with some house cleaning chores about specific duties and teams, then let them go to meet with their teams and get ready for the next formation.

Dodge, Garner and Reynolds headed toward the room on the south-east perimeter. After turning the corner they saw their hooch maid out next to the wire, hanging shirts on the concertina wire to dry in the sun. Dodge shook his head and had to laugh.

"You know you'd think they'd learn by now they're not supposed to do that." He trudged up across the bunker line and out through the killing zone to the busy little woman. She was wizened, cracked, with lines that traced her face like a road map. She shuffled along, flashing a vacant-hearted grin with brown stained teeth.

"Mamma san. No. No. You cannot put clothes here. You know that. We've told you before."

She looked confused, standing there complaining, "No *bic*? No *bic*?"

"Phil, she says she doesn't understand," said Reynolds.

"You bet your ass she understands. All these women know they're not supposed to be beyond the line of bunkers. They've been warned. We've got a few clothes lines around for them. I can't help it if some maids steal shirts every time the others turn their backs."

"All she wants to do is hang the stuff up where she can keep an eye on it. She does Kentucky and Pennsylvania's rooms too; she can see all this from there. Why not let her be, Phil?"

"Because, Jim, she could be out here just as easily cutting claymore wires while she's hanging clothes. How the hell do you think all these wires are cut all the time? Do you think a Charlie with an AK strapped over his shoulder comes in, walking around cutting? Huh? It's the maids, dummy. Do you want a hundred Charlies coming through the wires at you with the claymores cut?" Dodge grabbed the shirts, pulling them off the rolls of wire while yelling for her to get back on the other side of the bunkers. She was moving slow until he yelled he'd fire her if she didn't hurry. "You see her jump? You don't think she understands?"

They crossed the bunkers, and he tossed clothing on a bench, wagging a finger at her, giving one last warning. Then he turned and entered the team room to put on a cleaner uniform.

By ten o'clock everyone was back in formation. The Yards milled in an oblong block of men running north and south, facing west. The Americans were north, facing south, creating a corner of sorts. Both units faced the flagpole in the center of a ten-foot-wide cement platform. It had three steps and was tall enough for someone standing at the top to look out and address the troops.

They stood at parade rest, and were brought to attention by Donnally as a cluster of men strutted out the TOC's doorway. The Montagnard interpreter yelled to his men after Donnally started orders. Everyone was pretty motley looking, but lines were straight, and Garner figured that was enough.

Colonel Anders and Major Prosky, the executive officer, deferred to other men in the crowd. Then the colonel stepped up on the first level of the flagpole's platform and made an announcement.

"Gentlemen I have the privilege of introducing to you a man who is a major supporter of Special Forces in the United States government." The Montagnard interpreter on the side rattled off the introduction.

"He is a gentleman of steadfast faith, who understands the importance of the Special Forces mission. He has come here today to talk with you, meet with you, and learn from you. He has come to see front-line forces that conduct such vital missions for the war effort."

Garner muffled a smile at the turgid prose.

CHAPTER 23 • 189

"I would like to introduce to you United States Senator, Marshal Kilpatrick." At this, the colonel stepped aside and shook hands with one of the men in civilian clothes. As the Senator stepped out, Garner caught a glimpse of others behind. They were no doubt handlers of some sort, aides. Then far back, he recognized a face. It was Riggs, the bully from House Ten in Saigon.

The senator took the topmost step. "Gentlemen," he said expansively. "I came to Vietnam on a fact-finding tour and told my people I wanted to see the best Special Forces had to offer, and they brought me here today."

Garner decided God did not make such pretty teeth and that they must be capped.

The senator went on effusively, and Garner decided the man was probably pretty good on cocktail party circuits up on Capitol Hill. Hair was textured in a John Kennedy-type fluff up front, but sides were longer; so were the sideburns, in keeping with the times. His face was tanned, and he looked reasonably lean from many hours of workouts in the Senate gym, where blacks and Puerto Ricans were reduced to handing out towels to men of power.

Garner guessed the fact-finding mission also included stops in Japan and Thailand, and maybe Australia, with lots of duty-free shopping in between for the wife, who was probably back in Hawaii, waiting to join the great man at some safe, predetermined spot. He could imagine her making diplomatic parties by herself, possibly drinking too much and penning "Wish you were here" postcards, during her day at the beach.

The senator talked on, and Garner snapped back as the man spoke louder. It caught him off guard. There was little need to be so dynamic; the Senator already had a captive audience.

Garner listened to him drone on in the distance, and guessed the pretty man with every hair in place really knocked them over at the ladies' club, or PTA. He was good looking, probably on the make, and Garner bet women got downright slippery around the oily slink.

Then he noticed something strange, and started paying closer attention. Kilpatrick no longer addressed the Americans in part, but seemed to be talking just to the Yards. He talked of God, man and the universe, and the Yards stood there grinning like idiots. He was talking serious thoughts of war and victory, and the Yards just grinned.

Garner concentrated on the Yard interpreter rattling off behind the senator's words without a pause, confident, effusive and fluid, but something was up. It was only later that they got a better story from Dominique and others.

The senator might have supported Special Forces, but it was probably because of the image and elitism it represented. He was certainly not a kindred spirit.

A basic tenet was never talking down to people, or over their heads. Special Forces soldiers were primarily teachers, dealing with remote and primitive cultures. The senator was a snob who would no more squat in the dirt drinking rice wine than he would run down the halls of Congress naked.

Trouble started at the beginning. "You men are the bastions of democracy, the strong bulwarks of freedom!"

"You are all illegitimate sons who do not know your own fathers. You are the strong young bulls of freedom," the interpreter stated. The Yards glanced side to side, considering the confusing insult with frowns.

"I confide in my constituents every day, and I am proud to report to them that in this war there are men of such intrepidity and daring-do."

"This man has stomach problems, and he uses words I do not know, but he is an important man from the great United States. I will try to tell you what he says. Smile." They gave him smiles.

All at once they gave him smiles, all of them, big, white, gold capped, red and blue inlaid smiles. The senator was taken back. He'd said nothing funny. His clever lines were for rallies, and the times he wanted to be especially glib for a particular woman. These savages took the most rousing patriotic lines he had, and stood there grinning at him. He redoubled the attack.

"I tell you in all veracity that I contravene and condemn all those who say this war is futile."

"He, he likes the Montagnard peoples. All tribes are his friends. Smile."

"I tell you that the hegemony of North Vietnam will be stopped, and their rapacious grasp for power will be foiled."

"He hates North Vietnam. He, he likes the Montagnard peoples. Fuck Ho Chi Minh. He is dead. Fuck him. Smile."

Now the senator was caught. He'd said nothing about the newly dead leader of North Vietnam, but he caught the name as the interpreter tried keeping up. He eyed the dark man with black hair, and paused. The interpreter caught his slip, then twisted, smiling at the senator with a totally guileless expression. Garner and others muffled laughter, after catching the gist of what was happening. He considered the "Who, me?" look on the interpreter's face, and like other Americans, stared down at his boots.

"I am proud of you men, and consider myself lucky to be at the front lines with you, fighting the good fight." The flustered senator broke his remarks off at least five minutes early. He stepped down, shaking hands with the colonel. Then the entourage walked across the road to the club for refreshments. That is, everyone except Riggs. He climbed the platform, motioning to Donnally that he was taking over.

CHAPTER 23 • 191

"Men? My name is Riggs, Mister Riggs, and I need to speak with you about some policies in the field of intelligence gathering, that you men are not properly following. First of all when you are on a field exercise, you must use your cameras much more often and to better effect. By taking pictures of troop movements and enemy equipment you give us a clear—"

No one listened. The man was an imposter and a rear echelon clown, and no one listened. He gave himself away with terms he used. No one in the field in Vietnam called a mission a field exercise. That was stateside training garbage. He'd given himself away, and they slipped sidelong glances to each other, mouthing the words silently. He droned on for fifteen minutes, finally crossing the road and joining the others.

The senator had inspected Team Hawaii earlier, and Timmons, Wilks, and Harper, stood at parade rest by the TOC, with the rest of the team in their standard sterile field uniforms. Their loaded packs and weapons lay out in front of them. Timmons liked black, and had most of the uniforms dyed that color. The green headbands and camouflage, and especially the leggings, added to an image of the gnarly jungle fighter, and the senator was duly impressed. He talked with the colonel, downing three drinks before noon.

He was sorry he couldn't sit, and talk, and learn from the men, like he said initially. "I just wish I could." Schedules were tight, and he had a speech in Pleiku at fourteen hundred hours. They had to hurry, or he'd get in too late to make a PX run. After waving goodbye, he snapped Polaroids from the helicopter and went along his appointed rounds.

Word got around the senator thought these men ran Recon in the local area. He didn't know it was Riggs's job to keep him away from classified information about missions across the fence. Riggs briefed the colonel and others, and it got out that the man was a suspected security risk. He evidently liked to talk at cocktail parties, and it seemed there were several violations of information, untraceable to anyone else but him.

That night in the club, they were drinking to the bastions of democracy and toasting the bulwarks of freedom, while they laughed and hooted at the unfolding story. Dodge made observations about the rear echelon troops, saying, "Now you know why the words 'rear' and 'ass' are synonymous."

Then they turned and saw Riggs, the colonel and the XO coming in, taking a table by the bar. "The creep's job must have been to babysit the senator only while he was here. There's not much top secret at the B-Team in Pleiku," said Dodge.

"Probably keeping him over at the guest hooch and flying him out to Saigon in the morning," said Garner. "I wish Day was still here. He could tell us if a Blackbird is coming in with supplies."

They eyed the cluster from back in the corner by the latrines. The ferret talked with the officers, flashing a thin smile, showing plenty of teeth, but everyone at their table seemed tense. Officers had their own small club where they mingled and played cards. Younger ones felt comfortable mixing with the troops, but there was always that reserved strain, acknowledging the presence of a field grade in the main club. There was no masturbating Mo Jo when the colonel was around.

They sat with Danner and Adams, catching up on the latest rumors. Things were quiet and reserved. Then half an hour later, Riggs passed by on the way to the latrine, and the conversation turned toward him again.

When he reemerged, Dodge was wondering out loud "if that nurse packed the slimy bastard in the nuts for blackmailing Kidwell."

Riggs stopped short, catching the name from ten feet away. He swiveled, glaring at the faces in the dim light. Then it registered, and he came strutting, flashing teeth.

"You guys? I forgot about you guys. You too, bud," he said, staring at Dodge as he shifted around in his seat.

"That's not like me to forget someone I owe."

"What? Like you owe Kidwell for sliming around after his cousin?" Dodge asked.

"Watch your mouth, punk, or I'll have your ass for breakfast. I've got people who can fuck you up real bad. I've got people—"

Dodge was sliding the chair back, smiling. This was his home, his club, and he feared no outsider. He took two quick steps, pinning the thin man to the wall, leering drunkenly into his face. "You gutless little rear echelon shit heel. I ought to take off your head. You talk about missions and tell us how to do the job, and then come in and threaten, and try to blackmail us for your horny little prick?" He jammed the man against the wall, lifting him further. Garner saw Riggs's eyes go wide.

"Field exercise? Field exercise? Who the hell do you think you're kidding, jerk off. You've never set foot in the field, and you're bullying us? You're telling us how to do the job?" The man was dangling as if on a hook. Muscles rippled along Dodge's shoulders as he pulled back, throwing the man into the red bricks with a thump. Riggs started screaming, and Garner shouted a warning as the officers' table unraveled.

"Dodge! Sergeant Dodge!" the colonel bellowed. "Take your hands off that man. Do it now!"

Dodge gave him one more thump and dropped him, then stood at attention as the colonel chewed him out, ordering him out of the club.

Garner said, "Sir. Begging your pardon, Sir, but this man has been asking for a clubbing. He's used his power and connections to blackmail members of Special Forces to do personal favors for him. He was just threatening Dodge, and the sergeant overreacted."

"Quiet, Sergeant Garner. I don't want to hear it," the colonel said, then twisted toward Riggs as the man stretched his neck, complaining.

"I want that man up on charges, Colonel Anders. He attacked me, and I want his stripes. Damn it. I don't need to come out to shit holes like this and get assaulted by the garbage you people keep on the rosters—"

"Shut up, Mister Riggs. You are not in Saigon now," the colonel said. Riggs looked like he'd been slapped. "I only wish you were under my command so I could take care of you properly." Riggs opened and closed his mouth, then stood shaking with anger. "So now, are you going to threaten me, Mister Riggs? Are you going to try and stir a little sand in my career? Huh? Well let me tell you something. I've heard of your abuses and I won't tolerate them here. You come here and you mind your Ps and Qs. No, Mister Riggs, you can't hurt me. I'm too late in my career to be scared about promotions.

"Besides, I think perhaps you should be concerned about me! Isn't it one of your phrases not to screw around with people you don't know? Well, I know Sinclair, and I know Cap. Wilcox and Joe Waters. We sat together in foxholes at Tarawa. I suggest you go to your quarters for the night and be ready to leave when the driver comes to take you to the airport in the morning. You are dismissed, Sir."

Then the colonel dressed down the whole room for any acts of violence, real or considered. He closed the club for the night, and left.

Two days later, Sunday, they went back to the Yard village to do some fishing and drinking. Reynolds left for Pleiku promotion boards, and the rest of the team jumped in the truck, heading in the opposite direction. They bumped and jammed through Kontum traffic, and finally Dodge pulled over a quarter mile past the vegetable stand where they bought the first pig. He squinted in the glare of the morning sun working through the clouds, and sat appreciating the day. Then he looked out across eastern fields, considering a pack of dogs going systematically through a smoldering refuse pile.

"You see that, Ted?" he said, pointing at the dogs. "Survivors out there. They don't live by the hand of man anymore. They're feral, loners, joining together for the kill, or at least tolerating each other on the separate hunt.

"Good analogy for the whole war don't you think? Totally screwed-up country. Fighting for people who'd let you bleed to death on the street. They steal your money. They desert their army and want you to fight their war, and hate you for it at the same time. It's a feral country, Ted. Guys like Riggs fit right in. They hunt in the confusion and smoke of the burn, just like those dogs."

They watched the scabby-looking animals wander through smoldering debris, flushing rats, scenting rotting garbage.

"Country's not worth it, Ted, that is except for the Yards. They're worth a lot. You know, Dominique's chief called me to the Long House one time to drink, and he gave me a seat of honor, a beat-up nylon webbed aluminum folding chair. I wanted to sit on the floor with the others, but no. I was an honored guest, and got that pathetic chair." Dodge was talking to the steering wheel now, and the Yards in the back mumbled among themselves, smoking, rolling dice and laughing.

"The old man talked about different things. Asking me about the war, my folks, my family, my wife and, things. He asked about me as a person. Then he asked the sorriest question ever." Dodge looked across, and Garner watched his eyes turn moist.

"He asked if the Americans would ever leave Vietnam. He asked if the Americans would leave the Montagnards. He didn't know the term and Dominique couldn't translate it right, but I knew the old man meant to say 'abandon' the Montagnards. They gave me this." The friendship bracelet of polished brass shimmered, and filed markings of different abstract designs flowed around the ring.

"I almost lied, because I couldn't stand the truth myself, but I did right by that old man. I told him someday we'd all have to leave. That our country was fighting at home because of the war, and soon more of the fighting would be handled by the Vietnamese. You know he started crying? Not big tears, but his chin trembled and his eyes watered. He said through Dominique, 'Then we will be swallowed whole again.'"

"The Yards know what will happen when we leave, Ted. They know they're defenseless, and the gooks hate them. I told that old man the truth. I think it's the bravest thing I've ever done. I broke that old man's heart, 'cause he saw the future with the answer. Dominique!" he yelled.

Boxes scattered in the back of the truck, and the boy leaned into the cab. Dodge rattled off a phrase, and Dominique laughed and answered, "Yes." Then he turned, giving directions to the others, and Garner jumped as he heard bolts flying forward, loading the weapons. The still of the morning shattered with a hundred rounds fired just behind his head. He ducked as the firing stopped and the shouts began.

The truck rocked as the team jumped off the back and sides. Then they were in deep grass and mud, running to the five dogs they'd killed. Sporadic fire erupted as they found two others wounded. They were carried back and pitched in the truck. Fleas and ticks swarmed their thinly haired bellies. The rest of the ride was conducted in silence.

Garner gripped the meat with his teeth, and cut a piece away. It was tough as a jungle boot and just as tasty. No fat softened the stringy bundles of fiber. It was fully cooked too. Even the Yards knew different parasites lived in the dogs, and had to be destroyed before consumption.

The fish was better, carp of some sort, bony, but chewable. He cut another piece, realizing he was used to eating things that trappers might think twice about using as bait back home. Rice wine blurred it all.

They sat on the wooden floor of the Long House, eating and drinking, considering the pretty girls with pendulous breasts and large nipples, who served them. These women were much more endowed than Oriental girls, and their breasts shimmered as they went about their duties. They shuffled along, smiling with shyness and modesty, and found it difficult looking Americans in the eye.

Conversations were in Bahnar, and Garner kept a low profile, wanting to fit in. Finally, Dodge stood up and huddled with the Yards. He broke away and walked over. "If you're done, Ted, I've got something to show you."

He stood and followed. The Yards' eyes were wide, and smiles were forced. They walked to the truck, and Dodge climbed in the back, pulling a poncho cover off of three laundry bags. He dragged one forward, dumping it. Three bandoleers of ammunition and five grenades tumbled out on the metal floor. He watched Garner's face, and scooped it all back in the bag and passed it down to Dominique. Then he dragged the other two bags out, and also passed them down. "Come on," he said.

They walked back through the village, where women cleaned up after the meal. Dodge ducked and led them under the Long House, between log coffins stacked for future use and a jumbled wall of kindling. They stopped, back where the corner was dark and secluded. Dominique pulled back three layers of reed mats covered with a thin dirt layer, and Dodge reached down, grasping a knotted rope attached to a plank door set flush in the ground.

He pulled, and red dust sifted down like microscopic snowflakes into a black hole. More fell to the sides, and when it cleared, Garner saw steps cut into the clay. Each step was covered by a fitted plank. His scalp tingled, as if a thousand ticks were crawling through his hair. For the first time he was afraid of his own team, and the unexpected nature of that fear hit him harder than any experience he'd had in the field.

Dodge's eyes gleamed with the inner fires of a religious zealot, where all means are justified by whatever ends are deemed worthy. Garner questioned for his life. He puckered up to nine, as Dodge produced an OD flashlight and started descending the stairs, motioning him to follow. He did, and the Yards crowded behind with a lighted propane lantern.

The tunnel led down, and then straight back into the hill. The clay sides were hard, and cupped with the rippled marks of the entrenching tools that carved them long ago. Wooden beams and log supports held up a heavy plank ceiling, reminding him of Old West mining movies. Alcoves branched off, and he looked within as Dodge passed the beam of light. Each was filled, floor to ceiling, with boxes and weapons, some American, some Soviet. Spider webs clustered in the corners.

They passed five sets of alcoves, and the excavation ran out of clay, hitting bedrock. It didn't stop; it climbed. They passed two more alcoves, hitting bedrock again. It stopped, making a T intersection, and Garner guessed it ran along the sides of the mountain up above. They turned left.

Every fifteen feet, bamboo tubes the size of his calf came down through the roof by the sidewall. Water puddled the clay beneath each one. He sniffed fresh air. The hollow airshafts would never be noticed from above, as they blended with the surrounding stands. They passed two more alcoves crammed with damp proof ammunition cans, finally entering a larger room with ridgepoles down the middle. The smell of the lantern mixed with that of the damp earth. They stopped.

"What do you think, Ted?" Dodge said hopefully.

"Phil? I don't know what to say. I don't know what you want from me. What?" The sounds of breathing filled the room.

"I want your help, Ted. They want your help. We're stockpiling this for the time all the round-eyes leave. It's important. I'm finally going home in two months, and I want to see the work continues." His voice reverberated through the surrounding black.

"Phil, for God's sake, get a grip on yourself. Stealing this shit will get you Leavenworth if you're found out. Don't you know that?" He shut up. He was in no position to argue rights or wrongs, surrounded like he was ten feet underground.

"You don't get it do you, Ted? These people are the only ones worth fighting for in this whole damned country. FULRO isn't Communist. Oh it's got Commies in it, and even some of them high placed, but most are just Yards trying to assert their lives and make their own decisions."

"Phil, this is wrong." He turned.

"Dominique, don't you know you're just setting yourselves up to be slaughtered later on? Don't you know that when we leave, you'll never be able to gain independence? You're setting up families and villages to be killed in a futile gesture!

"You don't have tanks! You don't have helicopters! You don't have money to buy supplies with or a port to receive them through. You don't have a military infrastructure or any kind of coordinated government. Hell, the tribes don't even speak the same languages. Back before the Vietnamese bothered with the mountain regions you fought among yourselves!" He was getting mad at the coming waste.

"Phil, I'm surprised at you. Where's your head? You know damned well there's no chance they could win. All they'll do is set back any negotiated settlement with the government by thirty years and get a quarter of the Yards killed doing it. Damn, what a pity.

"Dominique, I'm your friend, and if Phil says you're not Communists then I believe him, but this is all the wrong way. I won't help you kill yourselves. I won't help you kill your families. You can't win like this. Do you understand?"

The boy studied Garner's face, and nodded solemnly. "Garnah, we know not too good chances to beat Vietnamese, but with help of Americans we—"

"No, get that out of your head. Individuals would like to help you fight, like Sergeant Dodge. Others would like to help like Larsen and myself, but help in other ways. Americans want to help the Montagnards, but our government will never come to help you in a fight. Never! You cannot win this way."

"Garnah," he said. "Maybe not, but we will try."

He felt totally alone, a voice of reason crying in the void. He wasn't afraid now, but a sorrow pressed down like the weight of the earth on the planking overhead. He whispered, and it echoed through the black tunnels.

"I'll try to help the village as best I can, but not this way. I won't betray you, Phil." The other man was steely quiet. "I'd never do that. I wish you could win. I really do, but you won't. Not this way. I'll help in all others, but not this way. I want to leave this place."

THINK

RECON COMPANY
SOA (CCC) 5TH SFG (ABN) 1ST SF
APO San Francisco, Calif 96499

SUBJECT: Policy & Information

TO: All Recon Personnel

SECURE YOUR VALUABLES BEFORE DEPLOYMENT

1. All 10s check your SCU personnel and find out who has successfully completed these schools: 01, Commo and Medic. Also, who has a certificate for successfully completing an Airborne Jump School. When you get this information let me know, and I will record it on the new manning board. This will save us all time and effort in the future.

IF YOU EXPECT RESPECT THEN SHOW RESPECT

2. Word from Saigon: All C and C personnel visiting Saigon must be in a complete military uniform to include berets. No other headgear authorized. Also, no weapons will be accepted for lock up at House Ten, if you stop there on the way to R&R. All weapons must stay in the compound.

HOW MANY WARNINGS DOES IT TAKE?

3. Today RT Arizona reported 7 of 8 claymore wires had been cut inside the wire. Have you checked yours 10?

DID YOU CHECK? HOW LONG AGO?

4. New promotions are being listed on the Recon Bulletin Board tomorrow morning. Take a look. Good news.

DID YOU SEEK OUT INFORMATION, OR WAIT FOR IT TO COME TO YOU!

5. (S-2) CAM RANH BAY - Explosive devices were placed in four wards of the hospital. (2 KIA, 54 WIA) Other explosive devices were discovered hidden in a latrine, 60 lbs of plastic explosive were found in a parked car, 10 lbs of plastic explosive were found in the gas tank of a motorcycle. Yesterday, a USAF Language School in Saigon was the target (12 KIA 62 WIA). It can happen here, lad.

ARE YOU ON THE WINNING TEAM?

6. (S-1) Personnel with an October DEROS can expect a 10 to 12-day drop.

WHAT DO YOU ACCOMPLISH IN YOUR SPARE TIME?

7. SSG Buker, SGT Stamp and SCU Trang, Tho and Wheam were KIA on Company operation today. Date and time of memorial service to be announced.

DID YOU NOTIFY THOSE WHO WERE ABSENT?

8. SSG Goldstein reported in. New 12 on New Hampshire.
   SGT Wilkens reported in. New 12 on Wyoming.
   SGT Hampton reported in. A Company.
   SGT Russell reported in. A Company.
   SP4 Montgomery reported in. A Company.

Make these new men welcome. Introduce yourselves. Don't wait for others to do so. This is a team effort. I expect team work!

PERSONAL PRIDE!

WILLIAM DONNALLY
1SG Recon Co.

25

The next three days were brittle in reevaluated silence. Dodge and Garner worked through drills, and Reynolds asked what happened, but neither offered an answer. Although each had saved the other's life, they groped for common ground and a new foundation of trust. There was a wounded sense of betrayal and unexamined assumptions, but each in turn understood relationships must change, not necessarily grow, but change.

They were fifteen klicks north of the Golf Course, just inside the border this time. The Annamite Mountains ran north and south, with hundreds of trails winding between the pressure ridges. From the air some border stretches were easily defined along the highest ridges, casting the longest shadows in the late day sun. Farther north, the terrain became jumbled, and even the maps admitted that the border was "indefinite."

Routes went hot and cold, and this time their mission was a linear recon. They were to insert at Tango-Six and head north, crossing trails and roads, and reporting on use and condition.

An old bomb crater was the jump-off point. Year-old bamboo shoots sprouted everywhere, and Huey blades snapped them into sticky splinters, slashing them down foot by foot. Twenty minutes later they were totally alone.

The ridgeline stayed on their right, and for two days they meandered north, crossing seven small trails and two roads, only one of which looked used within the last few weeks. At noon the third day, another ridge came in from the west, and they had to climb. Then it was down into a broader east–west valley that broke the mountain's spine as it wandered into Vietnam. They were coming down into the valley when they heard the sounds of trucks below.

Twenty minutes later, they sat seven meters off the road, counting vehicles and troops. The only reason they were able to get so close, was because of the engine noise masking the sounds of their approach. Under any other circumstance, it would have been impossible. The brush was just too thick.

Garner clearly saw the soldiers' legs through the thin stems of underbrush, but three feet up the branches and leaves exploded in an impenetrable jumble. He rested against his pack, facing the road, watching guards walk back and forth. He was proud to be this close, and felt like a voyeur. Then it happened.

One guard passing to the right suddenly stopped. He hesitated for a full five seconds, and then turned back. Was it a glint of metal? It couldn't have been sound. Was it smell? Americans smelled different. He sifted possibilities as the guard shifted back and forth in front of their position. Then the man knelt down, peering into the underbrush, looking right at Garner.

All of them had on heavy camo, and Garner squinted, hiding the whites of his eyes. The silhouetted face seemed to balloon as Garner stared, not daring to even blink. His weapon was cradled between his cocked knees, pointing right at the guard, but he couldn't shoot unless he knew for sure they'd been discovered. Fifty NVA would be on them in half a minute. He began shaking, but knew he had to wait and see how the man reacted. If he started pulling the AK-47 around, Garner would put half a dozen rounds in him. The standoff lasted perhaps ten seconds. Then it ended. The guard stood, backed up two steps, turned east and walked away.

"He looked right at me!" Garner whispered to Dodge.

All he got back was a nod, and a mouthed response, "He likes you."

Dodge took it light, but Garner demanded leaving, and signaled, "Grenades." If the guard backed away to save his life, it was doubtful he could keep the guilty secret long. They moved under cover of the trucks' engines, and within five minutes heard yells and shots behind.

They started to run, and tracked straight west for half an hour, parallel to the road, finally finding thinner brush as twilight turned to dark. Trucks were now few, with headlights taped down, showing only horizontal slits of light. The team crouched, looking for troops, and after fifteen minutes, crossed the dusty track, once again heading north.

By early afternoon the next day, they were several klicks away, and heard planes strafing the area behind, trying to flush a response from the now hidden convoy. Headquarters knew from prior missions about how long trucks ran at night before bedding down. They tried judging positions from coordinates the team gave.

The main ridge was again to the right, and late that day they climbed to a stony outcrop. It was a solitary finger of rock, pointing west into the valley. The view stretched two miles to the opposite ridge. They stood on the precipice taking it all in, reveling in the wind. Senses tingled, and they grinned for no reason other than the joy of living. Then Garner waved them back and down.

He'd been studying the valley with binoculars, and picked up motion on the far wall. He pressed the glasses against a stone base he was hiding behind, stabilizing his view. Then he felt his scalp begin to crawl.

The opposite ridge had a long horizontal slash of brown. It was a cliff face, ninety feet high and half a mile long. Toward the middle were several black holes, caves, and there was movement along one of the trails leading up to them. A line of men was climbing, two in front, half a dozen in the middle, and three behind. Nothing more registered, until one in the middle stumbled and fell. Others helped him. Then the trailing three came up from behind, and he saw the rise and fall of a whipping stick, and he knew.

"Oh, my God, Phil, there are POWs down there. Look."

Jaws dropped, and Dominique interpreted. Dodge took the glasses, pressed against the rock, and studied the line for clues. Two last blows fell, and the ragged group moved on. None were armed, except the ones in front and those who came behind. Dodge twitched violently, whispering, "Those bastards." The line staggered up the slope, then split in two and disappeared into the caves on the ledge.

The team moved back to sit and call it in. They couldn't be seen from any vantage point on their side of the valley, but those across in the caves could spot their movements. They sprawled across rocks, watching for the rest of the day, as others in Saigon considered the information they radioed in.

By late afternoon they confirmed at least forty guards were on the western ridge, and were resigned when they were told to leave the area.

Captured men would die in any rescue, and even if a large force could get in undetected, and assault the position, any prisoners left unfound would be murdered in revenge. Solutions were political, not military, and they were ordered out of the area.

The guilt of leaving Americans to such an uncertain fate bubbled over like a festering wound that night in the RON. They lay awake, under a cloudless sky bright enough to read by. Dime-sized lichens, glowing with a green fluorescence, peppered the surrounding jungle, looking like the glaring eyes of those they left behind across the fence. Lizards chided them with alternating accusations. "Fuck you, fuck you, fuck you."

"Who do you think they are?" whispered Reynolds.

"Pilots probably," said Dodge.

"Some could be CCS people," ventured Garner. "They lost some MIA this summer. What about those two whole CCN teams that disappeared?"

Dodge lay cocooned inside a slate-colored ground cloth webbed with black shadows and moonlight. He rolled constantly, and the webs ballooned and distorted along his length, the only clue betraying his presence.

He whispered, "Jesus, I feel gutless. I want to beat the faces of those bastards down in Saigon. We ought to go in and get them. I know one team's too small. We ought to load up the whole damned compound at CCC, and come back and get them all."

"I know, Phil," said Garner. "I feel that way too, but I also know to some extent they're right. Remember what you said when I first got in country, about jogging in formation down the road at camp? You said two or three snipers could take out the whole column. Guards would cut those poor guys down with a first hint of trouble. A firefight at the cliff base would be the end of all of them. I just can't imagine not getting them all killed if we tried it."

"If you were over there across the valley, what would you want?"

Garner paused. "I'd want them to try and rescue me."

"Same here. You've got to promise something, Ted."

"What?"

"Promise you'd never leave me in a way they could shut me in like that. Promise you'll do right by me if the time ever comes. Promise."

"You know I'd never leave you behind, Phil. None of us would."

"Hell no," whispered Reynolds, "we'd never do that. Never."

"No. It's not the leaving that's scary. We left McDaniels in the fight. He was dead three times over, and I wedged an M-33 grenade underneath him to get the first couple that tried searching him. Mac would have liked that. It kept them from parading his body and mutilating it. They skinned some guys down south you know. It's not the leaving. Just make sure I'm dead, that's all."

"What?"

"Just make sure I'm dead and set me up like I did Mac. I've got a special one on my web gear tabbed to do the job, but I've always been scared I might be unconscious or wounded somehow, so I couldn't pull the pin. You guys promise you'll do that for me, okay?"

"You're talking morbid bullshit, Dodge," said Reynolds. "Go to sleep, you're talking weird."

"No I'm not. Lots of guys earmark a special grenade. Just promise you wouldn't let them skin me out like some rabbit, or shove me in a hole like those guys across the valley. Promise, okay?"

"I promise," Reynolds said with haphazard easiness of sleep. "Now go to bed."

"Ted?"

"I promise, Phil." Dodge was sitting up now, looking at him in the twisting black and blue shadows. Garner said, "I haven't thought much about it before. I guess everyone thinks they'll live forever when they're our age, even over here. I once heard old age is when you count years you've got left instead of years you've had."

"I don't think about being captured. It's too scary. I've heard about the skinnings, and GIs with their dicks cut off and stuck in their mouths, but I haven't got a special grenade as a last resort. Not yet, anyway." He stared at the black silhouette ten feet away. "I guess I should. Phil?"

"Yah?" It came back at him like a croak.

"We split on some things, I know, but I won't let you down. I promise for you, if you'll promise for me. We won't let them get us. Okay?"

"Okay, partner. Okay."

Garner rolled to cover up, and never heard the sitting figure lay back down in the quilted quiet of the night.

Two hours after sunrise they were moving north again, burdened by the knowledge of the prisoners left behind. They moved along the ridge, through "wait-a-minute" vines and brush. Then they hit a quarter-mile-wide stand of bamboo, with the largest plants of their kind Garner had ever seen. They followed animal paths, and marveled at trunks as thick as a man's thigh. The tree-sized stems crossed and rubbed against each other eighty or ninety feet up, and winds gave voice to the stand. It was a creaking, screeching voice that jabbered warnings. Garner stopped Dominique when he saw fear in the other's eyes.

"Dominique. What's wrong? Why is everyone acting so strange?"

"The Donoi, Garnah. Donoi. It calls to us. Spirits of bamboo hate all men. We must leave this place, Garnah. Men cut bamboo. The Spirit, Donoi, hates man. This is old. Very old. Full of hate. Strong hate, Garnah."

The brown man looked over his head fearfully, and others hunkered down as Garner passed Dodge the word to move out of the grove as fast as possible. They crept under the creaking voices for another twenty minutes, and the Yards finally relaxed, only when they broke back into hardwood jungle of the higher mountains. Then they took a noon break, slumping in the sweltering heat. Clouds swept in, and they unwrapped ponchos while digging for a meal.

Dodge sat with his back against a tree, after talking to Dominique. He cradled his weapon and worked the can opener with faint tin snip sounds.

"Ted. The Yards are a pretty superstitious lot. Don't let it get to you. Their religion's animistic, and spirits are in every living thing. Dominique says bamboo stands are cut down, but grow back fast with the strength of the spirit. It hates the cutting, but the Yards use it to make almost everything they've got: buildings, drain pipes, shingles, baskets, smoking pipes, cups and even cow bells. They're caught, and the spirit stays mad. That stand we moved through is super old for bamboo, and the wind voices said the powerful old spook would do something terrible if we stayed around. They fear spirits a whole hell of a lot more than Charlie, let me tell you."

Rain pattered down through the canopies, growing to a roar as everyone flung ponchos, spreading them like lily pads, covering folded knees and packs behind. They sat, dozing for fifty minutes, listening to the rain. It didn't stop, and Dodge called in the sit-rep, saying he'd wait it out.

"Hey, Phil?"

"Yah?"

"You know those poor bastards. Those prisoners. I've been thinking about them."

"Me too."

"Well, you know, I wonder if it's fate or just plain, bad, dumb luck that put them there. Wrong place, wrong time. Like back home, you drive fifteen thousand miles in a year without any hassle, and then someone comes out of a side street and kills you. Bam! Five seconds either side of it, early or late, and you would have missed it, but instead you're dead. Why does it work that way? How many times did you miss the accident by being five seconds early or late, and never knew it?

"Those guys could just as easily be sitting here, or making love to wives in the middle of the night back stateside. Why? Is it destined to happen like that? Was it all mapped out, or could it have been different?"

"Hell, I can't believe anything's destined, Ted. There are odds you can bet on. That's why I gamble and make money at it, but nothing's got a lock. I remember a kid in school who knew from the seventh grade he wanted to be a doctor, a surgeon, and last I heard he was practicing in Denver. He was lucky, I guess, that he knew right from the start what direction he was taking. Hell, people say you follow paths through life. Maybe he did, but there aren't any for most of the rest of us.

"I've always thought of life like a huge, flat prairie, with no markings anywhere on the horizon, and no paths to follow. But you see, it's strewn with little pebbles, the things folks call 'life decisions.' You drift along in a reasonably straight line, until you step on one of those pebbles and turn your heel. It spins you off in a little bit different direction. Then you stay on that course until something else happens, and you twist on another one that changes it a little more.

"Two people going the same way, take different strides and end up spinning from one decision to another, from stone to stone, until they're so far apart it's impossible to think they started out together. It's like those guys down there in the valley. There's no grand plan putting them there. They just spun along, changing directions with each decision they had to make, and they ended up where they're at, just like we did. Just like we are.

"You can't worry about those kinds of things, Ted. Just make sure to keep your balance when you stumble on those decisions. You might not be able to direct the course you take, be it good or bad, but at least you can try to keep from falling."

An hour later, the rains filtered down to a drizzle. The jungle rustled as the drips pattered from canopy to canopy, and when it finally slowed, they packed up and headed out.

Two trails were crossed, well worn and slick, and they covered tracks by stirring sticks and brush in the mud. Jungle boots had easily recognized patterns on the sole. They continued north for an hour, and then took a late afternoon break.

Garner settled back, watching lumps of water gathering on leaf tips, hanging suspended until reaching some critical mass not to be denied. Each broke free, snapping into a pearl that splashed the mulch below. The air tingled, and a freshness filled the jungle. He thought he caught a whiff of ozone, but hadn't heard the thunder. He rolled to the right, quick and heavy, down the hill.

Whooosh KLAAMMMM! The rocket-propelled grenade came in off the back trail just as he recognized the movement for what it was. It passed a foot above where he'd been sitting and hit the tree, exploding in an eardrum-bursting roar. The shaped charge punched all the way through, making the tree lurch, as pulp absorbed the explosion. Wooden slivers pierced packs and flesh alike. Garner blew backwards, and his hands, which were covering his eyes, lit with fiery needles. Then it expanded, marching up his left arm and shoulder to reside in a pulsing purity of pain in his side.

Whooosh KLAAMMMM! Another rocket, maybe two, came in. Small arms rattled, and he came out of shock with Djuit shaking his fiery shoulder. "Garnah! Garnah! Come! Come! We go!"

He looked around. Members of the team were scurrying everywhere. He spotted Whean heading north, as Reynolds, Kehn and Kui fired into the jungle along their back trail. The M-79 sounded "Punk," and its sharp explosion cracked somewhere south. Movement came towards him, and he rolled as adrenalin dissolved the pain, like salt in a boiling cup of water. He was on the west, downhill side, and spotted encirclement twenty meters out. He locked against a tree, bringing three down in rapid fire. Others stopped and rolled, tumbling in the mulch, working lower downhill, trying to get around the side.

Dodge's whistle broke through the fire, and Garner turned at the signal to retreat while pulling two M-33 baseball grenades from his harness. He pitched them down the hill, and after they went off, ineffective rifle fire answered back as the flanking movement slowed.

Then it was up and out, and north, with covering fire as the team coagulated, running in line. He took mental notes, counting heads as he ran. Djuit showed red along the butt, but had no limp. Garner felt blood run down his shoulder, but couldn't find the wound. Pain was down and biding time, like a mugger waiting in the shadows with an ice pick.

He ran, tripping on Djuit, who was stumbling just ahead. Both of them went down, with Kui and Kehn piling in. They struggled up, and then went down again as heavy rifle fire came from behind. All of them rolled to the sides and started shooting from behind the nearest trees.

Again, figures moved, and he fired three-round bursts. The NVA were single minded, and he begrudged their tenacity for killing. "Let us run! Let us run, you bastards!" He screamed at the top of his lungs. His adrenaline pump was overflowing, and he locked his sights on them and fired as the rest of the team wheeled behind, firing over his head from cover. Then Dodge blew on the whistle again, and they all moved out. Garner turned, ran three steps, and stumbled into Dodge, who went down as he was hit with three bullets. Garner's eyes widened as blood bubbles frothed from Dodge's nose and mouth.

"Dominique! Djuit! Kehn! Phe! Carry Phil! Jim, get Covey and an LZ. Get us the hell out of here! Kui! Whean! You stay with me! You others, move out! NOW!"

They wheeled again, and Garner threw Dodge's pack aside, pulling out grenades and ammunition. He filled his pouches as others fired, and then threw grenades when done. Now, he fired as the others finished gutting the pack. Then he wedged a claymore in the mulch, popped the fuse and ran. Stock delays were twenty seconds for a running claymore. It burned, as the team retreated and the NVA advanced. He looked back and saw it go off as half a dozen neared.

Now Garner dug into Kui's pack while on the run, setting another claymore as they caught up with the others. The second explosion rattled the jungle, and Reynolds motioned northwest, down to the LZ. "Twenty minutes!" he said.

Dodge was limp, and stripped of gear as the four Yards carried him by his legs and arms. They panted, stumbling, dropping him on his side. "Phil! Phil! We'll get you there, Phil! Hang on, boy! We'll get you out!"

Dodge looked up with glazed eyes and whispered, "Go, tell, him, tell him. My son, my son."

Garner screamed. "No! No! Dammit! Jim, he dies if we don't stop. Give me the radio. You're a fucking medic! Work on him, now!"

He swung back, calling on the radio, spreading the Yards out in a crescent. "Covey, Covey. This is Operation Steamboat, over."

"Roger, Steamboat, this is Triple Nickel, Five, Five, Five, Over."

"Triple Nickel, we have wounded and must stop to treat. Popping smoke." He threw a yellow smoke. "I need azimuth, and direction to an LZ, and covering fire. Do you have fast movers or Spads for me? Over?"

"Steamboat, that's a negative for one zero minutes. I spy yellow smoke, please confirm."

"Roger, yellow smoke, Triple Nickel. What about the LZ?"

"Steamboat, you've got three hundred meters at three, zero, fiver, degrees. Over."

"Roger, what do you have coming in for us? Over?"

"I have Spads in one, zero minutes. Over."

Garner sat crouched, picking splinters out of his left hand as the first of three grenades came into their position from up the hill. The first one bounced right off his pack, and after catching it close to his chest, he had it back in the air, where it went off twenty meters downhill. Others rattled the sides, and he turned, checking with Reynolds as rifle fire started up again.

Reynolds shook his head, yelling, "He's gone! He's gone!"

Dodge's tongue was peppered with grit and leaves, falling slack between open jaws. Open eyelids showed syrupy eyes, and a red hole in his throat had frayed edges like a bloody filigree of lace. Dodge's skin was turning gray, as blood pooled deep inside and red corpuscles winked out life with oxygen starvation.

Garner studied the gray in surrealistic slow motion. He saw cells by millions winking out second over second. First were the outer layers of the brain, most sensitive, most needy. Then came the blood, where cell division was fastest and most frequent. Various tissues were dying off in rank, one by one, all the way down to the slowest cells of bone.

They were winking out before his eyes, and for the first time in his life he saw true death. It was the systematic shutting down of a marvelous machine, from the most delicate of parts to the most rugged recalcitrant. There was no coming back. As he watched, tissues threw irreversible switches, killing pieces bit by bit in the living power plant. The heart had stopped, but the last cells would not kick off their final electric charge for many minutes.

The dying eyes of his best friend reflected his own mortality, and he threw back a startling scream. Madness, and the illogical nearness of death, made his own invincibility all the more convincing in a self-delusional rage for revenge. He screamed for them to move and take the body, then gave the radio away and pointed out an azimuth. With a deadly cool, he went rolling to the side, heading for the hunt.

They moved down the hill, northwest, to the hole in the trees, and he ignored the soldiers coming down the ridge from the east. Instead, he scuttled southwest, to hit the flank he knew was coming. The team was breaking brush, and three minutes later he saw a stealthy column of men following the noise like a scent. Fifteen filed past him downhill, and never saw the two grenades he threw. Explosions lifted six men in the air, and he came in fast behind, taking advantage of the mistaken belief they'd been hit from the front.

They lay scattered, firing forward, and he rolled them like a rug, killing one by one with single shots masked by their own surrounding fire. He moved unchallenged, extracting magazines and revenge while stepping over bodies, marching forward. One twisted and saw him. He was screaming as he died, making the last three turn to face him. Bullets rolled them down the hill.

He moved north along the ridge, flanking those up top who threw the first grenades. Helicopters were coming, and their approach was answered by rifle fire, thirty meters out, in front and to the right. He crouched, moving closer, then stopped as the men passed in front like a puff of wind riffling down the hill.

They tracked the team, and he felt their eyes pass over him time and again, searching for signs of their flanking squad and the reasons for the explosions and firefight they heard. Twenty-five passed, and he let them go, as fear and pain started breaking through his adrenalin pump. His blood, and that of others, splattered his green uniform, and he shivered at the thought of all the carnage while gutting his pack of any remaining magazines and grenades. Smoke went in side pockets and baseballs hung from his harness. He moved forward, and then turned left and followed their track.

The valley filled with the sounds of rifle fire and Hueys. The track passed through thick brush, and the landing zone could not be far ahead. He crept around a curve, and stopped as he saw a group of NVA facing forward, just fifteen meters down. Their forward elements were firing, and he heard the team return it. Back elements were spreading on line, and if he was getting out he had to do it now.

Six grenades were on the ground where he knelt. One by one they went through the air in a ninety-degree fan, going off like timed charges of a road construction gang. His first magazine was dry by the time final explosions threw leaves and bits of gristle in the air. Then he was running, firing, screaming at the remaining NVA, taking advantage of smoke and the confusion as to the attack's direction.

He lurched towards the turbine noise, stumbling into brush, colliding with a man hiding behind the nearest tree. Garner gave him a horizontal butt stroke, catching his temple, bringing him to his knees. The NVA looked into the narrowing eyes of the bloody American. The pause was all of three seconds, before remaining rounds blew pulpy matter across the tree's roots. Magazines changed in rapid habit, and Garner ran screaming to sounds of the extraction. Door gunners fired in all directions, and he worked between the trees at a low crawl.

A first ship was up and gone, and he saw Reynolds fight to load the body. Garner screamed, and the other American turned, waving at the gunner to stop firing. Then Reynolds ran back to the wood line as Garner limped from the shadows and gathered in Reynolds's arms.

They crawled aboard with Phe, Kehn and Dominique, and the Gladiator gunner opened up again as they started climbing out. Garner groped for Dodge in the howling wind, saying nothing as he held on, cradling the slumped head, gripping tighter, ignoring everything but the pain, and the muggers charging from the shadows.

26

THINK

RECON COMPANY
SOA (CCC) 5TH SFG (ABN) 1ST SF
APO San Francisco, Calif 96499

SUBJECT: Policy & Information

TO: All Recon Personnel

CC 30th PRESIDENT?

1. The following information was put out at the staff briefing.

    A. No Montagnards will be permitted to leave the C&C compound for the next two weeks. Last night, our personnel fought with an ARVN Armored unit in down town Kontum. Several of the Armored Personnel are now in the hospital, and though the Yards apparently won the fight they have lost the peace for at least two weeks.

    B. One RF platoon, while moving down the Dak To highway, was hit by an enemy ambush this morning a few klicks from Kontum. An accurate report of casualties is unknown at this time.

    C. The weather is slowly clearing and we should be back to standard rains soon.

D. Another agent report stated that our compound may be hit by an unknown VC element sometime this month.

E. When walking through the compound during the day pick up any loose trash and place it in the appropriate barrels. Actions always speak louder than words.

SET THE EXAMPLE

2. SGT Thompson, Wyoming and SFC Kipple were medevacked to Pleiku. Both are reported in good condition. Both Stateside addresses are posted on the bulletin board in Recon H.Q. Write them if you have the chance.

FIRST VICE PRESIDENT?

3. SFC Dodge, IOWA, was KIA yesterday afternoon. Memorial services to be announced.

TAKE PRIDE

4. The subject for Monday's 10 session will concern "Message Composition" and a class on "Methods of Evading", by one of the 10s. 1500–1545.

FIFTH PRESIDENT?

5. The S-2 will conduct a class on Tuesday at 1500 hours in the theatre, for Recon personnel. The class will be on the new waterproof camera, which was recently acquired for use by the RTs.

LUCK IS A LUXURY

6. A. Nine 10s attended the last 10 "Exchange of Ideas" session last Monday at 1500. Remember 10s, these will be held in the Recon conference room. The success or failure of your next mission could well depend on your attendance.

   B. The topic was "Immediate Action to the Flank." The nine 10s present chose RT Texas's presentation as #1. RT California was #2, and RT NM was #3. Though you may not want to adopt a complete new method of action for your RT, perhaps you can adopt one portion to your plan and make it a little better. Try it out; practice it over and over until you have a highly polished method. Practice gives you and your team confidence, which in turn will lead to success. There will be a make-up period for those that did not or could not attend. Make sure your schedule's clear for next Monday's session.

WILLIAM DONNALLY
1SG Recon Co.

27

"I want you to look at this, Sergeant Garner." Donnally stood behind his desk, passing over a manila envelope. Garner started reaching with the left hand, but thought better of the pain, so he stopped and took it with his right. A wooden sliver the medics pulled out of him was over in the team room. It came in behind, through his pack, and though it didn't penetrate deeper organs, it skewered his rib and under arm muscles like a six-inch needle. He could work the arm, but the pain was bad.

The envelope was bulky, with a torn flap from overuse. On the front was scrawled, "Dodge."

Garner undid the clasp and pulled out its contents. There were bound wads of dongs and MPC, some camp pictures, a bar girl contract from Taipei, and another legal-sized envelope, unsealed.

"Open it."

Inside was a four-page letter, titled, "To Whom It May Concern," and it started off with, "Last Will and Testicle of Phillip B. Dodge."

Garner glanced over the handwritten letter, while Donnally started talking.

"Of course, personal valuables are stored in the safe when you go on missions. What with MPC changes and all. But this threw us. I felt, since you're mentioned, you should be made aware of it."

"I'm mentioned?"

"Yes, on the fourth page. He basically gave all cash he had to the Montagnards. He wanted you and Reynolds to split the flags and whatever other personal effects were left. He didn't have any brothers and sisters, and both parents are dead. He, mentions his wife though, and his son."

"Son? Son? I didn't know. He never said a word."

"Of course this thing probably isn't legal in the strictest sense, because it's not witnessed and formal and all that, but we know these were his last wishes, so the colonel decided to go ahead and distribute things the way he wanted.

Dodge names you executor, and swears he'll come back and haunt you if you don't carry out his wishes."

Garner was shaking his head and wiping his eyes. He read: "—you, because I know these things will be carried out. I have to depend on someone doing these things, Ted. I hope it's not a burden.

"Most of the jobs aren't too tough, and I hope the flags repay you for the time taken. One favor I am going to ask though, is that you see Jane and my son, Nathan, 'Nat', and that you tell them as much as you feel comfortable telling them about me. Nat is six now. He was born after we split, and really doesn't know that much about his old man. I've got packs of unmailed letters in my footlocker. The one favor I'm asking is that you make sure they reach my son.

"I know we carried different opinions on some things, Ted, but there's no one else I'd trust with this. We've saved each other's lives and the slate's clean, but I'm asking this favor as a friend. There's nothing else to say, because I don't know what kind of questions you'll have, and if the time comes you end up reading this, I won't be there to ask anyway. Just know I've appreciated your friendship, and never doubt you always had mine.

Phil"

Canada padded across her main room with a tureen of soup. Red and cream orchids bloomed in a wicker basket atop dampened moss in the table's center. Best plates and such were out, and she looked at Garner with the apprehensions of one approaching a tied mastiff that gave no clue as to disposition, either with a growl or a wag of the tail.

"Did you write his woman?" She placed the tureen carefully, lifting the lid and ladling soup for him and then herself. She sat across, expectant.

He came out of his trancelike state, looking at the food before him as if it just appeared by magic. "Yah. I wrote his woman. I wrote a bunch of guys too: Day, Larsen, Morrison and others. They ought to know. Larsen's made captain and Day's down in Colorado, chasing all the round-eyes, going to school." He sipped spicy soup, and realized she was a good cook no matter what the culture. He said nothing.

She eyed him while eating. It was like this all day. He'd been there five hours, coming in late Saturday morning, but instead of sweeping her up and carrying her to bed, he sat in the main room reading magazines over and over. He snapped about small things and paced from time to time. They never dared walk streets together, and as the day wore on, her pale green room began shrinking with a suffocating silence. The sun banked westward, and at the meal's end he straightened, saying, "Good," more to himself than to her.

"I'm happy I can make good meals for you, Garnah. I am glad you liked it." He looked up, questioning what she was talking about.

"Oh yes, Canada. Good meal. Good meal. Thank you." He reached into his back pocket, taking out his wallet, laying $200 in MPC on the table. "Change this over as soon as you can. I think there's another MPC change coming soon, and I don't want you caught with it."

"What is this? What is this?"

The shaking in her voice made him turn away, as he stood up and walked to his pack. "Here are some cartoned cigarettes. I bought six in Pleiku. Also, I brought some freeze-dried LRP rations. You're a good cook, but these are real handy, and I thought you'd like them."

"What are you doing, Garnah? I do not understand? The money?"

"I'm leaving, Canada. I've been lying to myself, and you long enough. No more. I'm leaving."

Her face crumbled.

"A good friend told me the bravest thing he'd ever done was breaking an old man's heart, because he found the courage to tell the truth. I've been gutless long enough."

"This is brave?" she wailed. "You come, for many months I cook for you, I love with you, and now you say, "No," and pay me money like some short-time girl downtown? This is brave? You hold me, love me, help me, and now you say enough, because you scared of me?" She was yelling in his face.

"You not brave. You fancy boy with big man's tong. You do not know me. I see! I see! You give me cigarettes and food? You shame me. I love you Garnah, but you scared of me like a little boy. Please do not do this. Grow up! Love me! I make you good woman! You can take me home. I can make you very good woman."

Her arms circled his neck, trying to pull him down to her tear-streaked face, but he broke her hold, throwing her arms down and away.

"No! No! No!" he screamed. "I don't know if it's gutless or brave walking away. I say I don't love you, but you're the best woman I've ever met. Maybe the best I ever will meet. No!" He warned her away with his hands. "All I know is that I'm not ready for this. I'm not ready to settle down. I've got too many things ahead to do."

"What?" she cried.

"I don't even fucking know right now. All I know is I can't do any of them if I'm, if I'm married! I want my freedom. When I get out I want to finish school. I want to travel. I want to taste hundreds of different women before I settle down to the one. I care for you, Canada, but I'm not right for you.

Maybe I am a little boy wanting all the fun and no responsibility, but that's my choice! I don't want to think about the future and worry over decisions affecting me for the rest of my life.

"Don't you think I know you want to leave the country? Don't you think I know you love me? I know. I know, but I'm not ready for love, commitment and all that crap. I don't want the pain. I don't want you."

He slammed through the door, not hearing her cries behind, and ran down the steps into the open street, where he stood gasping, deep, cleansing breaths of air. Then he walked away, catching her movement at the upstairs window, like a fluttering curtain. He broke into a noisy trot, with equipment jangling all around.

Two blocks away on the main street, he waived a motorcycle cab and went dodging and bouncing back to the safety of the compound. He was One Zero now, and Dodge's room was his. He put his equipment away and sat on the bunk, fingering the first thick packet of letters that Dodge had never mailed to his son. All were sealed and stacked according to the date written, almost three a week. He wondered what secrets, what knowledge and experiences they contained. What son should know a father through a pack of papers, dry, sterile, crumbling eventually with age?

He thought of his own family and its uncommunicative ways. He realized he probably knew less of his own father than Nathan would learn of his, through these scrawled precious pieces of paper. There was a distance in writing, actually allowing Dodge to get closer to a son he'd never seen. It could be like that, expressing thoughts and love on paper, thoughts that never formed to words, love that never transcended genial and distant pats on the head in passing.

The few times he'd tried talking with his own father were strained, narrow and one dimensional, littered with embarrassed answers of "Yes" and "No", to his naive questions on life. After several attempts, he settled into an easy truce with the old man, and neither pushed for hugs and such. It was love by definition, but not degree. Perhaps distance of the written word could give expression to the love Dodge felt for his son. He couldn't guess, but packed the letters carefully away and headed to the club.

The last of the steaks were grilled, but he passed them by, hitting the door with a thump. Inside, air conditioning gave a sticky chill, as he wound between tables to the bar where he found Danner.

"Bourbon, straight up," he said to the bartender.

"Hey, Ted, what are you doing here? I thought Saturday was your day to play downtown?"

He downed a shot and ordered another before the bartender turned away.

"I just broke it off with her. She wants too much. She wants me to marry her and take her to the States, for Christ's sake."

"So it finally came down to that did it? We were wondering if she'd put the screws to you for it."

"Who's we?" he said suspiciously, after killing the second drink.

"Hell, Ted, look around. Just about everyone. Is she coming in tonight?"

"I don't know. If she does, I don't think I can stay."

He picked up the third drink, and they wandered over to a table where Sardo and Adams sat talking. Danner broke the news.

"Don't tell me you ever thought seriously about bringing her home to the folks?" asked Sardo.

"No, I guess not, but I never really said I wouldn't. I didn't draw the ground rules firmly enough. I told her I wouldn't marry her, but I guess she just didn't believe it. God I feel ten ways shitty. She was crying her head off when I bolted."

"Not to worry, Ted. All these girls want to hook someone. Back in the States I heard stories of guys getting hooked up, only to find their women hit the ground running when they got back home. Lots disappear or start selling themselves again in a couple months. Can't change stripes."

"Canada's not a hooker, Tony. Watch your mouth, okay?"

"Fine, then go ahead and marry the kid and screw up the rest of your life."

"I could do worse. I could do worse. Mary!" He ordered another round, then another and another. By eight o'clock he had trouble focusing his eyes.

Don Timmons came booming through the main door, heading toward their table. "Hey, Don, I thought you were on Bright Light," said Adams.

"I am, but I drew first rotation back and got in late, so I hit the mess hall before cleaning up. I got news. Has anyone read today's *Stars and Stripes*?"

"Not me," said Danner, while the others shook their heads.

"Well get a copy. I read it cover to cover cause Dak To is so damned boring. Way in the back is a little article from Bragg. It says that an as of yet unnamed SF sergeant first class was arrested for assault in Fayetteville. He pistol whipped his wife because she was running around on him while he was in the Nam."

"So?" said Sardo.

"He beat her with a chromed nine-millimeter Browning High Power. The paper said it was a presentation pistol he got while overseas."

They rocked back in their chairs as Garner muttered, "Poor Snake. He leaves his wife for up to three, for up to three years, an' then gets mad cause she's p-poking other men. Jesus."

"No wonder he acted strange before going back. He must have guessed and didn't want to face it," said Danner. "Did he kill her?"

"No, I don't think so." Said Timmons. "It said she was hospitalized and he was in jail. That's all."

"Jesus, ain't that the way it is? Ain't that the way it is?" Garner wiped his face with his right hand.

Timmons looked at him, and Danner explained.

"He broke it off with Canada tonight. Teddy boy, is tying on a good one."

"Oh, well give me some time and I'll try and catch up, Ted." Said Timmons. "Oh one other thing, I heard that new guy, Randal, quit."

"Who, you mean him?" Garner pointed across the room.

Timmons turned, looking over his shoulder. "Yah, the new guy on Arkansas. He went to One Zero school down at Long Thon, came back, ran two missions and just quit today. What's more, I don't think they're going to ship him out. I heard he was going to act as launch site resupply, rear echelon."

"What?" Garner turned red. "Launch site resupply? Those are kinds of jobs res, reserved for Crispy Critters, after ten or eleven months. He's taking a slot that's gonna make others run longer than they have to. What justice is there in that?" He had the chair back, and almost fell out of it while getting to his feet.

"Ted! Ted! Let it be, dammit." Danner was pulling on his shoulder, but he broke away and wobbled across the room, standing behind the clean-shaven young man with bright blue eyes. Others at the table were all newer members that he didn't know beyond an absentminded, "Hello" in passing. The floor rocked like a ship's deck, and he braced against a table as the others turned.

"You, Randal," he said while fishing in his back pocket.

"Yes?" He turned with his arm draped lazily over the chair.

"Here." Garner threw a five-dollar MPC on the table. "I'll expect my leggings back in the morning. My supply has, has finally run dry, and I figure only people with the guts to go to the field ought to wear them. Don't you?" The boy turned red, but said nothing.

"Who the hell do you think you are, taking over a back slot with only two piddly assed missions under your belt? Huh? You're keeping people in the field when they ought to kick back their last couple weeks. Who the fuck are you anyway?"

"Ted. Ted. Knock it off." Danner came behind, pulling at him, and Garner tried a halfhearted swing that had no power. The bigger man blocked it, while others from his table surrounded and bodily lifted him out the doorway. He went screaming, "I'm not fucking done with that pussy sonofa, sonofabitch."

CHAPTER 27 • 223

Two days later, they got their new man. Reynolds was up, shaved and ready to go to Pleiku and the PX there, while Garner lay in the bunk, pounding with another headache from another hangover.

"Boom, boom." The rattling door on Reynolds's side exploded in Garner's head. "Boom, boom."

"Anybody in there?" It was Donnally.

"Yah, Sarge. Here!" Reynolds shuffled to the door in the other room, and Garner sat up as Donnally walked through the separating doorway.

"Garner, you look like you crawled out from under this hooch. You better be ready for training tomorrow."

He wobbled up. "Don't worry about me, Sarge. I'll be up to snuff." He stood there shaking his head, like he was trying to get water out of a plugged-up ear.

"This is your new man. Sergeant Marston, this is your One Zero, Sergeant Ted Garner, such as he is. Garner, Jake Marston."

"Nice to meet you." They said simultaneously, shaking hands.

Garner checked him out: taller, six one, thin, large hands with fingernails big and thick as nickels, good teeth in a wide, wide mouth stretched hard over sharp bones. The smile was cocky, cocky, cocky. Then the uniform: clean but not new, E-5, same rank, cloth combat infantryman's badge sewn above the left pocket, over airborne jump wings.

"Where'd you come in from?" Garner asked.

"I got jammed up with the Americal Division when I got in country. Finally got my transfer back into SF."

"How long?"

"Five months."

"See a lot of action?"

"A bunch. What of it?" The cocky grin came forward with the chin and the challenge.

"Nothing, nothing. It's just that rumor control says some units in Americal take ears after they sweep an area. How about it?"

"It's happened. So what? They're dink ears. Who cares?"

"Well, you take a dead man's ears and Charlie finds the body, maybe next time out he skins a live American. Ever consider that?"

"No. Cause I ain't gonna be the one they catch!"

"I see. We're the same rank. You gonna take orders from me in the field?"

"Sure, why not. I told the sergeant here I'll come along and play with you for a couple missions, but then I want a team of my own. I can handle it."

"I'm sure you can. I just want to make sure you keep priorities straight. Welcome aboard. Thanks for bringing him over, Sergeant Donnally."

"Then I'll leave you men to get acquainted." Donnally turned, shaking his head as he stepped out of the room.

Reynolds left and Marston started moving in. Garner shuffled around with his boots and pants but couldn't find a clean jungle shirt. He went to the outside door yelling, "Mamma san, *van*, Mamma san, *van*." The little woman was down by the latrine along the bunker line, hanging wash. She came running up.

"Mamma san, where's my shirt?"

She looked puzzled and rattled at him in Vietnamese.

"I said where's my shirt? You've lost three shirts in the last two weeks, and I'm getting damned sick and tired of it. Go get my shirts. Now!"

Marston walked through the rooms and said. "Maybe she doesn't understand."

"Oh, she understands all right." He motioned, pulling on imaginary sleeves for her. "She knows she's losing my clothes. The maids steal from each other's wash lines and sell them on the black market downtown. Now you skinny old witch, you took four uniforms out this morning, I want them back."

"*Co* take, *co* take. No *bic*," she said.

"Well you better get the guts to go after whoever stole them. Now go get my uniforms."

"No *bic*, no *bic*. *Co* take, *co*—"

He slapped her flat in the face and sent her reeling. Then as she stumbled up he menaced with his fist, saying, "Go get my clothes now!" She skidded away crying.

"God damned maids would walk off with the building if they could." He stalked away to the latrine for a shower, and fifteen minutes later his cleaned uniforms were folded on the bed.

First mission out with Marston was nothing much, a quiet area recon. The new man appeared to know his business, but he was cocky and smart mouthed, and felt that carrying the radio was beneath him. Garner took verbal challenges and gave them back, saying Marston could run his own team any way he wanted, but as long as he was on Iowa, he ran it Garner's way.

They talked with Donnally and got permission to go back on the Golf Course for the next one. Last time there was profitable, and Garner wanted to set up again in the exact same spot as before. "Besides," he joked, "we need a Christmas tree for the club."

They inserted and moved quietly for two days, dropping off two cases of Italian Green ammunition and a B-40 rocket. The third morning they were standing at their old ambush site, at the middle of the western side, looking out over the long grass. Radiating lines where the eight-inch shells bombarded the southern half of the field were gone, but impact points were still visible through the new growth. Garner explained the action to Marston, and pointed out that the cleared and burnt area was far enough away that they could still use closer grass for ambush cover. They sat, waiting like spiders in a web.

"Now look, we're in a perfect spot to nail a prisoner. I don't know about you guys, but I wouldn't mind going back to Taipei. So, we sit here and watch everything go by unless we just can't pass it up like last time. Okay?"

"Are you saying you're scared of making contact with Charlie? We're going to screw around out here, grab someone and haul ass, without nailing some bad guys. That's gutless."

"This isn't the Americal, Marston. This is Recon, and we shoot it up only when we have to. You better get a grip on that, otherwise no one, not Yards or Americans, will want to run with you. You want to run wild? Pull it with a team you control, not this one."

"I can't believe you, Garner. We've got more firepower than a platoon in World War II. You're just scared."

"You bet your ass I am, right down to my toenails. I'm not mincing words here. Do it my way or get another team. That's all, Jake."

Garner sat in the north wood line with Dominique, while Reynolds took the southern post sixty feet away, with Djuit. Marston grumbled and sat with the others back in the woods.

Just after noon, first traffic came south on the trail. It was a disciplined squad of twelve men. A two-man point was thirty meters out, with the rest scattered along behind at three-meter intervals. Weapons were low slung. They were on alert, and the team let them pass.

The next group was six soldiers coming south. Then four came north. By 1600 hours, seven sets of troops came along the trail, all but one moving south. Every group had too many members to try a capture. At best one man or two could be taken quietly. Any more than that would create a firefight. There was something about three or more men that bolstered spirits. In the face of overwhelming odds, one or two men would surrender, but if there were three or more, they'd inevitably try and fight their way out.

Marston argued that they should attack each unit as it came down the trail. "Come on, Garner, there's only five of them down there, and this is the seventh group you've let through. Let's just nail the first four and grab the last guy. It'll be dark soon. You said you'd like to get out today. Come on, let's go."

"No. I said I want this clean. No noise. We've got four more days to do it right, and we'll sit here until it comes along."

Reynolds reconfirmed with Leghorn relay site that things were quiet elsewhere and helicopters were ready if needed. Twenty minutes later, Garner jumped up. "Reynolds, come here!" The other man low crawled to the north position, propping up on elbows and working the binoculars' focus dial. "This may be it, Jim. You see it?"

"Yah. Let's do it," said Reynolds.

Far off in the northern wood line was a solitary figure walking swiftly into the open field. Garner said. "I want you on the radio calling a Prairie Fire. Marston will go out in the field with me. Don't take it wrong now, Jim. I need someone I can trust guarding my back, okay?"

Reynolds's look of shock faded, and he nodded understanding. Then he moved back down into the woods, calling Leghorn, while Garner talked to Marston, Dominique, Djuit and Kui.

"Remember, no shooting. We take him alive. How about extraction, Jim?"

"Leghorn says they're firing up the birds and coming out. They're jumpy cause we haven't caught the guy yet, but it's getting dark, and they understand we're scared of keeping someone overnight. They should be here in thirty minutes. We'll probably have to use strobes to get out on."

"Okay, let's move." Garner started out. "Keep the hell down."

Reynolds said, "Hey, Ted!" Garner turned. "Just remember, the words are, '*Cheu hoi, cheu hoi.*'"

Garner gave a thumbs up and chuckled, "You got it, boss." Then they moved out around the hill's southern slope, leaving rucksacks behind. Garner was crouched, moving at a trot, and several minutes later as the sun slipped behind the mountains, he spread the men out in line twenty meters west of the trail. They were at six-foot intervals, centered on Garner. When he was satisfied with placement, he motioned "down", and they disappeared into knee-length grass. He hoped their trail wouldn't be noticed, but nothing could be done about that now.

They waited and listened. Three minutes later, a light tread came closer. He'd told them he wanted surprise and the opportunity to confront the soldier just after he'd passed the ambush. That way when he was ordered to surrender, he'd turn and see five armed men, and he'd immediately see that fighting was suicidal. Timing had to be right. They were to cue on Garner, and stand quietly when he did.

Garner rose in a push-up position, and saw the soldier passing front right, with an AK on one shoulder, and another across the top of his pack. He lowered to his belly, counting to five. Then he stood, motioning others to do the same. Marston was southernmost, and as Garner muttered "Three" to himself, Marston stood up early.

CHAPTER 27 • 227

The soldier caught movement, and turned to see five enemy rising from the grass. He started running. Garner yelled *"Cheu hoi,"* as Marston opened up with two three-round bursts. The green-clad man twirled, then dropped to his knees and fell on his face. The rucksack and weapons fell to either side.

Marston rushed forward with his combat knife in his left hand. He was rolling the body over before the others ran up. As it came around, the floppy hat pulled off, and a cascade of black hair fell out, partially covering the face of a beautiful Oriental girl. She couldn't have been over fifteen, and Marston looked on dumbstruck, as she exhaled blood bubbles and began growing pale with death.

"You God damned sonofabitch!" Garner screamed as he lunged at Marston, who now hovered over the body. They rolled in the trail, as he knocked the knife away and beat on Marston's face with both fists.

"You want ears you sonofabitch? You want ears?" Garner grabbed the knife, rolled to the girl and cut the right one off all the way to the lobe. He sucked in hard with hysteria and again jumped on the dazed soldier, forcing the bloody gristle between his teeth. It took Marston several seconds to come out of the initial attack and realize what was happening. He tasted copper blood, not his own, and began fighting back.

Garner lost the knife while shoving the ear in Marston's mouth, holding it there with his left hand. They rolled and struggled, and Marston struck out, knocking Garner off balance, pulling away enough to spit the ear onto the trail. They fought on their knees, grappling while the Yards looked on, not knowing what to do. Finally, they rose together, shoved off and backed away. Then Garner came in with a right upper cut, snapping the other man's mouth shut. He was getting ready to attack again when Reynolds arrived, yelling for the stunned Yards to tackle him.

Reynolds held his weapon on Marston, and threatened him as he regained his strength and balance. "Back off and let it be, man. I mean it." Marston looked tempted, then stepped back, rubbing his jaw and the inside of his mouth. "Djuit, get the knife. Dominique, get the M-16s and AKs. Kui, you take the pack." The rest of the team sat on Garner as he cursed and shook himself to a silent calm. He looked over to the twisted body and saw her beauty marred by the missing ear, but she was not the angel in life that she appeared in death.

The pack was full of identifying papers. He found out later that her father was Deputy Political Commander for the Saigon sector, and two years before, when she was twelve, she operated under his guidance. Papers she carried outlined her life.

Lin Bao pulled her bicycle up on the sidewalk, out of heavy traffic jamming Tu Do street. She walked past the cafe, chaining the bike to a lamppost on the corner. Outdoor tables were jammed with GIs drinking Bau Muy Bau beer, and she smiled good-naturedly at crude advances.

"Hey, Chicky Chicky. You want good time? Short time? Come here. Give you five dollars."

She shook her head and smiled. "No short time, GI. I good girl."

"Shur, Chicky, Chicky. All VN girls are short time girls. How much?" The abusive soldiers were off duty and sloppy drunk. They laughed and slapped the tables, talking back and forth, eying the little girl with dark hair. She was a beauty, and the promise of her womanhood announced itself for all to see and appreciate.

"No, no, GI. I good girl. Mamma San teach good girl."

"Awright, awright, so you're a good girl. So take a hike then." They turned back to their drinks, but she continued smiling at them.

"Hey, GI?"

"Yah?" The one who answered hadn't been badgering her. He was a blonde PFC with a face drawn hard across the bones.

"Hey, GI? You watch bike please? No let cowboys steal. Okay?"

"Okay, babysan, we'll be around for a while. See ya later, cutie."

She fiddled in the baskets straddling the back wheel, then unhooked one, flashed the boy a smile, and walked down the street to go shopping. The second basket was wired to the back of the bike, and less than three minutes later, the hidden fifteen-pound block of C-4, wrapped in six layers of bolts, nuts and glass, blew out the entire street corner.

Seven people were shredded to unidentifiable chunks of meat no larger than a fist. Eight more died in pieces, and another twenty-two caught remaining shards, losing fingers and eyes. Americans and Vietnamese alike were butchered. She heard the explosion and was proud of her contribution when reading results in the paper. Her commendations were in the pack. She was no babysan.

Garner's breathing became more regular, and Reynolds ordered him back to the wood line. He accepted, quietly. The Yards picked up the weapons and the body, winding a slow trail westward, toward the wood line, following the exhausted team leader. Little thought was given about enemy troops coming up on them, and Garner knew it was a mistake not even heated moments could excuse. He looked north and south along the darkening trail, but saw nothing. Marston trailed behind, rubbing his jaw.

Fifteen minutes later, as twilight slipped to dark, they signaled helicopters with strobe lights and left. The second helicopter out had Garner, Reynolds, three Yards, and the body. Her pack was kept and her pockets were dutifully searched.

Ten minutes later, the crew chief moved to shut out the cold night wind, but Garner sat in the starboard doorway, waving him away. His legs dangled out, and he sucked in the frigid air at 4,000 feet. A three-quarter moon was up, and the clear night sky sparkled. The mountains below rolled on from ridge to ridge, empty and indifferent. No lights, no fires of any kind betrayed the hand of man. They glistened in the moonlight, while marching away to an indefinite horizon.

Somewhere, halfway back to Dak To, Lin Bao was released into the screaming wind. They watched her roll and pirouette in the star shine as she gathered speed, rushing to embrace the mountains she loved in life.

Marston was gone from the compound a week later.

28

THINK

RECON COMPANY
SOA (CCC) 5TH SFG (ABN) 1ST SF
APO San Francisco, Calif 96499

SUBJECT: Policy & Information

TO: Recon Personnel

"LUCK IS A LUXURY"

1. Latest intel; During the next ten days the moon will come into its low phase with 20% visibility. You can count on a 50% nightly alert status. Agents claim most larger cities in the area will be hit.

HAVE YOU FORGOTTEN ANYTHING?

2. Again, do not call Prairie Fire emergencies unless you absolutely qualify for one. If you can break contact and continue the mission do so. If you need heightened awareness of your on going situation call a Team emergency or a Tactical Emergency. Prairie Fire should be used for wounded or very heavy contact only.

DO IT RIGHT THE FIRST TIME

3. The monthly promotion board will be coming up next week. Personnel to attend are listed below and will depart this location at 1400 hours

on the tenth. Many slots are waiving time in grade and time in service. Good luck!!

To: E-7	To: E-6	To: E-5
SSG Dampier	SGT Garner	Sp4 Rollins
SSG Harper	SGT Sardo	Sp4 Randal
SSG Barker	SGT Cane	Sp4 Kilmer
SGT Smith, R.	Sp4 Smith, J.	
SGT Blackburn		

If you feel you qualify and your name does not appear, then check with your One Zero. One Zeros, bring complaints to me.

READY TO MOVE OUT TOMORROW

4. SGT Marston has been reassigned back to group in Nah Trang. SGT William Stamp is in today for Team Hawaii and Sp4 David Neal for Iowa. Make yourselves acquainted.

WHY NOT TRY IT?

5. We have more unit plaques in the Recon Orderly room now. If you qualify and did not get one at the Hail and Farewell let me know.

6. The next "Tips of the Trade/Lessons Learned" series will be published in the near future. Can you remember four of the ideas presented in the last? Have you put them to use? Did you just say, "That's a good idea" and leave it at that?

CHANGE TACTICS AND REPLACEMENTS MAY NOT BE NECESSARY

7. Those going on R&Rs. Don't forget, you represent the United States in a guest country. Conduct yourself like a good will ambassador should.

TIME IS PRECIOUS: USE IT WELL!

WILLIAM DONNALLY
1SG Recon Co.

29

Garner looked out the window at a broad expanse of outback, marching away toward the eastern sun. It rolled flat and dry, in a scabby combination of reds and browns. From thirty thousand feet, cotton-like clouds skimmed along the ground below. After fiddling with creases in his civilian pants, he went back to reading Australian R&R materials.

The fight with Marston opened up the wound where the wooden sliver pierced him, and a small infection started, but he said nothing of it. This was his official Rest and Relaxation, and slots were tight. He would not jeopardize it, so he worked almost exclusively with his right hand. The infection would take care of itself.

This time out he was alone. SOG had no control over regular R&R slots. People simply put in requests and took their chance. He lost. He was alone in a plane full of 150 strangers, going to a strange land. It was a scary proposition, and the atmosphere was tense. This was civilization they were going to, and all of them knew they'd changed in Vietnam, and the main question was about how to act.

Donnally hadn't given him a hard time for throwing Marston off the team. He'd met the new man, Spec. Four David Neal, just three days before. Not enough time for judgments, but from what he saw, Neal would do well. He looked like he wanted to learn.

Canada wasn't speaking to him of course, and refused to serve his table. He couldn't blame her. She stalked the club self-consciously, and began paying special attention to a relatively new man, a Spec. Four Bower, on New Hampshire. Garner couldn't tell if it was genuine or for his benefit, but he had to choke the thought down. She wasn't his. He'd chosen a path and the pain that went with it, but he was surprised it lessened every day.

Rage for Dodge was dying too, and he felt like a betrayer of the faith. Every day it dropped a notch, until it leveled as a throbbing ache. The face and crooked smile receded, until he brought pictures out to reacquaint his friendship with the man.

The plane shifted lower, and reds and browns were broken with slashes of green and blocks of white, as they approached the city. Then they dropped more steeply, and the pilot chattered on about the sights ahead.

There was Port Jackson coming up. White sails dotted the water, beating for the gate and the Pacific beyond. The concrete sails of the unfinished Opera House flared out on Bennelong Point, and straight on was the harbor bridge, connecting Dawes's Point with the northern suburbs. They flew over and lowered to the airport.

After officially checking through and changing money, they boarded busses for the center. It was downtown at Plunkett and Palmer streets, where they intersected with Sir John Young Circle, right in the middle of everything. There was a tour guide of sorts up front, giving lessons in Australian history, customs, money and sights. He went on about the many services of the R&R Center, and claimed as many as two hundred of Sydney's finest young ladies attended their smokers and mixers. Rumor Control said an Australian man's priorities were his mates, his liquor and his women, in that order, and that the girls went ditsy over the fawning attentions of the horny young Yanks. This wasn't Taipei and he wasn't scrambling for a woman, but he wondered how he'd act among the round-eyes.

After drifting through orientation, he broke out with several others, catching a cab to King's Cross, the night life district ten blocks away. There were standing invitations for Yanks to stay with Australian families, and although it was appreciated, he knew he'd drink, and smoke, and swear too much, and stay out too late to make an American ambassador of good will.

Instead, he pulled into King's Cross Rex, where air conditioned rooms were $10.75, with TV, radio, and room service. Downstairs was a restaurant, lounge, and cocktail bar, an altogether serviceable situation. As soon as he settled in and stepped outside, the feeling of being lonely in a crowd gave a hammer blow between his eyes. For two days it was altogether terrible. He wandered streets during the day and drank alone at night.

"Ey, mate! Le me buy you a beer, mate?" The man stepped up to his right at the bar and rubbed two days' growth with stubby fingers. His nails were cracked and broken, lined with inground dirt that came only from close association with heavy machinery.

"Ey, keep. Ow about two drafts for the Yank and Me."

"Thanks, Mister, but I've—"

"No buts about it, mate." The bar tender unconsciously brought beers and took the money. "I was bought many a beer by my American friends during the Second War you know. Never light in the pockets they were. Ere's to your health." He downed two huge swallows while Garner sipped. The man's eyes were loose, running liquid red around the rims. He groped in his left rear pocket for a nonexistent handkerchief, until finally giving up and wiping his lips with the back of his hand. Then he belched politely.

"By gor that's good ale, that is. Barkeep, another round for me and me mate. So, how do you like Sydney so far, Yank?"

"Well, I just got in a couple days ago and don't know anyone. I haven't had a chance to meet any Australians so to speak. You're kind of the—"

"Too right, too right. Glad you're enjoying Aussie hospitality." The pat on his back caught Garner off guard, and he jumped at the touch. They talked on for five minutes, and the man listened to Garner's answers about the war and the state of the world. He looked to be late forties, and road map veins at the end of his nose seemed to swell every time he raised the glass. He bought another round, talking ever louder. Then he put his elbows on the bar and hunkered down with the air of a co-conspirator.

"Say, mate, I don't suppose you could help a fella out could you? I've had a run of bad luck today, I have. Lost a potfull on the races over at Randwick. Could you spare a fiver, mate?"

It caught Garner in the middle of a swallow, and he choked it down as the mug hit the bar with a slap. Adrenalin pulsed through him, but for some reason he wasn't mad. Instead, he was hit by one of the most profound sorrows of his life. He brought his hand out of the pocket so fast the bum flinched, but instead of hitting him, he pitched five dollars on the counter and trudged out of the bar.

Williams Street was busy with shoppers in the early evening. He wandered west, and for the first in a long, long time, felt totally alone. Back home leaves had fallen, and snow was coming, a muddy, ugly time of year. Down under the Southern Cross however, it was early summer, and the night air was brisk, crinkling the insides of his nose. Australian hospitality had drained him for the night, and as he wandered west, hitting Palmer Street, he made up his mind and turned north. He'd spend time with his own kind at the center.

The main lobby was awash in light, and the second-story balcony was full of men and women, mingling, talking, laughing. He stopped to take it in, when the blustery matron approached.

"Good evening, good evening. You're just in time for the mixer. The band started ten minutes ago, and everyone's upstairs dancing."

"Oh, it's tonight?"

"Yes. We have one every Tuesday and Friday," the American woman burbled. "If you didn't know about the mixer, perhaps I should ask; are you taking advantage of all the Center's services? We want to make you boys happy, here so far from home. We have water-skiing, sailing, horseback riding, big-game hunting and deep-sea fishing. We have camera tours and cruises, skydiving and sport parachuting—" She was slavering with delight at being so helpful.

"No thanks. I've almost broken my ankles on parachute landing falls."

"Well, we have surfing, night clubbing, a floating disco party, and a moonlit harbor cruise."

"Well, now being a stranger in a strange land, where do I get someone to take on a romantic harbor cruise?" he asked sarcastically.

"We have many of Sydney's finest young ladies upstairs waiting to meet you handsome young men on vacation."

"Oh, they must provide the one recreation you left out of your list of things to do, screwing." He walked to the wide staircase covered with red carpet. Halfway up, he stopped and turned. She stood there with her jaw unhinged, dangling loose and wobbly. "You didn't deserve that. It's been a tough month for me, I'm sorry." He turned and climbed.

The balcony opened on two sets of double doors and a ballroom beyond. Dappled shadows floated by, and as he entered the darkness swallowed him whole. Off to the right were three layers of intimidated soldiers hugging a long bar. They twisted in the muted red light, reaching over shoulders for drinks that bolstered confidence. They sat, and stood, and talked, and stared across the room, working up collective nerves.

In the center were couples dancing on the hardwood floor. Mirrored balls twirled high above, shooting layers of fractured light in ever widening clockwise circles. Everything turned surrealistic in the roving glitters, and off to the left in the darker shadows, were the girls.

They formed a block, a British Square of sorts, as solid and formidable as anything Napoleon ever faced. He shriveled at the thought, but kept on walking as adrenalin pumped through him again. It made him mad, and he cruised the outer edges like a shark off the coast, finally locking onto one with mousy brown hair, wearing a plaid dress. Her eyes were large, dark, and growing as he neared. She stood with her arms in front, hands clasped, fingers intertwined, palms together, unconsciously protecting delicate parts beneath her dress.

"Excuse me, Miss, but would you care to dance?"

"Oh, why, yes, thank you." Her voice came high and rich, like bells across the valley. He raised his left arm, but dropped it with the accompanying pain, and they walked to the center of the floor without touching. Then they turned and started swinging to the beat. The arm threw him off balance, and he felt like there was concrete in his shoes. They danced two fast dances, and then the beat shifted to something slowly romantic.

"I'm sorry. I, ah, I don't know what the rules are here, if I'm monopolizing your time or something."

"Rules? There aren't any that I'm aware of. Why?"

"Well, would you like to dance slow?"

Then she understood. "Why yes. Of course I would." She stepped up, and he held her hand and waist like eggshells. Then she moved in closer, and he caught fragrances of femininity and soap. Memories mixed with emotion and he backed away, but too late. She brushed against the erection, and he felt her stiffen in the dark. The secret was out.

He whispered to himself, "What the—"

Then he said, "My name's Ted. Ted Garner."

"I'm Janice Grady. Nice to meet you, Ted."

"Nice meeting you. I, I'm sorry I'm so tense. It's just that it's been a long time since I've been with a round-eye, a lady."

"Well that's what this is all about isn't it? Kind of reacquainting you Yanks with civilization, so to speak."

"Yah, I guess. It's just that it's hard, difficult."

"Yes." Her laughter came jolting out as her stomach muscles spasmed. "I know."

They danced in embarrassed silence, and he barely kept from bolting for the door. Finally, the song ended, and he gathered enough control to get to a table and order drinks. They sat there during the band break, talking about things of no importance.

"Great, great grandfather O'Grady was the first of my family to come over. Of course he was a prisoner in the penal colony then. The family claims he was an Irish patriot, but I've heard others say he was nothing but an unsuccessful second-story thief."

He laughed, and drank in the liquor and her tinkling giggles from across the table. Tensions wanted to break, but his body wouldn't allow it. Finally, he started stretching his neck, twisting his head, trying to loosen up.

"I beg your pardon, but what are you doing?"

"I'm sorry, Janice. It's just that it's been so long. I'm pretty tight. I'm starting to feel hemmed in a little."

"Here, let me help." Before he could protest, she was up and back behind him, probing taut shoulder muscles. He sighed as her fingers went deeper. Then she pulled his shoulders back, and he winced in pain.

"What? What?"

"I have, I have an injury under my left arm. Look, thank you, Janice, but this is getting too much for me. I'm feeling kind of, strange. I think I'd better leave."

She walked around in front. "You have a wound under your arm?" He nodded. "You're feeling a bit claustrophobic?"

"That's about right. It's got nothing to do with you. I'm just not used to this."

"Well then, let's go take a walk," she said.

He stood up, caught her checking him out, and remembered his outrageous Aunt Jean, who told him once that all women are incorrigible crotch watchers. They walked across the dance floor as the band struck up, and he groaned as the lead strummed a chord and started singing. They reached the stairs, and he almost ran down as the lead started singing about wanting to go home. They bolted out the door arm in arm.

Her lips traced side to side over the puncture wounds, where the slivered piece of wood passed through his body. Tensions drained away, and he drifted, thinking about the loneliness of the last two days. He'd watched amazed, as people led what looked like normal lives. He had a war to go back to, and it hit him that he'd changed so much, that the war was his real home, and that the beach, this city, this woman, and the trappings of so-called normal life, were the things to be afraid of.

The next morning, sunshine pushed all his fears away. Janice called into her work and took a few days' leave, and the first thing she did was take him to Bondi Bay, where they stripped to swim wear and soaked up the sun. He played in the shallows with her, but protected the crusted wounds from immersion in the fiery salt water.

The next morning they visited the zoo, and later took a tour of the harbor. The sails of the Opera House flared open, looking like they'd pull the whole thing into the bay, to collide with the ferry, where they stood wrapped together on the fore deck. Her hair wisped back along his cheek like a mane, and he understood why so many talked of emigrating from America to Australia.

At night they walked dreamlike around the town, to dinners and movies, dances. It was a clean city, and they strolled the botanical gardens without concerns of muggers and such. They wandered hand in hand along the water to Mrs. Macquarie's Point, where lights of the bridge and Opera House glinted silver on the water.

For five days they played, and then like any dream, it ended. Sunday morning they stood at the bus that would take him to the airport. She held him close but loose.

"Well, what can I say, lady love. Thank you. It was fun. I, I ah."

"Shush," she instructed. "No sad goodbyes, Teddy, all right?"

"Okay, but give me your address so I can write." He was stunned with the answer.

"No, love. No address. Remember? No regrets you said, and I agreed. No writing of letters and promises of things that will never happen." She patted his face. "What will I do if you go back to that awful place and get killed or maimed? I want to remember you and the week, our week. Just for us, all right? Let's not muck it up."

They stood and kissed deep, and parted. He worked along to a window seat, and waved goodbye to a dream world that would never again in his life come quite so clear. Within the hour, they were up and gone for the long stretch to Manila.

Saigon was a hop after refueling, and after staying the night at House Ten, he changed back into familiar olive drab for the Blackbird flight home. It was a milk run, and after four stops they finally hit Kontum, where he walked off the back ramp to the waiting grins of Danner and Adams, and a quickly popped beer.

"Hey boy, how was round-eye heaven?" asked Adams.

"It was clean, affordable and fun. And the natives were friendly."

"Well, tell us all about it, boy?" said Danner, and he did.

They crossed the bridge as he finished a brief sketch, and Danner said, "Well, you made the list, that's first, so you're a staff sergeant. The second thing is you missed the party two nights back. Colonel had Girl Night in celebration of promotions, and let all the ladies in Kontum come into the club. There were women everywhere. He wouldn't let them on the secured side of the compound though, where the team rooms are. Man you should have seen people scrambling for shadows and cover. The mosquitoes in the bunkers bit a lot of bare asses that night."

"Anyone hit while I was gone?"

"Yah," said Adams. "Buker got it in Golf-56 and Carter medevacked. Stewart's walking wounded. Oh, and that guy Randal, the one you chewed out. He got it at Dak Pek."

"What? He was resupply."

"Yah. They got shelled. He took a frag in the left front pocket. Lungs bled and he drowned. Nasty."

"Ohh God," said Garner.

"I don't know if this means much now, Ted, but that new guy Bower is evidently hot to trot on Canada. I don't know if he's dipping her, but that's the rumor."

Garner twisted the aluminum beer can and crushed it flat. "I hope he makes her happy," he said.

Two weeks later he was on the ground in India-Six doing another area recon. Neal worked out well. He took instruction without getting his back up, and he offered insightful advice when asked. Garner decided to put him up for promotion as soon as possible. Time was winding down, and he gave Reynolds more and more command. They walked the woods for a week, and saw two sets of troops and a recently used bunker complex. Things stayed quiet and they came back out without incident.

The second day of stand down they decided to host a feast at the village, and began gathering supplies while they sent Dominique to the chief to ask permission. Word came back, "Please, come drink with us, come eat with us. A hundred times welcome."

It was Reynolds's third feast, and as they sent Neal on errands in the jeep, Reynolds said, "It's an experience you'll never forget." He drove downtown with the mess hall sergeant, and Garner and Reynolds retired to the club to check their lists and have an early afternoon beer.

They sat drinking, making their plans for half an hour, when a rowdy bunch came punching through the door from the bright sunshine outside. Three men called out to anyone in the room, and then lurched toward the bar more by feel than by sight.

Garner called out, "Dravos, you turn up more often than a bad penny, boy. What are you doing all the way up here?"

"Hey, Ted, is that you? Hey come on over, guys." Dravos skirted tables with Sardo and Kidwell, and introductions with Reynolds skimmed around.

"I heard they got in a load of plaques," he said while sitting down. "I told you guys, I wouldn't leave country without one."

"You still snoring?"

"Snoring?" Kidwell joked. "He rattles rafters in the Americana. We're roommates down there. Jeez, you should hear him."

"Kidwell, tell me what ever happened to the sonofabitch Riggs, and your cousin?" Garner asked.

"Wow, did he get nailed. We heard he caused trouble up here, and we heard about Dodge. That was too bad. He was good people."

"That he was."

"Anyway, I told her all about Riggs, and she set him up. They went out with a bunch of her hospital friends, who were in on it. He was hitting on her pretty hard to break away and leave, but they wouldn't let him do it. She played up to him all night, then when it got time to go, he leaned on her pretty hard. She was in the street and chewed him up one side and down the other, and said there was only one way he'd ever get into her panties. She reached around behind and underneath her skirt, and pulled them down and stepped out of them. Then she walks up and stuffs them in his chest pocket, and says, 'Have fun.' Man what a cousin."

"I'll bet Riggs hid in his hole for a month or two," said Garner.

"No such luck," Dravos said. "He's out around escorting teams for truck driver snatches. Saigon wants a prisoner, cause there's been a lot of rumor of a new offensive sometime in the spring. At least that's what we heard from some guys from CCS Riggs was down there what, three weeks ago?"

Kidwell nodded yes while lowering the beer can. "They said he'll be coming up here too. CCN has already gotten orders, and rumor had it they tried a truck driver snatch last week and killed the guy. Riggs is just running around to reinforce the mission order, kicking ass and making himself obnoxious in general I believe."

Dravos broke in. "You might want to sound warnings up here about him, Ted. We heard he got in a pissing contest with a CCS team and threatened them all. Claimed the Yards were Communists or FULRO. What a clown."

"He'd better be careful with that," Garner said. "People might be willing to nail him for stirring up that kind of trouble." He put the drink down and turned quiet. Camps were loaded with FULRO sympathizers, and he was finally one among them.

He'd given Dominique the two captured AKs the girl carried. They would be stacked with others underground and come out again someday when the Yards began their self-destructive revolt. He wondered how much Italian Green ammunition was unknowingly stored at different villages, and how many bright, good-natured Yards would have AK-47 firing pins and bolts blown backwards through their skulls. A terrible waste was coming, and he downed the drink.

They talked on, and Garner told of the girl and Marston. Dravos listened quietly, and added to the core of thought. "One of our Earth Angel Teams brought in a prisoner once last summer. We have a reward system like you guys up here, but with only two Cheu Hois on each team it's kind of tough to get prisoners. Anyway, they brought back a Cambod girl. Caught her working in a field or something. I always thought it was a wuss thing to do, going after a girl and all.

"Well, they brought her in and we turned her over to the folks down in Saigon. About six weeks later I caught my counterpart, Mr. Peters, drinking. He splattered a bottle of beer against the wall and said he'd heard SOG turned her over to the ARVN cause she was just a farm girl with cow dung between her toes.

"Peters said the ARVN had her in their secret service compound for a week, gang raping her. Then when they were through, they popped a cap on her someplace out in the woods." They all stared into their drinks. "At least that's what he told me the rumor was. He was kind of upset."

Garner didn't want to hear any more. He swallowed down the last of his bourbon and said good night early. Two hours later, before others got back, he was rolling, pivoting on his bunk. He jolted, shouting gibberish. Then he screamed and screamed, and woke in sweaty shivers, with his hands tucked down between his legs, protecting his groin.

Vague images darted in and out, and as he came out of hyperventilation, he tried recapturing the dream, but found it gone. Thin wisps of smells, and sights, and fears were left, but it was gone. He dropped back into bed, exhausted, as echoes of fear skimmed the roughened edges of sleep.

Two days later, on Sunday, they loaded up assembled supplies and headed out the gate. Garner wasn't as successful as Larsen in getting gifts to distribute. They brought cases of food, and of course the chief was always presented something, this time a new green uniform, but larger boxes of clothes and toys were lacking. There was no apparent shift in the tribesmen's attitude, however. They were greeted with open arms and ushered to the long house with characteristic hospitality.

They drank stick after stick and laughed among the loops of men. Garner relaxed, washing away his fears of going home with alcohol, like he always did. These people were more natural now than ones waiting in the States, and he finally understood and mourned for men like Snake Martin, Billings and others. He was outside the world of telephones and ice cream, living fast and scary, and he liked it and feared it, but he knew he had to leave one day, and that was scary too. He drank another stick.

"Garnah! Garnah! Reynols! Reynols!" Dominique called, and motioned for them to stand.

"*Trung Si* Garnah, *Trung Si* Reynols. Team Iowa has helped this village many times, many ways. You are as brothers to Bahnar, and we welcome you." He urged them to step forward, and Dominique came to Garner as Djuit stepped to Reynolds. Neal was far too new to be included.

"We welcome you as brothers, and even when you go far away we hope you will think of us and remember brothers of the mountains." Dominique spread the brass ring, pushing it over Garner's right hand, retightening it on his wrist. Djuit did the same for Reynolds, and they all bowed and laughed in the excitement and warmth of their acceptance.

THINK

RECON COMPANY
SOA (CCC) 5TH SFG (ABN) 1ST SF
APO San Francisco, Calif 96499

SUBJECT: Policy & Information

TO: All Recon Personnel

PERSONAL PRIDE

1. All RTs WILL make three scheduled radio contacts daily. This is for your own protection. One RT, which was inserted yesterday, passed a "Good Day," but then no further word was received for 22 hours. An aerial search was made during the night and again this morning. One platoon was preparing to enter the RT's AO to commence a search when at approximately 0930 hours today, a standard SIT REP was received reporting NEG enemy contact, NEG, enemy sightings. Any comments?

WITHOUT PRACTICE YOU WILL NEVER SUCCEED

2. RECOMMENDATION: Have contests on changing magazines. You will be surprised at what you see and the results. Also simulate dark and do it blindfolded.

YOUR FLAG: IS THE TOP STRIPE RED OR WHITE?

3. CAMERA ISSUE: There are two times scheduled for camera issue. They are: 1500–1600 the day prior to insert, and 0730–0800 the day of insert. Upon completion of mission, return the cameras to S-2 ASAP.

DID YOU TURN IN YOUR ONE ZERO AID KIT?

4. Too much ammunition and C-4 is being left unaccounted for from this compound. Your Montagnard members are not allowed the use of this material other than on a mission basis. Several have been stopped the last two months from leaving the compound with cases and equipment. This is absolutely forbidden. Keep an eye on your troops.

WHEN IS (WAS?) FLAG DAY?

5. Yesterday a One Zero reported that his claymore wires had been cut inside the bunker. When was the last time you checked yours?

THINK MEN, THINK

6. The "ladies' night" was a success in that there was no violence in the club. The colonel has promised to continue the "Invitations" once a month as long as you behave yourselves.

WHO IS GOVERNOR OF YOUR STATE?

7. The club is offering a $100 reward for any live "fuck you" lizard brought in. If possible we will build a cage, but it must be able to swear properly before doing so.

COVER TRACKS

8. Black 10 jackets will be made for those personnel leaving the unit this month, on a first come, first served basis. Report to S-4 section as soon as possible for a fitting. Next week, personnel departing the unit next month, are to report to S-4 for fittings. It is requested that if you already have a '10' jacket, that you not request another. The unit will embroider your name and unit on the one you now have if you so desire, at no cost to you

WILLIAM DONNALLY
1SG Recon Co.

31

A week later they got Bright Light, and trained one last time on the rappelling tower and helicopter bodies at the range. His Hail and Farewell was coming up the week after, and Garner started concentrating on turning the team over to Reynolds. They conferred on tactics constantly, and checked sheets of Lessons Learned from time to time. Finally, they flew to Dak To, and he knew it was the last assignment he'd have with the team. He fingered the brass band on his wrist, and enjoyed the windy flight in silence.

They were back to the winter dry, but a front came through, and darker clouds hugged the mountains. Winter was approaching, and teams coming out of the field advised others to take heavier sleeping gear.

By late in the week, two teams had been extracted and three inserted. Of those three, Illinois was shot out the first day and had to go back to Kontum and plan for a fast reassignment of a new area. California came out after the third day. They were inserted and slept in cold that got down to forty-five degrees.

All the Montagnards had bronchitis and were coughing, making noise. The only team left in was Washington, and on Thursday afternoon they came screaming out on a Prairie Fire emergency after a three-hour run and two aborted attempts to land and rescue.

"Here they come!"

Eight Americans and fifteen Yards boiled out of the barracks, tower and adjacent areas, to watch six Hueys turn south and fly along the runway. They approached with characteristic "Whop, whops," and landed in a whirlwind of power. As soon as skids touched the lumpy pavement, the team unfolded from the bellies of the middle two. Garner ran up with cold beers.

Everyone patted backs, dancing around the team as they trudged across the ditch. Thompson, the One Zero, looked haunted. His eyes were dilated, and he sucked at the beer greedily. Fear was still leaching out of him.

Garner yelled above the helicopters' turbines, "Damn, Jimmy. You got out on a thin one today!"

"I didn't think we'd make it out. I sure didn't want to call on you to come and get us out again, Ted. Last time with Miller was bad enough."

Confusion reigned, as everyone talked at once and Thompson finished the beer. He walked to the barracks with the others, shucked his rucksack and web gear, and sat with a thump, his back against the wall. The Montagnards drifted away with their beers, and sat under the tower, telling their own stories.

Two with traces of blood showed off puncture wounds on their arms and legs. Grenade shrapnel would be found after careful probing, and the stiffness and pain just now breaking through the adrenalin rush would get much worse. They drank the beers and told their stories, but took the pain without comment.

"Jesus! This was the worst yet. They ought to nuke Juliet-Nine. We moved out at noon and hit a bunch on a sweep lookin' for us. Johnson here stitched two of them quick." He looked up into the new radioman's eyes. "That was good shootin', Johnson. This was one hell of a mission to break your cherry on. Like mine was."

Johnson flushed, and watched his team leader work off rattled nerves by talking it out.

"We couldn't shake 'em, couldn't shake 'em. No chance to lose 'em and sit on a cold LZ. No chance. They worked us around, and I could feel 'em trying to herd us toward the road? Covey, thank God, got us an LZ north. We flashed him on the run and found it ten minutes before the choppers came in.

"Then all hell broke loose. God, thank God for those Cobras. Man, they came in ripping along the LZ's edge. ALL around us. All around us." He looked at Reynolds. "Charlie was yellin' at us too. Chung, the interpreter, says they were yellin', 'Fuck Americans' and all stuff like that. Man they were pissed.

"The Hueys, oh God. Man, those Gladiator pilots have brass the size of grapefruit. The LZ was super small. Man, they came down on a dime while Cobras were workin' out. Then, after we're on, they goosed the power and we popped out of there like a champagne cork. POW. Hahaaa. Oh, God."

He looked up at Garner and said, "Ya know, Ted? There musta been fifteen or twenty of 'em out in the clear, gettin' shot at. They came right out of the woods trying to get us. They wanted us that bad. Brave, dumb, bastards.

"Casings were flying everywhere. The M-60's goin' nuts. Casings down my back, burning. Jesus. I went through six mags myself while we were coming out. It happened that quick." He snapped his fingers, then went quiet. Thompson took a deep breath and another drink. He closed his eyes and lowered the half-empty can, holding it with both hands. Aluminum crackled and popped.

"You got out, that's enough," Garner said. "You've got wounded. Let's get you back home."

He walked to the commo building and Gable reported in. It was early afternoon, and normally Hueys would stay on station and not return to Kontum for several hours. However, with the recovery of Washington, they had the unusual situation of not having any teams out.

Wyoming was supposed to go into India-Three, a southern target, but it was fouled with dirty weather and the day was getting on. Kontum said to bring everybody home. He brought beers to the Huey pilots and gave them the news. They made some small talk, then boarded and cranked up as Garner walked back, looking for his One One.

"Jim. Everyone's going back for the night."

"Us too?"

"Sure. There's no sense keeping the whole team here with no one in the field. Have a drink and watch a movie tonight. Better than sleeping on cots. Hah?"

"You're not coming?"

"Nah. I can't. We need security here for the commo shed."

"You want me to stay instead?"

"No, no, you go on. You can owe me one. You too Neal!" he yelled at his radioman twenty feet away. Turbines were building.

Neal turned. "What's that?" he asked.

"You're going back tonight."

"He says we owe him one, Dave."

"You want me to stay instead?"

Garner laughed and said, "No, no, get out of here before I take the two of you up on it and stick you with it!"

With that they skittered away, gathering the team and their packs. Five minutes later, the wounded Yards, walking stiffly now, were helped aboard, and all three teams jammed the doorways.

Four Hueys and two Cobras increased power, kicking up dust. They took off in line, then curved around and headed south; just twenty minutes after Washington landed, Garner was left alone, waving to the rapidly disappearing whirlwinds.

He stood in the long shadows, regarding the bank of clouds far off to the southwest, which prevented Wyoming from going in. It was perverse, how essential luck was in surviving such a war. Any war. It seemed there was a constant stream of danger they swam through on a daily basis, but the actual dying came about almost as an afterthought. Wrong place, wrong time. A war conducted like a thousand traffic accidents.

Tonight, Wyoming would drink, watch a movie, eat good chow and maybe play some cards. Tomorrow they could be dead, covered by ants sucking up their juices, somewhere on the jungle floor. He turned from the strip and walked to the barracks.

He watched lower halves of the troops through the stems of underbrush. Two feet up, branches and leaves exploded in a jumble, trapping three years' worth of dead growth. He sat against his pack, facing the road, watching guards as they passed back and forth, not ten feet away. He was proud he was this close to the road. Like a voyeur, he watched, listening and waiting for the trucks and the number count. Then it happened.

One guard walked past to the right, stopped, turned and came back. Did a glitter of metal give him away? It couldn't have been sound. Was it smell? Americans smelled different. No *nuoc mam*. Old Spice instead, crazy thought. He sifted possibilities, but couldn't find an answer. It didn't really matter now.

The guard stopped in front, hesitated, turned, hesitated, then knelt down, peering deep into the darkened underbrush. Garner had on heavy camo, and squinted, closing whites in the corners. It didn't help. The nondescript Oriental face grew larger as his fixed sight went telescoping to it. Then the guard began pulling his weapon around.

Garner groped with his M-16. It was in his hands, thick and heavy, remote. He pointed at the silhouetted face and pulled the trigger, but nothing happened. An empty "click." He pulled the ejector back and let it fly, jacking in another round. "Click!" The AK-47 would start at his groin, and work across his belly and chest to his head. Garner squeezed the third dead round, and was digging in his heels, scooting backwards like a crab as he started screaming.

Then, he was out of it, staring at the rough board ceiling, shaking with sweat. The face was gone. Both hands were tucked between his legs, protecting his groin. He shuddered, forcing himself out of hyperventilation while lying quiet for five minutes. The terrors were distilled through repetition, over and over again. The face was never distinct, but Oriental.

Then, came the grinding trucks and the yells outside.

He worked off the cot and made the doorway as a first lieutenant came past the gate, ignoring a "Restricted Access" sign that cordoned off their little compound.

"Excuse me, Sir! May I help you? Excuse me, Sir. You can't come in here!" He walked toward the young officer, wiping sleep from his eyes. "Sir! Stop!"

The first lieutenant stopped, startled. He was preoccupied, not paying attention, and began collecting himself while eyeing the man in front. "Who the hell are you?" He spit.

"Staff Sergeant Garner, Sir. Ted Garner, Sir! How may I help you?"

A staff sergeant yelled at an officer? Garner saw the message hit home and words take shape before they ever exploded from between his lips. "Who the hell do you think you're talking to, Sergeant?" He advanced into the compound, past the sign. Behind him, outside the wire, twenty or more dirty-looking grunts clustered around three trucks, looking at one another and the bloody cargoes in the back.

"Sir. This compound is off limits. Stop!"

The officer reared back five feet away, coiling like an eastern diamondback. Garner stood temptingly close.

"Sergeant, you better get out of my way or I'll have you court-martialed. How the hell dare you talk to me like that? I've got wounded and dead. I'm going to use these buildings until I get transport out of here."

"No, Sir, I can't let you do that without contacting my people and getting permission."

The lieutenant stepped forward.

"I mean it, Sir. Those are my orders." He studied the officer, deciding he was a jackass. "Sir! You must have a top-secret clearance and a 'need to know' designation, in order to come in here. If you give me a direct order, I will of course obey it. However, I will contact my people as to your name, rank and unit. They will contact their superiors in Saigon who will no doubt contact yours. They will not be pleased.

"Sir. Give me a few minutes to get in touch with them and ask for permission that you use these buildings. I just need time to sterilize the barracks, but I'm sure they will gladly grant permission for its use. Please, Sir. Let me do my job, otherwise things will get difficult, very, very fast."

The officer looked like he was going to roll right over him, but then took note of his uniform, and stopped sharp. Garner watched the officer examine everything about him, and then saw flickers of uncertainty cross the man's face. He looked for patches of identification. There was nothing sewn on Garner's green jungle jacket: no rank, no name, no unit insignia, nothing. The jacket was old and worn, and it wasn't that patches had been cut off. They would have left shadowed outlines on the faded fabric. No, in this case patches were never put on to begin with.

He stood there analyzing the unfamiliar situation as Garner read his thoughts. Was the man who had the impudence to yell at him actually a staff sergeant? Yes, probably. There was no hesitation in his answers, no fall back, but also, no fear. Why? Enlisted men should never talk up. Who was he? Longish hair, at least for the Army. Full moustache not to Army trim. Poor commanding officers no doubt. Who the hell was he? Could he be a threat, a danger to the promising West Pointer's career? Possibly. He had to find out more before taking the initiative. He would wait.

"Contact your people, Sergeant. Now!"

"Yes, Sir!"

Garner turned on his heel, smiled as he walked to the commo shed and made a call to Kontum. The answer was of course what he thought it would be. Police up everything classified in the barracks. Sterilize it, and give it to them for the night. He went through his list, checking everything in the compound, and came back to the officer standing in the late afternoon sun.

"Yes, Sir. You have permission for your people to enter and use that building." He turned and pointed to the barracks. "This commo building and tower, however, hold classified materials, and your people should be instructed to stay away from them."

The tall officer turned, beckoning his men. They were engineers, ragged and dusty. Two were walking wounded; two were on stretchers with a medic hovering nearby. Behind, one of the trucks had bodies sprawled across the metal bed, big green and rusty red, Raggedy Andy dolls.

Standing next to them, taking in every detail, was a big man in civilian clothes: late forties, early fifties, some belly, no soldier, small green butt pack (not military issue, easy to see), cameras, lens cases slung around the neck. He'd been watching the confrontation, and Garner felt a heated stare. The question was there to see. Who was this man in sterile green? He came forward, away from the sour-smelling bodies that occupied so much of his attention.

Garner stopped him at the gate, but the lieutenant waved aside objections.

"Sergeant! This man is with us, and he will enter this compound. I don't want you to give him a hard time. Understand?" The officer was in his face. "This is Mr. Sean McLeary, a well respected photojournalist for *Life* magazine. He is a guest, and General Terry has asked that he be treated with the highest respect and courtesy. Do you understand me?"

"Yes, Sir. I understand you're ordering me to allow a photojournalist inside a classified compound. Is that a direct order, Sir?"

The blond officer rolled back, sputtering twice before yelling back, "Yes."

"Sir, may I go and secure my materials?"

"Go."

With that, Garner nodded, acknowledging McLeary's presence, then turned and walked to lock up the commo shed. The world would explode around him if photos were published, showing Laotian/Cambodian maps on the walls inside. Once that was secured, he made another barracks pass, making sure there were no field maps or other sensitive materials lying around. He gave the officer a wave, walked to the cooler, grabbed a beer, and made his way to the field tower where he sat on the steps, blocking entry.

The engineers clustered while the officer barked orders to offload the bodies and bring them inside. Most of the soldiers milled about. They were young, and the large M-14 rifles made them look awkward. Boy soldiers. The M-14 was a beautifully crafted weapon, but it was obsolete, created to hit a target five hundred meters out over the Russian plains.

It was a beast, firing a 7.62mm round. The recoil could knock a man's shoulder out of its socket. No combat units carried them any more, only backup ground personnel. This was probably the first contact any of them had with the enemy, and three were dead.

"Tough." He muttered to himself. Then he tipped back the beer and sucked down two gulps.

McLeary snapped pictures everywhere, and some of the boys posed in typical Charles Atlas fashion. Finally, he broke loose, threading a path over to Garner.

"Lieutenant Phillips is a little strung out. His Engineers got hit by snipers, halfway between here and Dak Seang, and I've got pictures of a couple of his people getting killed. It's really got him bugged. He doesn't want me around, but there's no choice. He's got his orders."

Garner eyed the big man and then squinted in the setting sun. McLeary's ruddy face was freckled, and capped off with a mop of fire-engine-red hair. A big mick out of Boston, he guessed by the accent. Were the broad smile and meaty hand extended toward him real, or a guise to worm in and expose classified information?

He guessed both, while taking the hand and shaking firmly. A reporter could be friendly but would always troll for news. He reminded himself to be alert.

"Garner, Ted Garner."

"Good to meet ya, Ted. What kind of work do you do?"

He got to the point fast, and Garner gave his best smile.

"Oh, a little of this and a little of that, and none of it anyone else's concern. Sorry, Mr. McLeary, I don't mean to be rude, but if you want to talk, it'll have to be about something else."

The big man chuckled in response. He'd obviously learned to take rejection. It was a requirement of the business. "It sure seems there's a lot of spooks running around this country. People wearing civilian clothes with GI haircuts, and people wearing sterile uniforms with long hair. There's a pot full of you kinda guys."

"Don't know what you mean, Sir."

"Okay, okay, I'll move off it. It's just that I don't see people pop off to the likes of Phillips very often."

Garner looked over at the officer sputtering orders sixty feet away. "Maybe I was out of line, but the guy's a jerk. Why didn't he come down the road with an escort? Hell, engineers still have M-14s. They're not combat people."

"We had a VN command with us when Charlie blew out the tires on the first truck. They ended up hiding in a ditch and didn't fire a shot."

"You got pictures of that too?"

"Yah. I'm sure we'll run it sometime next month."

"The little bastards."

"Yah, look."

Garner followed McLeary's finger. Bloodied bodies were carried to the barracks.

"Charlie's snipers are pretty good aren't they? Sure messed up Lieutenant Phillips's day."

"Not to mention those three," Garner responded.

Phillips rounded the building, walked to the airstrip and watched the medevac helicopter come in. He yelled for his men to bring the wounded forward. They would fly to Pleiku, and the hospital there. Then he turned on his heel and walked toward them as Garner stood up.

"Mr. McLeary. Would you like to accompany the wounded to Pleiku? I'm sure the hospital facilities there would be of interest to you."

"Well, Sir, I appreciate your invitation, but I think I'd like to stay with you folks for a while longer."

"Sir?" Garner said. "Aren't you going to load your dead?"

"No," he snapped back. "They'll fly out in the morning after graves registration people do whatever they have to do." He turned again to McLeary. "Are you sure you don't want to fly to Pleiku?"

"No, Sir, but thanks for the offer." The big man's face beamed, and Garner imagined the officer getting as red as the Irishman's hair. It was just a glow from the setting sun, but he smiled at the thought.

They said some small goodbyes and McLeary headed for the gate and the trucks beyond. Engineering units surrounded the secure airfield and just about owned Dak To, and they would report in to stay overnight. Garner walked them back to the trucks, where Phillips turned on him.

"Sergeant, you'd better straighten up your act. I'm pushed for time right now, but if I ever have a chance to nail you I will. Don't ever think you can talk to an officer with that offensive tone of voice."

McLeary and the grunts turned toward the tirade. Garner listened to another minute of it, answering with an appropriate "Yes, Sir," and "No, Sir." Finally, the officer, fully satisfied, turned and headed for the waiting vehicles. Halfway there, out in the open, Garner yelled, "Sir? Sir?" The man turned and looked at him.

"Sir, is it true your men were hit by snipers rather than a full side assault ambush?"

"Yes, what of it?"

Garner snapped to attention, bringing up a crisp salute, while staring hard at the officer. It took a moment to register, and when it did, Phillips went apoplectic, but there was obviously nothing he could do about it. He almost threw a return salute at Garner, then turned, glanced nervously around, and barked orders to his drivers.

Garner lowered his hand and watched McLeary give a beefy wave while disappearing in a tower of dust. He turned and walked back to the buildings and the bodies.

Graves registration people arrived after dark, as a three-quarter moon climbed the eastern sky. The night glittered. He showed them to the barracks, then quickly excused himself and walked back to the tower, sitting on the step, drinking more mind-numbing beers. Eventually though, he was drawn back to the open doorway, and forced himself to watch in thoughtful silence.

Two men were busy at work on the three bodies lying on the floor. One bulb glared from the ceiling, muting colors and accenting shadows. The dead second lieutenant was a young black man, six three or four. He lay with arms across his stomach. A hole the size of a thumbprint punctured the left side of his neck, and blood tracked a trail down.

The other two were white privates, draftees going home, he guessed. Boots had crisp edges. They'd been in country maybe a month. One's entire chest was covered with blood, but no holes were evident in the dark green shirt. The second's left arm was ravaged above the elbow, and gray flakes of bone littered the sleeve. Blood stains dotted his abdomen.

All three lay with open mouths, as if caught in the middle of a sentence by a surprise punch to the stomach. Skin was waxy, and crusted with dirt. Eyes were half open, glazing like jelly, showing the dark lower rims of the iris. Jelly eyes staring to space and God.

The two soldiers went about their jobs, checking dog tags, filling records and listing personal effects. This was their business, and after months of it, he guessed their souls were numb to what they saw.

They unfolded body bags, glancing silently at Garner as the noxious smells of the heavy rubber hit him in the doorway. He reeled, pulling back, but was drawn again to the light, stifling the urge to retch.

The Spec. Fours placed each body, like an offering, onto a deep green rubber bag, then wrapped the sides around and zipped upward from foot to head. The sets of eyes disappeared behind those rubber curtains, and Garner had a vision of flailing arms, clawing fingers, wide stares and noiseless screams, crying for escape from the void. He turned from the light and walked to the quiet airstrip, sucking up the blue, night air.

Eastern hills across the strip stood out against a sky studded with a tapestry of stars. The moon glared at him as well, and he studied the double shadows his body threw against the ground: black against steel blue, against silver blue, texture upon texture. Finally, without clarity of thought, he unlocked the commo building, and laid down on the cot where he'd been born a physical man almost ten months before, a lifetime ago.

He lay, hands clasped behind his head, contemplating jumbled thoughts of life and love, the physical versus the ethereal, what's supposedly fair and unfair. He saw so much of it, while understanding none of it.

Mortality crowded in, pressing at his temples, until he felt the rhythmic thumpings of his heart and the coursing rush of blood within his veins. He drifted, sensing the watchful glares of those pleading, jelly eyes, as he broke repeatedly through a thin sleep, to listen to the night.

32

By 7:30 the next morning the bodies were loaded onto a helicopter bound for Pleiku, all properly tagged, registered and ready for shipment home. Garner wondered when families would get the news. Get them on ice and ship them out. Everyone likes an open-casket ceremony, but few from Vietnam got the luxury. He shook his head at the thought, as teams came back in from Kontum.

Iowa and Wyoming were joined by Montana, with Benson, Altos and Carver. They would try and snatch a truck driver far, far north, in Tango-Seven, where CCC areas of reconnaissance almost overlapped those of CCN in Da Nang. Deep targets meant neither planes nor choppers could stay on station long. They were exposed areas that everyone hated.

The prediction that Dravos made in the club came true. Riggs got off the helicopters with the teams, and Reynolds groaned as he and Garner watched the man approach. He was the same as before. Sharp eyes hinted at a level of viciousness brought to the surface in an instant, like a fox killing chickens in the coop.

"Well, here comes old, 'Field Exercise.' I wonder what the hell he wants."

"Stow it, Jim. Be cool."

"Welcome to Dak To, Mister Riggs." Garner walked toward the smaller man, but did not raise his hand to shake.

"Well, Sergeant, do you think you can insert a team today, or is a little rain going to hold up things again?"

"I can't say. That's not a decision I can make. That's between Covey riders and the chopper pilots. We just baby-sit the compound while we're on Bright Light, but your team is going up north. It's been pretty clear there. Trouble yesterday was with a southern target."

"Well." The man tipped his face upward and studied cloud structures. "It doesn't look bad. I see no reason why they can't go in."

"Yes. Covey should be on station within a half hour or so, but I think you're right on that. Like I said, the trouble's been down south, not where your people are going. I take it this is the first time you've been at this launch site?"

Riggs eyed him. "Yes, what of it?"

"Nothing. Just welcome aboard. Please let me know if there's anything you need or if you have any questions."

"You." Riggs finally recognized him. "You were on that team with that smart ass who got blown away about two months ago. Dodge. He was—"

"That's right, Mister Riggs. Dodge. He was my friend. Excuse me." Garner turned and walked towards the barracks, to tell others about strange events of the night before.

At 10:45 Wyoming got the word. Garner stood by the commo door smoking his ninth cigarette, and since Gable was sleeping off a hangover, he took the call.

"Dusty, Dusty, this is Ranger Bob, Dusty, Dusty, this is Ranger Bob, Over."

He walked five steps from brilliant sunshine, past the cot, and keyed the mike as he sat down. "Ranger Bob, this is Dusty, what have you got for us. Over."

"Dusty, I've got high and broken for you. You're clear for your people today. Over."

"Roger, Ranger Bob. I'll confirm with our people here and call you back. Over."

"Roger, Dusty, I can stay up here a long time. I got plenty of gas. Ate downtown last night. Over."

"Ah, Ranger Bob, know the feeling. Will get back to you. Out."

He checked with Ricketson and Bell, then with the Gladiator chopper pilots and Kontum. In less than three minutes he confirmed clearance for liftoff. The day could begin.

Ricketson sniffled and spit as he reached down, picked up the sixty-pound rucksack, throwing it across his shoulders, over web gear loaded with grenades, canteens, and two hundred rounds of ammunition. He swung his arms beneath the straps and pulled them tight with the slack ties.

Like everyone, he stood, popping on his toes, making the sterile pack jump, while simultaneously pulling even tighter. It wrenched his shoulders back and made them ache, but the pack became a part of the man: no rattles, no jingles, no slipping, no sliding. It was riveted in place.

The whole team was slinging, adjusting, and bouncing, and Garner thought back to Janice, and Australia. Ten buxom girls running out of heavy surf in Bondi Bay, snapping, shifting and moving skimpy bikinis so they were comfortable and covered all the necessary places. That was another world, in many ways more frightful than the one he'd come to know so well.

Finally, with a wave, Wyoming turned from the assembly area and trudged out to the helicopters. They were off.

Riggs sniffed around the compound as the day wore on. Garner tried to steer clear, but it seemed like he was everywhere. Iowa stayed in the barracks, and Montana sat under the tower, waiting for the fleet to return so they could be inserted in the afternoon.

"Sergeant Garner."

"Yes?"

"That's 'Yes, Sir.'"

"I beg your pardon, Mister Riggs, but are you telling me that you are a military officer?"

"No." The ferret stood looking edgy.

"Yes, Mister Riggs, how may I help you?"

He studied Garner for a second and continued on. "Tell me. How long does an insert like this normally last?"

"It depends on target distance and the number of LZs available. Sometimes they draw fire from every hole in the canopy and can't land. That happens a lot up north, where there are more mountains and fewer holes."

"Well, just because they get fired at from a landing area shouldn't prevent them from going in? Cobras and gun ships can lay down suppressing fire, and the team can jump off on the run. That shouldn't be too difficult."

Garner's eyes went flat. "Ah, well, don't you think the team ought to have at least enough time to get in deep and hide? It's been shown they don't accomplish much if they're running from the start.

"Sometime back, Snake Martin's team jumped off under fire, and knew they were in trouble when they saw a flagpole on the clearing's edge. They landed in a battalion-sized bunker complex, a damned parade field, and because of heavy fire the helicopters had to get out fast, leaving them on the ground. This was before I got here.

"Anyway, Snake got on the radio and said he had three wounded right away, but that no one should worry because he had the enemy surrounded from the inside. It took twenty-three sorties from Pleiku over two days, to give enough support so he could get back out. Mister Riggs, these are only eight to ten men. Besides, if every LZ is hot, doesn't that in itself represent important intelligence?"

"Sergeant, that type if intelligence is good, but it doesn't replace actual on-the-ground experience. They need to get in, hot or cold."

"I hear what you're saying. Excuse me, I'd better listen in on the radio."

"Go ahead."

With that they separated, and Garner walked to the commo shed where he found Gable sitting up, feeling much improved from the night before. By noon, Wyoming had been successfully inserted and the ships were back to pick up Montana. Ranger Bob refueled and headed north to find an LZ, and because of the distance involved, would no longer be in direct contact with Dak To. Instead, he talked with Leghorn, the remote radio relay site deep in Laos that would pass on messages in both directions.

Riggs paced back and forth, pondering something as the ships landed and took on fuel. Then, when everything was ready and Montana was loading onto the center Hueys, he came to Garner, saying, "I have authorization to go along as an observer. A number of people have done this, right?"

"Yes."

"Good. Contact Kontum and let them know I've decided to go out and watch the launch from a gun ship."

Then he turned and walked under the swirling blades to talk to the lead ship's pilot. He climbed in and sat between two door gunners, as they led the insertion. Montagnards in the middle two ships waved and smiled like kids on their first Ferris wheel ride. In three minutes they were gone. The second insertion was under way.

The afternoon wore on. Garner felt like he was waiting for something to happen. He was pensive and a bit paranoid, and was playing cards with Gable, when the call came in at 3:45p.m.

"Dusty, Dusty, this is Leghorn over."

Gable picked up right away. "Roger, Leghorn, this is Dusty. Read you five by, over."

"Dusty we have problems, partner. Ranger Bob says he's got a gun ship down, and another bleeding smoke. We'll need a Bright Light. Looks like they're down across the fence. Over."

"Christ." Garner stuck his head out the door, yelling, "Neal, get in here. We got trouble!"

Gable said into the mike, "Leghorn, where is Ranger Bob now. Over."

"Dusty, he says he's circling south of the crash site, and has about another hour's worth of fuel. Then he's got to haul ass. He's calling Triple Nickel to see if he can fuel up and take his place, over."

Neal ran in from the barracks, and Garner gave him the news. It was as bad as a Bright Light Team could get, a downed helicopter across the fence. On insertion, Montana evidently off loaded all right in a medium-sized valley with steep walls. The ships took tracer, .51 caliber antiaircraft fire from upper sides of the mountains. All four ships were hit after dropping the team, and one went down nine klicks south of the target area.

One of the remaining ships was in desperate trouble and turned immediately toward the border, but the other two hovered over the crash site, and one dropped emergency ropes with sling seats, called McGuire rigs. The second ship stood guard, returning fire from all quarters. If anyone was alive and conscious, they could reach the ropes, tie off and be pulled out for a terrifying ride back to Dak To.

"Dusty, Ranger Bob says he sees people coming out on strings. Over."

"How many, dammit."

"Wait one." The pause seemed like an eternity. "Two people. Over."

"Leghorn, that means we've got two birds left on the ground. Over."

Garner took the mike from Gable and said, "Leghorn, this is Bright Light, does Ranger Bob see any LZ nearby, or do we rappel in. Over."

"Wait one, Bright Light. Over."

Garner started hyperventilating as his heart pulsed like a drum roll. A search and rescue hadn't been conducted for all the time he'd been in country. Perhaps, if there was a close landing area, he could take the whole team in, use compass and flash mirrors to get directions to the site, and come back out intact. If there was no LZ within a mile or so, they'd have to rappel down, find survivors and either come out on McGuire rigs or escape and evade to a distant LZ. It was nasty business.

"Bright Light, that's a negative on the LZ Ranger Bob sees solid canopy for ten or eleven klicks. Maybe one south, over the next ridge in another valley, but he says it looks swampy. He thinks you'll need strings for an insertion. Over."

"Shit!" Garner went wild, pounding the opposite table, making C-ration cans jump. "Okay, Neal, let's go."

"Bright Light, Ranger Bob says also negative on two birds." Both Garner and Neal turned toward the radio. "He says there's a strap hanger with the ship. He makes it three on the ground."

Garner slumped and Neal muttered, "Crap, Riggs."

They stalked out of the commo building toward the barracks, when Gable yelled after them. "He says ETA fifteen minutes, Ted. The smoky chopper landed at Dak Pek."

Garner's mind was spinning with possibilities as he yelled over his shoulder, "Okay." They hit the barracks at a trot, and Jim was shaking his head from a nap he'd woken up from. "Jim, you're my radioman. Get up, dammit!"

Neal looked like he'd been slapped, because of the apparent lack of trust from Garner. He turned with his mouth open.

"Neal, we can't go in heavy and expect to bring out three more men on strings. The choppers can't hover long at this altitude with that weight. I need Jim. He's a medic for Christ's sake. We don't need two Demolition/Engineers on the ground. Okay? I don't have time for hurt feelings. Okay?"

Garner guessed Neal had mixed feelings about going, and guilt swelled up, but he'd also know Garner was right. He took a step back nodding. "Yes."

Montagnards clustered around the commotion. "Dominique? Dominique?" The young man stepped forward, quizzical. "Dominique, your English is best. You're my interpreter and a good shot. You come too, okay?"

The boy looked around the room at others and grimaced a smile of sorts, and nodded, saying, "Okay Garnah, I come. We play *beaucoup* on Charlie's head. Okay?"

"Okay, good. Now, we'll have to rappel in on the crash site, down through the trees. Do you have any questions, any problems with that? You remember the training well enough?" He got nods. "Okay, let's get outside, get our rigs on and pack up."

They hurried out to the tower and took their packs apart. The two Americans and Dominique unraveled coiled ropes of their rappelling harness, and began looped them around their waists. Then rope was brought back around the butt and out front between the legs. Ends were tied off at the navel on the initial loop of rope. A large metal D ring snapped around the knot, and finally another ring snapped through the first.

On rappelling, the drop rope would be turned around the link three times. Loops of rope provided friction that could be controlled as the soldier descended. The left hand guided the line and the right hand controlled the slack. If the right hand was held down and behind, friction increased, and the descent slowed or stopped. If he held the slack rope high, friction released, and the soldier fell like a stone. It was a delicate balance. Since the rope burned, they tucked leather gloves into the waistbands of their web gear.

They gutted surrounding packs, taking extra grenades, magazines, canteens, and one machete, along with two days' food. Sleeping cloths, the extra shirt and rain ponchos were kept, but everything else abandoned. Since the radio was the heaviest component, Jim carried little else, just the medic kit and ammunition and grenades. All other survival gear was carried on the body or on the web gear, including small survival radios that made their pants pockets bulge. Packs could be shucked if they had to run.

They were bringing everything together when the helicopters blew in. One flew across the strip to the fuel depot, where it was immediately attacked by a refueling team. The second was high, its human cargo slung 125 feet beneath, at the end of a web of twisted ropes. One man clung there, and was lowered to the waiting arms of every other available person on the field.

"Jesus, there's only one guy," Neal muttered. "Leghorn said two."

Garner shifted, adjusting his pack. "Neal, go find out what's going on."

He took off toward the descending helicopter as Garner continued checking preparations. Finally, Garner reached into the pack, pulled out the World War II leggings, strapped them on and started lacing. The helicopter landed briefly, and the trailing ropes were cut away. Then it crabbed across to the fueling depot and joined the first to land.

People, pulling the ropes away, surrounded the man on the ground. He stood, then staggered, and was half carried to the shade of the commo shed. Garner watched a door gunner massage circulation back into the man's legs. Then, Neal ran up as refueled helicopters blew back across to the west side, and settled down in front of the tower.

"He's one of the pilots. Says they got hit by a B-40 rocket or something. Tail blew off. They spiraled in." He panted between takes.

"Any alive?" Garner checked snap links.

"He says they couldn't find one gunner, and the second fell out of the loop as soon as they started lifting out, broken arm, shock, something like that."

"What about Riggs and the other pilot?" Garner talked while watching door gunners bring four new rucksacks full of coiled nylon rope to the rescue ship.

"Riggs is all busted up. He couldn't come out. The other pilot got weak and slipped forward, out of the McGuire rig, halfway back to Dak To. Tried to hold on I guess, with the loop behind his back and under his armpits. Circulation probably got cut off; his arms went numb and he fell off. Four thousand feet."

"Bad end." Garner looked over to Jim and Dominique. "Thanks, Neal." They shook hands. Quick smiles. "See you."

"Yah, yah," Neal stammered and looked around self-consciously.

"Let's go."

The three of them trudged, weapons in hand, to the rescue ship. The crew chief and door gunner finished tying the last of four new lines into the rope ring that looped through metal clasps on the helicopter's floor. Then he looked out at Garner and gave a thumbs up sign. They climbed aboard and barely settled in when they started rocking back and forth, ever faster as the turbine built to liftoff power.

They dragged, bumped once, and then were up and off, canting forward, heading south along the runway, building speed and altitude. They were up over the wire, banking right, up and up, until a quarter mile later they'd completed the loop and were heading north and west into the green mountains deep in shadow.

Garner watched them float upward, then turned left, examining the tail of rope coming out of the rucksack's open mouth. The knot was tight where it attached to the ring on the floor. Coils looked clean, laid freely, untangled, down and down, around and around inside the pack. It was like looking down the inside of a threaded tube, the coils of rope cut circle after circle, and somewhere at the bottom, beneath 125 feet of nylon, was a padded loop.

He motioned to Jim and Dominique in the other doorway, to check their lines and make sure they were free of knots and tangled coils. When packs were dropped, the coils had to flow out like water, free and clear all the way to the jungle floor.

He turned back satisfied, and watched Dak To disappear far back to the right. Then he glanced to the Gladiator crew chief on the M-60: helmet on, everything flapping in the roaring wind at 4,000 feet, big smile.

The 57th Assault Helicopter Company crews died for teams. They stayed on target longer than was called for. They hovered down and used their blades to splinter bamboo and trees. They fired up all their ammunition in support of getting teams out. One had no function without the other. Recon depended on them to get the job done, to get them out; to get them home.

Now, as he looked at the gunner's hopeful smile, he knew it was time to return the obligation. Garner closed his eyes and rattled in the cold like a piece of ice in an empty paper cup.

Ten minutes later, four Cobras caught up and trailed back to the right. He dozed in the freezing cold as they all flew in tandem, north and west, crossing the border at an angle. Half an hour later he jerked awake, and puckered up to nine when he felt the subtle shift that always marked first sight of the target, and adjustment for the coming free fall spiral down.

He edged to the door, looking forward into the blast of wind, and saw a silver glint, which was Covey skimming through clouds far ahead. Then there were two, and he felt another ten-degree shift, westward. Both Coveys were there, one fresh, one nearly spent. They were giving directions, matching coordinates with the pilots in the bubble up front.

Sides of the popcorn clouds below were golden pink to the west and steely blue to the east. Mist was building along deeper folds of earth, and could be easily mistaken for fires. Pilots took their time. Then he felt a tap on his shoulder and looked around. The gunner motioned loosely, and concentrated on instructions being given over the head set inside his helmet. He pressed the gloved right hand against his ear, shutting out the rushing wind. He listened and then talked into his mike. Then, as he stared at the floor, he nodded to accepted instructions.

He looked past Garner, pointing down into darkening mountain folds. Garner followed, looking out again as the ship lurched more westward and dropped. Three klicks ahead, at one o'clock, was a wide valley, green and solid. It was a tributary that ran west off the second, north/south ridge of mountains inside the border. He strained his eyes, and there, down in the blanket of green, was a tiny tear, a small brown cut on the northern wall, near the ridge. Thin mist or smoke coiled around. It would have been easy, so easy to miss.

They banked west again, looped right and flew east, coming in out of the setting sun. Forward airspeed slacked, and he was prepared for the drop when it came. They tipped forward, falling out of the sky like a fistful of hail. He snapped three loops of rope around his D-ring, and as they plunged toward the hole, he imagined they were racing downward with the sun, to the eastern valley already flooded deep in shadow.

33

The crash site was not clear. The Huey had angled in through the trees, and there was a brambled canopy above. Only glints of metal, smoke, and a gash of red earth betrayed its presence. After the drop from 4,000 feet, the rescue helicopter crabbed closer at treetop level, looking for an opening. Finally, they had to take the best of bad, and the pilot hovered over a scattered break. The gunner turned, giving Garner a signal to go ahead.

He checked across to Dominique and Jim. They raised rucksacks to their chests, and dropped them through the cleanest holes within the canopy. Then they pulled on the leather gloves, climbed out on the skids, turned, leaned out and went jumping backwards into the unknown.

The free fall was clean, and as Garner slowly pulled slack rope behind his back, he felt friction heat building in the glove. Descent slowed, and he flipped upside down as he knew he would with the pack's weight behind. Down through the bramble he fell. The door gunner's face was growing smaller as he looked up past his legs to the whirling machine above. Upside down. How ludicrous he thought, and then it all stopped in terror.

Sixty feet down, his right hand caught a clump that couldn't be seen from above. It ripped around his side to the metal ring, stopping him short, leaving him looking at a tangled knot of nylon and twigs at his waist. The pack of rope had fallen to the ground, but halfway down, a loop was caught. Not much, but it was enough. He hung there in the wind like a spider on a thread, tearing and pulling at the knot, but gravity was far too strong. The clot of metal, wood and rope pulled tighter within itself.

He dropped his pack and M-16, and was dimly aware of the other two descending as he grappled with the knot, trying to release it. Nothing helped. Then he looked around in desperation. He couldn't go up, he couldn't go down. He looked from twig to branch to the tree and started pulling himself along, hand over hand until he hugged the barrel-sized trunk to his chest.

There was no choice. He looked up through the fluttering leaves at the gunner, and brought his left hand slashing across his throat five times in rapid fire. The signal was made. The face above disappeared, and he clasped the trunk as the 1,500-pound tensile strength rope was cut loose from the ship. He slid down the trunk like a shot, dumping out on the ground thirty feet below. He was ripped and torn, but finally stood with nothing broken. His Omega watch had been ripped from his left wrist.

"Ted, dammit! Are you okay?" Jim yelled as the helicopter stayed on station right above them.

"Yah, ahh, I think, God, what a ride." He checked himself.

Dominique ran up while scanning a full 360-degree circle. The helicopter's roar was like a beacon for Charlie. Patrols had to be coming.

Garner staggered around, reslinging his pack and checking the weapon. "Let's sweep the area."

They were twenty meters west of the crash, and spread out on line, with Garner in the middle. Except for a few strewn pieces, all that was left was a seven-meter, oblong scar of magnesium/aluminum ash. He couldn't see how anyone survived, but sitting nearby against a tree, was a man, rocking slowly back and forth, staring at the white powder before him. His dull eyes took no notice as they approached. His right arm was obviously broken, and he cradled it like a baby with the left. A red gob of fatty tissue oozed out of a gash on his lower left cheek.

Jim went to him, tearing off his pack and digging for medical supplies next to the radio. The other two continued searching, and finally heard a weak call for help. They found Riggs on his back, his face contorted, racked with pain.

"Are you shot?" Garner yelled above the helicopter's roar. His face hardened as he knelt down.

"Oh, Jesus, no." The man moaned. "Leg's broken, maybe pelvis. I don't know. Jesus, it hurts."

"Can you manage a sling?" Garner knew the impossibility before the answer was panted back at him.

"No. No. No."

Reynolds ran up as Garner turned to Dominique, pointing along the hillside. "Keep looking for the other door gunner. Go." Then he turned towards his One Two. "What's up, Jim?"

"The guy's close to shock, but I gave him morphine anyway. We can get him out. How's Riggs?"

"Bad. Shoot him up. I need the radio."

Reynolds moved to the stricken man as Garner took his pack. "Covey, Covey. This is Bright Light. Over."

"Bright Light, this is Triple Nickel. Over."

"Triple Nickel, we've got two men hurt here. One can ride slings if we tie him in, but we've got a broken hip with the other. He can't sit. We need a stretcher to tie him into and pull him out with. Over."

"Roger, wait one." Garner checked the darkening sky and wondered how long they'd have light. "Bright Light, chopper pilot says no stretcher on board. He's having trouble hovering. Sun's almost down. He thinks they're being fired at, but can't see muzzle flashes. Over."

"Triple Nickel we can't hear any fire here on the ground. We're too close to the ship and the turbine is too damned loud. Can you have Cobras move off half a mile or so west, and either hover or rip up some jungle so we can confuse Charlie on the crash site? Over?"

"Roger, Bright Light. Good idea. Will do. Out."

Garner jumped to his pack, pulled out the machete and cut two saplings the size of his wrist. Then he pulled out the extra jungle shirt he carried and went to Reynolds's pack, doing the same. He buttoned them and turned the sleeves inside out, so they made reverse tubes down inside the shirt bodies. Next, he slid the nine-foot poles down the sleeves, and brought the shirts butt up against each other. It made an uncomfortable, but reasonable stretcher.

Reynolds came back up the slope. "Ted, I shot Riggs up with morphine. He's resting easier. He's busted up pretty high on the right hip."

"Okay, let's get him on this thing."

They took the stretcher and lifted the groggy man. "Okay, Jim, go help Dominique look for the other door gunner." Then Garner turned back and heard the radio call.

"Bright Light, this is Triple Nickel. We're making noise like a landing west of you, but your chopper pilot says he's been hit several times now. He's getting nervous. He can't see where it's coming from. Can you help? Over?"

"Covey, that's a negative. We still have one man to locate and have to tie off a stretcher. We've got another one sitting here in shock. I hear no gunfire, but what the hell, I'm yelling at you. We're too close to the chopper. Tell him to hold on. We're beginning to tie off. Out."

He watched Jim and Dominique sweep downhill twenty meters away. They were looking everywhere, in trees, in brush, all along the cindered ship's path. Then he left the radio next to Riggs and ran to the gunner sitting by a tree. He pulled the man up and guided him over to the packs of rope. The man was listless, saying nothing as he sat back down and was tied in tight to the padded loop.

Garner pulled off the triangular bandage he wore around his neck, and made a sling for the man's broken arm. Then he brought new rope up around his waist, between his legs and then tied off on the edges. He did it again for good measure, and then pushed the man's right wrist through a slipknot strap called the "dead man's loop." If he managed to fall out, the strap would tighten, and he'd dangle below the chopper by his hand.

The other two came back, shaking their heads. Suddenly up the hillside, less than sixty meters away, automatic weapons fire exploded. They ducked and dodged, and Garner ran for the radio.

"Covey. Get the chopper out of here. They're taking fire just north, up the hill. Have Cobras hit the hill. Get the chopper out. Do it! Over!"

The hovering machine moved straight up. The rope tightened, stretched, and then the door gunner popped off the ground, bouncing like a giant's yo-yo as he climbed through thin branches.

Reynolds and Dominique scrambled back to Garner, reslinging their packs, picking up Riggs and moving downhill, as waves of Cobras came west along the ridgeline, firing mini-guns and rockets.

They moved down into increasing gloom, away from enemy patrols using the noise of rescue to finally locate the crash site. They moved south and east, down the hill, until helicopters were distant and the rattle of antiaircraft fire stopped far away. They moved until they found a clump of brush in the dark, thick enough and large enough to hold breathless sounds of panic and of fear. Then they sat listening, and finally slept a fitful sleep that held no dreams for them.

Garner snapped awake as Riggs moaned, stirring in his sleep. Dawn was coming, and he spotted a leech on a branch two feet away. It swayed back and forth, checking scent. Then it locked onto him and started coming with a standard inchworm rhythmic hump. He reached out, plucking it from the twig, examining it closely. It was a mucous-covered tube of bundled fibers, with a sticky stump of a foot on one end, and a rasper-filled sucking mouth at the other. He crushed it and watched internal organs dump out the bottom as he pitched it to the side. "Jim, Jim." He kicked at the nearby man and watched him jump.

"Huh? What?"

"Let's go."

As usual, Dominique was awake, aware, waiting for them. They checked the map, but it was little use. There was no landing site nearby, so when they stood and picked up Riggs, they simply moved down and east as a tenet of faith.

They moved slow, and carried the litter as gently as they could. The extra man acted as point, with his weapon at the ready. Garner checked his watch and rotated every twenty minutes. They hit small trails, and crossed like moving shadows. Two hours later, they heard a Covey drone overhead, and finally stopped.

"Covey, Covey, this is Bright Light. Over."

"Roger, Bright Light, this is Broken Bottle. Lots of folks are gonna be happy to hear you guys are still around. Over."

"Yah, thanks, Broken Bottle. Couldn't talk on the run last night. We've got a man on stretcher and want to get the hell out. Come north three klicks and we'll give you a flash. Over."

"Roger, Bright Light. Coming north. Out."

Signal mirrors hung around their necks, inside the shirts, where dog tags would have been if they'd worn them. Jim pulled his out, moved to a crack in the trees, aimed through the mirror's center, and hit the plane dead on with a brilliant flash of reflected sunlight.

"Whoa. Roger, Bright Light. Got yah good there. You've moved off a bit since last night. You say you've got a man on stretcher. What about the other one? Over?"

"Couldn't find him. He might have burned, or he could have been thrown in the trees, hung up. Couldn't find him. Sorry. Over."

"Too bad. Dusty might want you to look again. Maybe you should sit tight till they decide. Over."

"Broken Bottle, you can tell Dusty to shove your code name up their collective ass. We've got our hands full and are walking out of here. They'll have to get someone else to look. I just want an azimuth to shoot and a distance to the nearest hole. Over."

The plane flew east, and Covey came back laughing. "Yah, Bright Light. Can't blame you there. I agree you've got a full plate. Wait one. Over." He came back on line thirty seconds later. "Looks like the nearest is north and east, where we dropped those folks off yesterday. Over."

"Negative. We can't climb the ridge like this. Besides, with our luck we'd trip over our own people and get shot up. Fly more east. I don't have a kak card so you'll have to give it to me in the clear. To hell with it if Charlie's listening. Over."

"Okay, Bright Light. You've got a hump in front of you. Tell you what. You know Mister Heinz and all his flavors don't ya? You know, like his steak sauce? Over."

Garner laughed into the mike. "Yah, Okay, Broken Bottle. I know Mister Heinz. What's he got for me. Over."

"Well, if you subtract forty-six from Mister Heinz, you've got the klicks, and if you add forty-one or forty-two, you've got the azimuth. How's that. Over?"

"That's great, Broken Bottle. That's appropriate. Come Saturday, maybe we can share some Mister Heinz back in camp. Over."

"Sounds good to me, Bright Light. I'll try to get back midday. I got to check on other folks right now. Good luck, partner. Broken Bottle. Out."

They looked around as Garner checked the compass. He gave Dominique the angle with his hand. Ninety-eight degrees and an eleven-klick hump was what they faced. Garner shrugged. Then he and Reynolds stooped to pick up Riggs, and finally headed out. They moved all morning, wearing slowly down as the man on the stretcher bitched and moaned at every bump and turn. They changed off frequently, stretching aching shoulders, mopping sweat filled eyebrows. Riggs complained every time. Then they took a break at noon, and on the final bump and bitch, Garner drew the line, as all the bile stored up in him spilled out upon the ground.

"Look, you sonofabitch," he whispered. "I want you to shut up from here on out. You understand me?"

Riggs was startled, taken back, then whispered. "Who do you think you're talking to you four-stripe punk? I'll have you busted when we get back. I'll have y—"

"I'm telling you now." He pointed down. "We're in deep shit here. We don't need noise. We don't need whining about the pain. Chew on a stick and bite it in half if you have to, but no more bitching, or by God I'll make you sorry.

"We're out here 'cause some rear echelon Saigon commando wanted to go for a joy ride. We might have found that other guy back there if we hadn't had to waste our time with you. At least he was there for a reason. He was doing a job. He deserved to be found. Don't mess with me on this, Riggs. Shut up and take the pain, or we leave you."

He turned, took four paces and sat facing away as he dug into the pack, looking for a can of anything to eat. All was quiet behind him, but as he cooled, he felt the ferret's eyes upon his back, and he sat certain sure that some vengeful plan was forming.

Then he kinked and stretched, and laid against a tree while working the can opener, but nothing helped. Tension wasn't broken, and all of them were tight. Broken Bottle came back, confirming they'd moved five klicks. Then he was gone again. "Other trouble," he said, and they were up and moving.

By one o'clock they'd moved another klick, and sat prepared to cross the fifth trail of the day. They were on a bend, looking, listening, when Dominique scuttled back and tried to duck. Two men were on the trail. Behind them was a girl.

The men saw Dominique five meters in front, and as the first one brought his weapon up, Garner blew his brains out with a single shot. They splattered on the girl. Then he stepped out as the body crumpled and the others raised their hands in surrender. Her woven basket clattered down and to the side, spilling cups, and bags of rice.

The team crossed, pulling the other two along. They dragged the body off the trail and scuffed the dirt free of blood and tissue. Then they gathered all and moved deeper into bamboo to sit and analyze the situation. Garner searched the boy. He had on loose pajama clothes. Civilian clothes. He searched the stark-eyed girl, and felt her soft and supple underneath. Then he broke the attendant thought and cursed the involuntary erection building fast. He sat them down and asked in general, "What now?"

Jim said. "We sure can't let them go."

"Of course not," Riggs replied. "They're prisoners. We'll take them both to Saigon for interrogation. They could be valuable." He shifted on the ground, wincing with pain, but held his tongue.

"I don't know," said Garner. "Dominique, ask them who they are and what they're doing here."

Then, as the interpreter moved toward them, muttering low, Garner said to Reynolds, "The dead one was NVA for sure. There's no mistaking that." He held up the green, cloth-covered helmet with the star emblem circled by a wreath. "But these two don't seem to have anything on them indicating who and what they are." He groped through the packs and her basket as Dominique continued his quiet questioning.

"It doesn't matter," said Riggs. "They were with an NVA. They must be Commies. We take them back."

Garner ignored him while talking to Reynolds. "One shot. Anyone who heard it would think it's someone hunting, right? Don't you think?"

"Yah. We cleaned the trail. If they're missed, it should be tough to spot the crossing."

"Yah, but we can't afford the bet. We've got to move."

"Agreed."

"Dominique, what have they told you?"

He scuttled back, and Garner considered the two people squatting on the ground. She looked fawn-like, hunted, scared. The boy was tense and alert.

"He do not say too much, Garnah, but he looks plenty mad to me. He speaks Vietnamese. She Lao girl I think. Her talk, her, her words are not same,

same as Bahnar, but close. She say she is from village down below other side." He pointed southwest.

Garner examined her Polynesian features: wide face, roundish eyes, dark skin, with a button nose, full lips and pointed chin. She was young, maybe fourteen, just budding into womanhood. He rubbed his palms together, turning the thought aside.

Then he considered the boy: eighteen, nineteen, lanky, not an ounce of fat, tough sinew, taut from hard work, but work of what kind? His Oriental face was passive, but Garner sensed a flow of rage behind the eyes.

"Dominique, have him show me his hands."

He translated, and the boy held them out.

"Palms up." Garner showed him and he rolled them over. They were soft on the palm and fingers. "No callous. He's no farmer, but what is he? And he doesn't come from her village. He's Oriental, she's certainly not."

"She say she go to village over top ridge, in next valley. Mother's mother lives there. She say she know dead NVA. He was guard along the road. They buy rice sometimes. He say he take her over ridge to help. She never see this man before. He knew the guard. They meet down below and walk this way together."

"So, we've got Little Red Riding Hood and a guard who's shinning up to her, no doubt trying to get into her pants, and then we have a mystery man. This is too much for right now. Let's pack up. Maybe we can still get out today. If we can't there's tough decisions ahead."

Garner hobbled them both with rope, so they couldn't extend their stride any more than three feet. Then he pressed them both into service, each carrying a pole at the front of the stretcher. He traded everyone off every half an hour, and when they weren't carrying, they were tied together with a six-foot length of rope. Whoever the free man was at any given time, brought up the rear and guarded them. They hit the valley floor by three o'clock, and made much better time as they continued east and slightly south. The risk of discovery was greater at any valley bottom, but they were rushing for the hole now. Garner didn't want to think about hard choices to be made if they had to spend another night.

By five o'clock Covey was overhead, giving a last fix to help them find the clearing. Then he called Dak To for an extraction, and ten minutes later they broke through a jungle edge to look out over a field of vegetables and irrigated rice. It was almost a hundred meters across.

"Dominique, ask her about this."

She came forward, talking quietly.

"She say over other side further east, is camp. Maybe half a mile. Pretty big she say. A road comes through this valley, south of here along the stream, hidden, going east."

Reynolds said. "They must use it to supply guerrilla activity around Dak Pek and further east. The shell that killed Randal probably came down that road."

"Well, let's just hope everyone's asleep today and it's nice and quiet." Garner turned and tied the prisoners behind at the elbows. Then he went to the wood line, looked out over the well-tended field and sat down, waiting for extraction. The sun canted to the west and would be setting soon.

Fifty minutes later they cocked their ears. The girl looked terrified. Hueys were coming. Garner pulled a red smoke out of his pack and laid it aside. Then he stood up, tired and stiff, shaking his head with a decision. He turned to Reynolds and smiled.

"I don't think they woulda paid us on this one anyway, Jim. I'm gonna let them go if it's all right with you."

"What?" rasped Riggs. "You can't. That's not your decision to make. I'll get your ass for this if you do, Garner. I mean it, dammit!"

Garner watched him leaning back on his forearms, trying desperately to sit up, and finally gave the man a look of sad exasperation. "Riggs, what are you gonna do to me? Put a letter in my record jacket? Screw up my DD two-fourteen file? Make me a civilian? Write a note to my parents? You gonna send me to Vietnam? You're in no condition to call shots here." He noted that no weapon was within reach of the man on the ground.

"I don't care who you are in Saigon. Out here it's my show." He thumped his chest with the right thumb. "You see, Riggs, I've seen too many heartless guys like you. I'm too damned close to it myself, but now it's gonna stop."

"No, we take them back. They might be valuable."

"You don't understand do you, Riggs. He might be VC. I don't know. I don't much care, but he doesn't have a thing on him to make me think so, or to make me want to screw up his life any more than it already is, and as for the girl? Well what are you gonna learn from her? That she sells rice and flowers and maybe a piece of ass to truck drivers on a side branch of the fucking Ho Chi Minh Trail? What? What are you gonna get out of her? Maybe a truck count going east for last week? What?

"I'll tell you what she'll get, though. She'll be flown three hundred miles away from her family, friends, home and village. You'll pump whatever piddly assed information she has out of her. Then you'll turn her over to your VN counterparts.

"You think they'll fly her back up here first class? No. They'll pump her for information like you, but they'll try to do one better and get more when there isn't any. So they'll work her over till they're satisfied they're wrong. They'll pump her for information. Then they'll probably pump her full of dicks, and finally drag her out into the woods someplace and pump her full of holes. No. It stops now."

"You're deranged. We don't do things like that. Never. Never. We take good care of prisoners. It'd never happen like that. Oh God, I wish I could get up."

Garner rasped, "It's happened. You may not like it, but it's happened. It stops now. Not this time. I'm going home. You can keep your war. I've killed one girl too many. No more."

"That wasn't your fault, Ted," said Reynolds. "That damned Marston did her in, not you."

"I was in charge. She was my responsibility. I can delegate authority, Jim, but the responsibility is always on the One Zero."

"So you guys killed that courier. By-God, I should have known. You jackasses screw up every opportunity without even coming close to trying. I warn you, Garner, you might be leaving, but I'll get you for this. I can screw up your team if I can't get to you. These SOG camps are loaded with FULRO sympathizers.

"We take these prisoners back like I say or I'll turn in a report stating your whole Goddamned team is FULRO. The ARVN will have a field day with them. They'll drag 'em out of the compound and—"

The bursting dam started as a trickle that suddenly exploded, breaking through any remnants of civilized consideration. He stood struck dumb, listening to a stiletto voice carving words somewhere in the distance, but he heard none of it. The rush of emotion overwhelmed him, and he stood against its force for just an instant before being swept up, letting it carry him through the torrent.

Dodge, Canada, the Cowboy, the Yards, the tunneled cave, all the killings, and the girl, especially the beautiful, dead, mutilated girl, they all washed in, howling along canyons of his mind like churning boulders in the rage.

They were scouring sides, eroding edges, crumbling and dissolving any final restraints, until the flood of rage washed unchecked through his entire being. He started shaking, and the venomous tirade from Riggs went unchecked, until Garner brought his weapon up and sighted into the other man's right eye.

"Dominique, say 'yes,' and I'll kill this man right now." He shook, but the weapon didn't waver.

Riggs went absolutely white and groped for words, but couldn't find them as he stared into the small black hole that would send bullets through his brain at over two thousand feet per second. He sputtered and trembled as Dominique and Reynolds came up.

"Don't do it, man," said Reynolds.

"I'm listening to Dominique, Jim." Garner said it dreamlike, but steady.

"Garnah. Will this man do this thing?"

"He's mean enough to, Dominique. Do I shoot him and leave him?"

Dominique studied the squirming man mouthing, "Please," over and over. He pondered the offer for ten seconds. Finally, "No Garnah, no. I know why you do this for me, but no. Not this way, okay?"

Garner hesitated, stiffened, hesitated again, then slowly pulled back. "Okay, okay, but I'll tell you something Riggs. You owe this man your life. You're medevacking stateside with that bone break, and I'm coming home right behind you. These people are my friends, and if I hear that you've done anything to them, I'll find out who you really are, and where you are, and I'll cut you into runny pieces. I can do that. Do you understand me? Say you understand me."

The squeaked answer came back between thin lips. "Yes, Yes."

Garner turned and walked to the squatting prisoners, who were now tied with their arms behind their backs. He motioned for them to stand. "Jim, get on the horn with Covey and bring the choppers in." Then he led them back into the woods and turned them both around.

The girl's eyes brimmed with terror as she watched him unsnap the knife taped upside down on his web gear. He pulled closer, and she looked up past his chest into a killer's face. It was powerful, hard, giving no clues. His hands were full, with the blackened blade in the left, and the rifle's pistol grip in the other.

He came in, pointing weapons to the sky as he pressed them to her ears and smelled her fear of rape. Then he pulled her to him, kissing her forehead with increasing pressure. It was a release, a benediction, a prayer. He pressed harder, shaking as his teeth cut the inside of his mouth. He tasted copper. Then it was over.

He backed a step, and she looked up startled into weather beaten eyes that offered no answers to her questions. She was lost. He turned her around and sawed with the knife, cutting the cords that made her hands puffed and numb. Then, turning her back around, he said. "*Di di mao*. Go. Go. *Di di mao.*" He motioned her away with the hand holding the blade.

He turned to the boy and cut his lines, and was surprised when he looked back and saw her still standing off to the side, wavering with uncertainty, unable to sort out the conflicting signals of her mind.

"*Di di mao*, girl." He moved over again. "*Di di mao*. What do I have to do, kick you in the butt?" He smiled.

Then he caught a flicker out of the left edge of his vision, and would have muttered a groan of resignation and sorrow if there'd been time.

Where did it come from? He didn't know.

Hidden deep in the crotch? He couldn't guess.

How did I miss it? He'd never learn, but it was there.

The folding three-inch blade was in the boy's right hand, making a looping curve from behind and to the left. It slashed in, and had the power to lay his neck three quarters open, but he shrugged to the right, raising the arm so it hit his shoulder, where his neck had been an instant before.

It lanced through his shirt, skin and muscle, skittering around the bone of the upper arm while passing out the front. Her screams started before Garner's own, and as his knife dropped from the useless left hand, he brought his rifle up across his chest, releasing the safety with his thumb. The boy's momentum carried him forward, and his contorted mouth screamed his curses as it met the muzzle.

The first round blew off his jaw: second was in the gums, third on the cheek, fourth at the temple, and fifth in the crown. The entire front of his face disappeared in a blinding flash of gore. Garner vaguely heard her screaming something over and over, as he glimpsed her disappearing into brush on his right. The body fell at his feet, disgorging a pump of blood and tissue over his boots. As Dominique ran up, he started a slow collapse, while raging at the body and bleeding wholesale.

"You sonofabitch! I was letting you go! Why? You knew it too! Dammit, you knew it too! Why?"

Reynolds ran up, cut the sleeve away and dug inside his pack as Garner finally sat in stunned silence beside the body. Reynolds used seven safety pins to close the wound. Then he wrapped it tight with gauze and tied it off.

The shock was easing off, and Garner felt the first wave of pain as Reynolds gave him a shot of morphine, and pinned the spent cartridge to his collar. He struggled up, with Dominique under his right shoulder, and considered the oozing humanity at his feet, while listening to echoes of the girl yelling far off and away. Then they heard building rifle fire and the rapidly approaching helicopters. They would not get out cold. The shots and the screaming had seen to that. They worked back to the wood line as Riggs began yelling and laughing at him.

"See what happens, you bastard. He should have killed you. I wish he had killed you. You can't give these people a break. I'm gonna bust you when we get back. I'm gonna go and—"

Garner shrugged loose of Dominique, took two steps, and kicked the man's broken leg as hard as he could. Riggs gulped for air and began screaming nonstop. He gulped and screamed, gulped and screamed, until his wails became part of the sound and fury of the descending helicopters.

Garner said, "I don't want to hear it any more, mister."

Jim threw smoke, and the Huey came down while Cobras ripped around the edges of the field, firing mini-guns. They picked up Riggs and hurried out of the wood line to the ship as it landed. Rifle fire and explosions rocked on all sides of them. There was movement on the other side of the field. Green uniforms were running. Muzzle flashes. Door gunners rocked with six hundred rounds a minute, shooting out the molten insides of the M-60 barrels. Casings flew, and the machine guns clapped their ears like slaps from the palm of an open hand. Then they were up and out, and the gunners pointed their burning weapons progressively downward and back, until finally stopping.

They smiled big smiles, like kids at the park, and Garner settled in, letting morphine do its work. Ten minutes later came sunset's twilight sleep. The roaring turbines and the liquid air rocked him with a tranquil peace. He was out and crumpled with his cheek against the icy metal floor.

34

The Pleiku hospital offered refuge, and six painful days were spent sleeping the long sleep of those who go too long and see too much. The body needed time, and finally had a chance to use it for purposes of healing flesh and soul. Garner fought to stay in country, and get back to Kontum long enough to pack his things and go. The Army liked to rush, and temptations of "mind over matter" were very strong.

However, the logic of his request finally settled in. His time was winding down, and they'd discharge him out of Fort Lewis when he hit stateside. If he medevacked now, he'd simply process into somewhere else, and stand in lines, get issued clothes, and have to deal with altered orders, and basically spend his two remaining weeks of Army life at busy work. The doctors wanted rest instead, and sent him back to Recon, thirty miles up the winding road.

Donnally met him at the door with a careful handshake. The green sling around his left shoulder and forearm was far too intimidating for a slap on the back, but he looked tempted.

"Well, Ted, did you come back to kick around any more intel officers?" Donnally smiled wide, showing crooked teeth.

"Good God, Sergeant. If everything's out, why did Riggs drop charges? He did, didn't he? That's what Williams told me on the way back here."

"Well, let's say conflicting statements mixed up with morphine, and the fact you guys saved his butt, was enough for higher-ups to convince him to forget it. Besides, Jim Reynolds told everyone you tripped after getting knifed. Your interpreter, however, got a real charge out of it, and it got around you gave the guy the boot on purpose, but he changed his story when Reynolds told him it could get you in trouble. It's over with."

"Good." He leaned against the doorjamb. "But I was wrong, Sarge. Riggs wasn't the enemy. He was right, the sonofabitch. He was right. They were Cong.

He tried to kill me. I shoulda brought 'em back. To hell with it. I screwed up bad. I endangered everyone. I was responsible again for everything. Maybe I should be charged with something after all. That bastard Riggs was right. I'd like to kick his ass, but he was right."

"Well, you let it get to you. You had a lapse. No one got hurt but you."

"Tell that to the kid I killed," Garner said. "Well, what now?"

"Now? You've got what, ten, twelve days to DEROS? That shoulder isn't going to do Recon any good, and no one else wants a gimp. You can shuffle papers here for the captain and me if you want. We gave the team to Reynolds and assigned a new radioman two days ago. You're out of it."

"Okay." Garner wheezed with resignation. "I guess I'll go move my stuff out of the team room."

"Already done. You missed your Hail and Farewell, but I've got your One Zero jacket and plaque right here. As far as bunks go, I've put you with Williams, the orderly, over at building seven."

"Hah, okay, he didn't say anything about it coming in. We hardly spoke. We'll make good Crispy Critter bookends for you."

Donnally laughed, then cut it off with the next thought. "Ah, Ted. I'm sorry, but you've been out six days now. Wyoming and Illinois got hit bad. We lost Cummings and Ricketson. Bell was medevacked. He's okay."

Garner found the chair, staggered, and sat heavily, blinking through the tears. "It doesn't stop, Sarge. It just keeps on going." He held his right hand out in front, and watched it tremble, unashamed.

"Oh, God, I've got to get out of here, I'm losing it. God help me, I love it and I hate it. I'm losing everything."

Donnally came around, put his arm on the good shoulder and waited with him in the silence.

Later that day he was back in control, picking up forgotten items at the team room. He made goodbyes to Reynolds, Neal and most of the team. Dominique and Kui had gone off to their village and wouldn't be back for several days.

He popped pain pills, finished the move with Williams and went through collected mail. The letter from Day, back in Colorado, drew a smile, and he imagined the campus, the girls and the mountains his friend described. Then he looked at the enclosed forms and considered them.

He wrote the folks of course, his sister and brother. There was no woman for him now, but he simply shrugged that thought away. She would come. They said Bower was checking with authorities about marrying a Vietnamese national, Canada, and he hoped the man was being straight and fair with her.

Then he filled out the forms Day sent, addressed the envelopes and dropped the many pieces at the mailroom.

Over the next week the story was pieced together in the club, since the danger had passed. Drinks were bought, toasts were made, and cards were played. A chapter closed and was added to an oral history that would die eventually with those who told it.

It was hard working up courage to confront Canada with the rumors, but he did, and she confirmed them. "Yes, Garnah. He is a good man. He loves me and wants to take me back. I am happy."

"I am happy too, Canada. Phil told me once, that people drift through life in a straight line, and only change course when they stumble on decisions, like pebbles in the road. They come to points where they have to make choices, and because of that their lives spin off in new directions. They lose balance, but survive it if they're strong.

"Canada, I've been spinning from stone to stone, and when I saw I had to come to a decision about us, I got scared. I'm sorry, but I got scared. I couldn't see my direction, and I hurt you, and I'm sorry." He mumbled on while holding her, and searched in his heart for his feelings, but found them numbed and lacking. Then he bent, kissed her forehead, and turned away without looking back.

He did the best he could for Donnally, but it wasn't much. They said his arm would heal in five to six months, but he'd have to work at regaining any semblance of his former strength. It was cut across the muscle bundles and would never really be right. Finally, the last day came and looked surprisingly like all others from before, but it was the last.

He'd said what needed saying to those few remaining who counted, and now the only thing to do was leave. The stranger in the mirror was crisp and hard. The beret sat level, flap down to the right. Not like some pie plate. The crest was centered exactly over his left eye. His mind wandered, and he continued checking the stranger out while reflecting back upon a simple gift of truth distilled and crystallized throughout the year. He'd been granted far more than just the gift of life, he'd been granted the gift of sight.

They say it's not possible to explain the color red to a blind man. There's simply no reference point to start from, no base of knowledge, no understanding. Like others of any war on any side, he'd been blind to the immediacy and sweetness of living. Now at the end, he reveled in the deep abiding love he had for every day he was granted.

Only fear and the presence of death opened his eyes, allowing him to see the quickening colors of life with such clarity and appreciation. Now, as he prepared to go, he hoped the lessons, the knowledge gained, would stay ever present in his mind like a bright and shining diamond. That each day would sparkle with the understanding that it was unique, never to be experienced again. But he looked at the man in the glass and admitted he knew better.

Safety and the dullness in everyday living would cloud the visions like cataracts, and colors would shrink and blur, but not disappear entirely. Remnants would remain so that many years later, as an old man viewed by thoughtless others as an unimportant relic, he at least would know a truth behind the bravado phrase of Recon, "You have never lived until you've almost died." He would always hold a secret shared by precious few.

He rubbed his shoulder and adjusted the sling. Then he took three pain pills and swallowed them down with a fast beer. He knew it was too much, but it hurt so bad. Finally, he was ready. He turned from the stranger, stepped to the sun-blasted doorway, and walked outside. There was time before the flight, and he dropped his duffel and laundry bags in front of Recon. It was early. Police call was over and teams were now collecting, working out their training schedules for the day. He turned to the club, but came up short when he heard his name from behind.

"Garnah, Garnah!" It was Dominique and the team, and for the first time in a week, his face lit up.

"Dominique!" They came together, giving each other a careful hug. "Dominique, I'm happy to see you before I go."

The dark boy grinned and asked, "Garnah, you no forget Dominique, okay?"

"How can I, my friend." He raised his right hand, and the brass band of friendship on his wrist jumped, sparkling in the sunshine. "You gave me my first woman. You saved my life. You ran to me when I was in trouble. That girl, she could have grabbed my rifle instead of running to her soldier friends, yelling for help."

Dominique looked puzzled. "No, no, Garnah. She good girl. She yell to warn you. She yell, 'No, no, stop,' when that man swing knife. She scream to save you, then run away yelling, 'Thank you, thank you,' because you let her go. She not run to Cong. You did good, Garnah. She not Cong."

His mouth bobbled and he stood blinking in the sun like he'd been slapped. The dark man looked over his shoulder at the waiting team. "Now we go and train some more, Garnah." He winked. "New man on radio. You go home. You be safe."

Garner came back to the present, awkward and stumbling. "I, I wish the same for you, my friend." They shook hands, and he said goodbye to all of them again. Then they loaded on the waiting truck, and he watched them drive off as he crossed the road.

The club was dark and cool. Only three new members crowded a bar side table. He stood in the doorway drinking it all in, and as the pills began working on his pain, his eyes and ears distorted with the echoes of ghosts both living and dead.

In his mind the silent jukebox jumped alive with a Mamas and Papas song, and he scanned a sea of faces. Timmons and Miller pored over music selections, and turned with smiles as he passed. Their voices were foggy, but he knew they said hello and goodbye at the same time. Miller's skull puffed out in the back, showing dull white matter.

The wood and red brick walls closed in, and he roved between chipped tables and wobbly chairs. Colonel Anders stood up to shake hands, but thought better of it and just continued smiling as he sat back down. Sergeant Billings stood up two tables away, swinging the chair around his head two times. Then he jammed it to the floor in front and sat down, straddling the back with his legs. He gave Garner a thumbs up nod and a big grin, then reached down and started scratching Mo Jo's ears.

At the bar, Tony and Duke Danner argued back and forth about relative merits of the M-16 and AK-47, while Kilmer limped towards them on remains of his water rotted feet. Then all three turned, regarding him thoughtfully. They turned back, ordering more drinks across the bar, and from the shadows came three North Vietnamese soldiers wearing pith helmets and bloody uniforms. Their sallow faces had hollow eyes, and they said nothing while pouring drinks, slopping edges, letting them run over. Canada and Beetle Nut Mary came forward, taking them to tables.

He crossed, catching Hamilton coming out of the latrine buttoning his fly. Hammy laughed a hollow echo at some joke he'd heard, but he'd already forgotten what it was. Randal told the joke and came behind, stopping in his tracks, staring at Garner. Words tried forming in apology for the insults he'd given Randal for quitting Recon, but they stuck in his throat as a small red spot on Randal's left chest pocket grew. Randal spit blood and started coughing. Garner turned away.

The club was filling up now, and catcalls, toasts, curses and drunken cheers filled the foggy air. He moved among the tables, and all faces turned as he passed. Friends he knew, faces he remembered, names he never learned.

Some laughingly threw beer cans, but they missed and clattered to the concrete floor without a sound. He reached the pool room door and stepped within, as Marston and Reynolds played a rack. They argued back and forth as the Q-ball careened around the table. It looked like bloody gristle, and they stopped in mid-sentence, looking up at him. Marston scowled, while Reynolds nodded and gave a thin smile.

Then, far back somewhere, he heard his name. It came again, louder, punching through the distance. Was the voice familiar? An arm turned him around, and he gave an unconscious yelp of pleasure and recognition as he starred into the face of Dodge. "Dodge, you dumb, dead, sonofabitch." Dodge laughed a crooked smile and said, "Garner. Hey, Sergeant Garner!"

Dodge mouthed the words, backed away and started melting. He turned into a stranger calling Garner's name.

"Sergeant Garner, are you okay?"

He was a Spec. Four, young and new. The shock of tight curly brown hair was identical to Dodge's.

"Ah, yah. Yah. I'm okay. Sorry, you caught me daydreaming. Pain pills and beer got me kind of screwed up. Not paying attention." He glanced around and considered the vacant pool table.

"I'm James, Bill James. Captain Wilson over at Recon told me to take you to the airport by 10:30. I asked around and some folks said they saw you come into the club. It's after ten, so I thought I'd better hunt you up. You don't want to miss your plane out of here." He stood there with a bright smile and eager look.

"Yah, thanks. I can't miss that, can I." He shook his head, trying to clear his thoughts.

They walked out through the club, and he glanced at the three huddled men. Then they stepped out into the theatre, and he could almost hear the movies, the gunfire and the chairs scooting forward toward the strippers. Outside, they crossed the road, and the driver loaded the bags into the truck. Garner stood in the hard-packed staging area, studying details of the compound, fixing them in his mind one last time.

"You ready, Staff Sergeant?"

The boy he didn't know sat behind the wheel.

"Yah, I guess, let's go."

He turned, awkward and lopsided, twisting his heel, catching a larger piece of gravel that threw him off balance against the truck. He hit it with his wounded shoulder, and howled with the pain. Garner dropped and sat on the running board as he rubbed his arm through the sling. Then he started laughing. It started low and gruff, but grew thinly higher until he clutched his shoulder and punched back and forth with the power of it.

"Are you okay? Are you okay?"

"Yah, yah." He said while continually rubbing his shoulder. Then, he reached down with his right hand, wedged the offending golf-ball-sized chunk of limestone out of the surrounding matrix, and examined it while climbing in the open cab. He propped his left knee on the seat and remained standing up. Next, he grabbed the windshield's upper edge, scanning one last time as they wheeled through the gate to the airfield. Several more new members crossed to the club, waving absentmindedly as they concentrated on their conversation. He grunted at the roaring muffler, smiling at its longevity.

They passed the bunkers, the wire, the Green Door and the shacks. The compound began shrinking, and not too far ahead was the bridge, the airfield, Cam Ranh Bay, the long flight home, and eventual discharge.

He knew the nightmares would continue, but not that the formless face would take on the paradox of the deep-set eyes and pointed chin of the screaming girl he'd saved. She'd smile a dazzling smile while pulling the trigger, making him dance like a paper doll on a string. Eventually, with time and healing, her visitations would decrease from two times a week to one, and then somewhere out in time she'd take her final bow, leaving his life in peace.

He'd taken Day up on his offer of being roommates, and had sent appropriate papers back to the University of Colorado, breaking the patterns of his prior life forever. "Live it bold!" Dodge would have said.

He had an appointment to keep in Anchorage, but after that, there would be girls to chase, education, goals and careers to pursue. Adjustments would be made, family deaths would be mourned, and concessions and compromises would be battled.

Then, somewhere out in time he'd grow enough and find the woman. The one woman. The one to commit to. The one to finally end the chase, and children would come flowing like sweet water from mingled springs of love and laughter. So many visions marched to the future in jumbled profusion. He marveled at the clarity and formless knowledge of it all. It was there to see so easily. He smiled.

Looking back, the compound finally disappeared in dappled blurs of tan, white, brown and silver. He fondled the stone in his left hand, and considered all the twisting, turning choices of the future. Then he slipped the rounded pebble in his pocket, turned into the wind that whipped his eyes, and quickly brushed them back and to the sides before the driver noticed.

THE END

Team Iowa. Left to right: Whean, Kehn, Phe, Djuit, Kui, and Dominique.

Iowa Team leader Phile Rice (left), Raymond Harris (right), and Team member Djuit (middle). Djuit MIA 19 October, 1970.

Epilogue

I've stated this is a work of fiction, and that characters are compilations of many men I've known. One variation of that is that Team Iowa was very real, and still is for me.

Whean was the quiet one, shy, turned inward but friendly. His cousin, Kui, spoke up for him because he was just the opposite. He laughed a lot and flashed a buck-toothed grin.

Kehn was smallest, but built like a fireplug, just as short and just as tough. He enjoyed Americans the most, and liked to hold hands often. There was nothing shameful in it. All SF understood the friendship and affection behind the gesture. It was common.

Phe was tallest, wiry, a leader. Others looked to him for guidance.

Djuit had a Beatle haircut and wraparound sunglasses. His skin was dark and smooth. We joked that with his good looks and glasses, he looked like a Riviera playboy.

Dominique, the interpreter, tied the team together. He'd get drunk and complain and say he'd quit, but pay was good and he had his wife and child to think of.

John Gunnison came up from CCS in mid-1970, and for some reason took over Iowa with a team of Chinese Nungs he brought along. The team of Montagnards I knew was spread around, most transferred to Arkansas.

I left Vietnam and went to finish college. Later, I heard from friends that the team had been hit. On October 19, 1970, they were attacked two miles inside the Laotian border, and tried to run. Several were wounded, including Kehn and Djuit. The One Zero, SSG Peter J. Wilson, known as "Fat Albert," was covering the rear, helping Djuit. He directed the One One, SGT John M. Baker, to lead the team and move east to an LZ. Then he turned again to help Djuit, and continued fighting a rear guard action.

The team was split. Baker heard a mayday call on the emergency radio and another firefight behind. Staff Sergeant Wilson and Djuit were never seen or heard from again.

I didn't know Pete Wilson, but Djuit was my friend. I found out about Dominique's murder thirty-nine years later, but what ever happened to the others, God can only know. They were good kids, and many times I wake up in the dark and miss them.